The Morality of Abortion

Legal and Historical Perspectives

The Morality of Abortion

Legal and Historical Perspectives

Edited, with an Introduction, by John T. Noonan, Jr.

John T. Noonan, Jr., Paul Ramsey, James M. Gustafson,
Bernard Häring, George Huntston Williams, John M. Finnis,
David W. Louisell, contributors

Harvard University Press / Cambridge, Massachusetts

© Copyright 1970 by the President and Fellows of Harvard College
All rights reserved
Third Printing, 1972
Distributed in Great Britain by Oxford University Press, London
Library of Congress Catalog Card Number 70-129118
SBN 674-58727-8
Printed in the United States of America

Contents

Acknowledgments

An international conference on abortion was held in Washington under the joint sponsorship of the Joseph P. Kennedy, Jr., Foundation and the Harvard Divinity School, in September, 1967. This book is not the proceedings of that conference, nor the papers of that conference, but it is one outcome.

Without the original sponsorship of the Foundation and the School, the preliminary work for the book would not have been done, and without the continuing assistance of the Foundation, the book would not have been published. To both institutions I offer my thanks. I have a particular sense of debt to those who had the vision to see the need for a scholarly conference on abortion, the late Samuel H. Miller, then Dean of the Harvard Divinity School, André Hellegers, professor of obstetrics and gynecology, the Georgetown University Hospital, and Herbert Richardson, professor of theology, St. Michael's College, University of Toronto. Above all, I am indebted to Ambassador Sargent Shriver and Eunice Kennedy Shriver for their interest in assuring an examination by experts of the values involved in the American debate over abortion.

John T. Noonan, Jr.

Introduction

Educated American opinion today accords an acceptance to abortion which even a decade ago it did not enjoy. Estimates of its actual practice in America vary enormously; the highest plausible projection is 1000 percent greater than the lowest; and the range of probable error is too extreme to permit confidence in the guesses made. But the shift in influential sentiment is palpable. Respectable, serious, committed persons have contended that the planned termination of pregnancy has a social utility and humane character not appreciated by earlier generations. Response to these contentions among groups likely to determine attitudes toward abortion has ranged from benevolent tolerance to passionate conviction. Abortion, once regarded as a secret and loathsome crime, a medical disaster, or a tragic manifestation of human weakness, has been justified by the draftsmen of the American Law Institute, defended by the American Medical Association, applauded by the American Public Health Association, championed by Planned Parenthood–World Population, and publicized by the *New York Times*.

In America, as has been more than once observed, moral issues become legal issues, and legal issues become constitutional issues. What is right must be legal, and what is wrong must be unconstitutional. Discussion of the desirability of abortion has focused on the amendment of laws against abortion. Pressure to amend the laws against abortion has become a challenge to the constitutionality of any restriction on abortion. The Deans of all the medical schools in California, the American Civil Liberties Union of Southern California, and some fourscore professors of law, teachers of gynecology, and practitioners of obstetrics drawn from all parts of the nation have asked the Supreme Court of California to assert the constitutional right of a woman to have an abortion when she seeks it and the constitutional right of a physician to perform an abortion if he finds it medically appropriate. In *People v. Belous,* by a vote of four to three, the California court in September 1969 avoided ruling on these claims by finding the old California abortion statute, which had been applied in hundreds of cases, too vague to be understood by an unlicensed physician performing a clandestine abortion. *Belous* stands as a landmark in the swift change in which the established statutory regulation of abortion has appeared in a new light.

Analysts of law, typified by the great English jurisprudent John Austin, have sought a purity for their subject by purging law of moral value. To the embarrassment of such analysts there are few if any issues of substantive law where considerations of the purposes of human beings have not determined the outcome. Important legislation has inevitably incorporated judgments about who are persons, who have responsibilities to whom, what standards of behavior are moral between human beings. The Civil Rights Act, the Securities Exchange Act, the Social Security Act are merely prominent examples of the normal process of legislators enacting their moral ideals into statutory prescriptions. They are striking instances of ideals imposed on recalcitrant minorities who had rejected with passion the majority claim that one class of beings had human rights or that fair behavior between two economic classes was required or that one group owed aid to another group. With equal inevitability, constitutional litigation has been determined by the moral convictions of the judges. From *Dred Scott* to *Brown v. Board of Education* great principles about human nature have been the stuff of constitutional decision. What is a constitutionally permissible balance of interests, what is fundamental fairness, who are the persons who cannot arbitrarily be denied life, liberty, or property — these questions cannot be decided without moral judgments. Rightly, the American instinct has yoked the constitutional to the moral. With abortion as the issue, the moral and the constitutional are tightly tied together, for the moral decision determining who is human is decisive for constitutional adjudication.

If legal judgments on abortion cannot take place without moral conclusions about human persons and purposes, moral valuations depend upon the law to a substantial, if not equal degree. Moral judgments are not made by disembodied spirits, nor can they be formed in interior private spheres of mind so insulated from society that the social judgments embodied in law cannot touch them. Moral notions are partly formed by the teaching of the law. Austin's analysis would have it that law is only a system of coercive sanctions keeping the bad man from external actions harmful to the community. A fuller view of the functions of law understands that the law channels action and, channelling, shapes conduct and inculcates attitudes. The public teaching embodied in the law tells the uncertain man — and on many matters we are all uncertain men — what is right to do. Legislation which enforced slavery, for example, systematically formed American moral judgments about blacks. Court decisions which required desegregation shaped a new conscience for blacks and whites. Law prohibiting abortion had taught a view of life and responsibility, and the law cannot be abolished without substantial impact on the moral consciousness of Americans.

Hard dilemmas have always existed in some situations where abortion could be a solution. Most classic has been the case where the life of the mother could be saved only by taking of the life of the child in the womb. The casuistry of theologians and the common sense of lawmakers agreed that, with these alternatives, no legal obligation could be imposed on the mother to prefer the child's life to her own; if she made the choice of self-sacrifice it was in obedience to a higher law of love than common morality or law could enforce. The tragic split of emotions that maternal feelings could produce here became a rarity as gynecological advances virtually eliminated the necessity of abortion to preserve maternal life.

No less old a problem was that created by rape. Must a woman suffer the psychological trauma of bearing and giving birth to off-spring literally forced upon her? The issue was acute in ancient embryology where the male seed was thought of as maintaining some identity in the woman's womb; it is no less acute in contemporary America where over 12,000 rapes are reported annually, and emotions aroused by racial consciousness sometimes have added to the natural repugnance to be physically reminded of the ugly origin of a pregnancy in violence. As false delicacy ceased to inhibit immediate medical examination in the event of assault, it became standard practice to sterilize the uterus at once to destroy spermatazoa, and even if recourse to a physician were delayed for several days it remained possible for a uterine curettage to be performed

Introduction

without violation of the abortion law. The increase of trust in
prompt medical measures seems likely to make the dilemma caused
by rape almost as rare as the dilemma caused by pregnancy physically threatening the mother's life.

Involuntarily, in a third situation, a mother was put to a cruel
choice: where it became known during the pregnancy that there
was a substantial chance the baby could be born deformed. The
prediction might be based on the malfunctioning of a drug, as in the
case of thalidomide, on the effect of inherited genes, or on the presence of a viral infection such as rubella. Vaccines could be developed to eliminate the most dangerous infections, as they have been
developed to prevent rubella; stricter drug control could eliminate
gross mishaps; acceptance of sterilization could reduce the transmission of abnormalities in cases where the chance of transmission
was very large. Yet no measures were certain to eliminate the problem altogether. The gravity of the problem could also vary widely.
Sometimes, as had been the case with rubella, only a very broad
spectrum of deformations could be pointed to as possible, and it
could be said with certainty that two out of three babies would
not suffer even the least serious of these disfigurements. The modern case of a predictable, severe deformity has joined the classic
cases of threat to life and rape as a rare instance where a harsh
choice was made whether an abortion were performed or avoided.

These cases often dominated popular and theological discussion
of abortion. Generous human impulses would always be torn by
them. Yet they have not had a dominant part in the change of educated opinion which has occurred. Creation of this change has been
the work of forces both more specific and more profound. Specifically, one force has been the desire of medical men to have autonomy in their professional judgments. In the hard cases doctors
did not want their exercise of discretion subject to review by a
court. In the borderline area where an abortion not immediately
necessary to save life might be necessary to preserve health and to
keep life from being shortened, doctors wanted a free hand. Some
physicians stretched the statutory exception and performed operations unnecessary to save life but necessary in their view to keep a
mother sane or to give her peace of mind. Such operations, performed within accredited hospitals, were never punished by the
criminal law. Physicians performing them were conscious at times

of hypocrisy in their practice. Private, paying patients were far more likely to receive an abortion on psychiatric indications than patients in the public wards. As administered by the profession itself, the rules on abortion were applied more laxly to the rich than to the poor. Conscious of discrimination, conscious of hypocrisy, conscious of constraint by extra-professional criteria, doctors sought change in the law. The decision to abort, they maintained, was a professional medical decision which should be made by the medically competent.

This modest proposal to vest mastery of a technical decision in the technically trained would, still, by itself, have generated no strong current for change. The demand could appear special and parochial and even self-interested. It might have had no greater claim to credibility than other self-proclaimed needs of the American Medical Association. What gave the demand wings was the population problem.

"The population problem" consisted essentially of three problems — one, the absolute increase in the population of the world at an annual rate approaching two percent; two, the relative increase in areas whose geography, economic efficiency, social structure, and governmental organization together or singly prevented the adequate feeding, housing, and education of large numbers of new persons; and three, the particular increase in population of the United States. Population problem one was the long-run problem of the earth; population problem two was the present problem of several islands and underdeveloped nations; population problem three was an American problem with a racial cast. In each situation the growth of population was an obvious factor in creating major challenges to existing patterns of human life. In each situation, the growth of population was focused on, and reproduction was viewed as the key variable to control. Reality appeared in such a way that attempts to change other variables in each situation would be described as utopian. What appeared to be most malleable was not man's capacity to leave the earth, to overcome island or national boundaries, to share more fraternally, but his capacity to reproduce.

The view of the world as a whole, or parts of the world, or the American way of life, all being overwhelmed by an increase of human beings, generated enormous interest in ways to curb the danger. Despite the demographic history of Western Europe in the nineteenth century, it was assumed that the encouragement of sexual continence and the postponement of marriage were too ineffective, too burdensome, too unenjoyable to be taken seriously as means of restraining man's malleable reproductive capacity. Only measures which permitted sexual intercourse while inhibiting birth were regarded as solutions appropriate to the magnitude of the triple problem.

Until the 1960s, "birth control," promoted as a way of restricting population, was more accurately described as "conception control." Official literature of the planned parenthood associations stressed contraception as a way of avoiding both birth and abortion. It became apparent, however, that known means of contraception were unsatisfactory to achieve a reduction of population growth in many areas. Coitus interruptus required motivation and discipline often lacking in the male. Diaphragms were expensive and required fitting. Progesterone pills were effective only if consumed in obedience to a prescribed schedule of dosage, and their safety was not unquestioned. For poor, little-educated, slightly motivated persons, none of these methods was highly desirable or efficient. The one spectacular success in meeting a population problem was Japan's reduction of growth, and this success was achieved less by contraceptive means than by the massive spread of abortion. The most efficient mechanism for preventing reproduction was the intrauterine device or I.U.D.; and uncertainty continued to exist as to whether it prevented fertilization or implantation; its status as contraceptive or abortifacient was arguable. Technological developments and the limited effectiveness of unquestionably contraceptive means thus combined to make devotion to contraception alone appear as a kind of fetish, indefensible and inexplicable except by reference to the history of thought about abortion. In 1968, Planned Parenthood–World Population publicly changed its stand and endorsed abortion as a means of population control. The action marked formally a transition which had already occurred. Abortion was now put forward as a rational solution to the crises connected with population growth.

Without the appeal to a serious public larger than the membership of a single profession, and without the zeal of a dedicated organization, the efforts of physicians to obtain professional autonomy would have had no great impact. Together, the divergent interests of physicians and those concerned with population control brought disciplined power to bear upon the abortion statutes and effectively spread a message favorable to abortion through the American communications media of newspapers, magazines, and television. Yet educated opinion could not so swiftly have been swayed toward an acceptance of abortion by organizational tactics alone. This opinion responded because the appeal addressed to it touched two deep contemporary currents: the trend to reject all codes of morality as exterior, authoritarian, and absolute, above all, to reject sexual codes as the most odious; and the trend to control one's environment and life through rational planning.

The desire to be free of a code of morality fed on a distrust of any abstract formulation of an "absolute," a conviction that many such formulations in the past had actually harmed human beings, and a disbelief in the existence of any authority capable of promulgating universal rules. Translated into practical judgment, this viewpoint perceived every law restricting sexual behavior as an arbitrary imposition of another's will on the sacred sphere of personal liberty. Statutes regulating abortion fell within this global rejection. Such statutes meant that intercourse between the sexes could not be engaged in freely without preparation unless a woman was willing to risk being forced to bear a child. Justifications for such statutes could not interest those who saw in their necessary effect an affront to a liberty especially prized. In Aesopian language the statutes — no more ancient than other parts of Anglo-American criminal law — were attacked as "antiquated": the meaning was that they were intolerable infringements on a new and cherished freedom. A rational purpose for the statutes was even difficult to imagine. Although ancient law made by male-dominated societies had maintained that the fetus was part of the woman, and modern tort law had just recognized the fetus' independence, the American statutes were often pictured as made by men and animated by a special misogyny, as though a conspiracy against womankind had designed the punishment of the risk of pregnancy as a condition for coitus. Unrestricted access to contraceptives was not enough to remove the curse of the law: many persons lacked the knowledge, many persons resented the effort involved, and many persons acted in the confident belief that while others became pregnant through intercourse they would not. A sure means of "backstopping" omissions or errors was necessary. In a society where all other legal restrictions on adult heterosexual relations had been repealed or abandoned, the existence of laws exacting the possibility of uninterrupted pregnancy as the price of natural intercourse appeared as an unbelievable anachronism. Not accidentally de Sade had been the first Western champion of the right and pleasures of abortion. Abortion was necessary if sexual revolution was to succeed.

Paradoxically, the desire to be free from external control imposed by another's code did not conflict with the desire to control one's circumstances through planning. The desires were reconcilable if the planning was done by the individual himself. With every technological advance, with every step in the mastery of the environment, the wish not to be subject to irrational accident, the wish to determine one's future, became stronger. To have one's energy and resources dissipated, one's plans spoiled, by a pregnancy that it lay in one's power to end seemed senseless self-denial. Viewed as a technique available at the personal option of a woman, abortion maximized both freedom and planning.

To be sure, if the planning were done by one person or agency for other persons or groups — if abortion were viewed as the tidy way of eliminating such incorrigible social problems as illegitimacy, juvenile delinquency, child neglect, and mental retardation — then planning would conflict with the freedom to have children. *A fortiori* there would be conflict if abortion were used as the sure means of controlling population within limits determined by a national policy. But this potential conflict remained a possibility not taken seriously by individuals who could not in any event believe that their own desired family sizes would conflict with any governmental plan. From their perspective, the harmony of sexual freedom with rational planning was manifest. A child who was not planned was spoken of as "an accident." The comprehensive category of "unwanted children" was created. Abortion, then, appeared as the surgically certain way of eliminating accidents, the completely effective way of preventing unwanted children. Through abortion the individual's control of the consequences of his sexual freedom was affirmed.

The desire for professional autonomy and the desire for efficient means to control population had given focus to forces in the culture wider than the special aims of organized groups. Converging, the desire for sexual autonomy and the desire for rational planning of one's future combined to shape the American response. College students, journalists, lawyers, physicians, professors, and opinion-makers came to share the attitude that abortion was acceptable. That attitude is examined by the authors of this book.

The stumbling block for those who reject abortion is the limit which the most humane, most libertarian, most autonomous of ethics must set: the right to life of another person. Absolute abstractions may be impossible, misleading, or harmful to human welfare; but the life of another person is not an abstraction. Belief in a transcendent source of authority and sanctity may be required for reverence toward those regarded as the image of God; but simple coexistence with other humans demands that the lives of some not be open to sacrifice for the welfare and convenience of others. If man can be recognized at all in the multiple forms of humanity, the notion of man necessitates respect for the human person's right to live. One person's freedom to obtain an abortion is the denial of another person's right to live.

To answer that the fetus is not human is to join issue. Proponents of abortion, for the most part, have not cared to make this contact with their opponents. In the appeal to principle, they have seen an obscurantism originating in religious dogma. For them, in this context at any rate, the question, "What is a man?" need not be answered. They are content to bypass what strikes them as fruitless speculation of a metaphysical sort. The relativity of morals, the subjectivity of knowledge, the lack of agreement on ethical principle, all these cautionary epistemological axioms, are deployed to turn off discussion of abortion by those who pronounce with conviction on the morality of war, the rights of conscientious objectors, and the wrong of capital punishment. In not responding when the question of humanity is raised in relation to abortion, they make their own decision as to who is human. "How long can a man turn his head and pretend that he just doesn't see?"

Fetology and child psychology, tort law and constitutional law and general jurisprudence, the Gospels and Hellenic Judaism and patristic Christianity, philosophical argument and pastoral dialogue, and, above all, a view of the human person point to an attitude to abortion different from the one now so strongly championed with such indifference to the fundamental question. Having shared the assumptions and the experiences of their contemporaries, those writing here have asked if these assumptions could not be challenged, if these experiences could not be vicariously enlarged. At a time when abortion is the cry, when the orthodoxies of the hour make questioning of the postulates underlying its imminent acceptance impertinent, when the well-informed managers of the media know that abortion will sweep all before it, it is not too late to face the central issues.

John T. Noonan, Jr.

Berkeley, California
March 25, 1970

The Morality of Abortion

Legal and Historical Perspectives

JOHN T. NOONAN, JR.

An Almost Absolute Value
in History

What determines when a being is human? When is it lawful to kill? These questions are linked in any consideration of the morality of abortion. They are questions central to any morality for man.

In answering such moral questions the temptation to invoke historical determinism is not unknown. A species of behavior is said to be right because it inevitably will be practiced and accepted in the future. "Trends" are hypostatized into forces like older theological conceptions of the divine will; they are supposed to exist independently of human volition and to legitimate by necessity the human acts which they require.

Such use of history, I suppose, appears exploitative and dishonest to most men who have tried to discern the thought of the past. In looking at the data and documents of another age, one does not encounter irresistible trends moving with mysterious authority to foreordained results. Order in human history is the pattern made by the historian in his choice of categories and selection of events. What he encounters is a record of human thought with no greater necessity to it than the result of any meeting of human minds.

The rejection of necessity in human development is not a rejection of continuity, recurrences, and even direction in human experience. These philosophical notions, or something like them, appear as preconditions for the perception and organization of historical "facts." Something like organic behavior may be postulated in the experience of groups of men. Ideas do have implications which are sometimes worked out. No value can be pursued alone without its single-minded pursuit endangering other values, so that balance is the condition of stable phases. Human groups mature. To suppose that these characteristics of human behavior constitute suprahuman forces is to replace history with ideology. To ignore the organic character of human experience is to reduce history to chronology.

History can record insights gained by human beings, insights which once generalized by education are taken as a part of the mental outlook of the persons subject to such education. Such is the insight into the connection between being human and being free. Once men have seen that the determination of their own potential humanity can be injured by the domination of others, they insist on their freedom of action and of thought. The pursuit of freedom as a single absolute, however, is unworkable because the maximum conceivable freedom of action for one man necessarily involves the right to dispose of other men; and any society committed to freedom as a human good must move dynamically toward a balance where freedom for one man is not achieved at the expense of freedom for another.

In the conflict over abortion, the desire of many women to be free from restraints imposed by men and the desire of many contemporary human beings to be free from the domination of sexual codes established by others give dynamic power to any proposal to reject all limitations on abortion. In a society peculiarly conscious of the difference made by age, it is easy to define one class by age so that it is not regarded as even human, so that then there can be no objection to elimination of members of the class whenever a member of it interferes with the freedom of those who are human. In this case, then, there is no need to balance the gain in freedom of some humans by the loss to other humans.

The question remains, Can age be the determinant of humanity? Behind this question, the questions are repeated, What determines when a being is human? When can human freedom be vindicated by killing other human beings? In this chapter I propose to examine these questions as they have been answered in the context of a religious tradition concerned with them since its inception.

The impatience expressed by proponents of abortion with a view asserting the humanity of the fetus sometimes incorporates an elitism which assumes that everyone — that is, every enlightened person, everyone in the ruling group — knows who is human. The elite may become franker and say, Even if the embryo is human, we can distinguish between human lives. Some lives are more valuable than others. To sacrifice a poor, undeveloped life for a rich developed life is a decision which morally can and should be made. More probably, the expedient of the rulers of *Animal Farm* will be adopted, and some lives will be recognized as more equal than others. To any variety of this viewpoint, a religious teaching which asserts the basic equality of men must seem irrelevant; but it is difficult to extricate the aspirations of the modern world from the assumption of basic equality. A teaching anchored in this assumption may be stronger than the very strong attraction to believe that some lives are more valuable than others.

The teaching of a religious body may invoke revelation, claim authority, employ symbolism, which make the moral doctrine it teaches binding for believers in the religion but of academic concern to those outside its boundaries. The moral teaching of a religious body may also embody insights, protect perceptions, exemplify values, which concern humanity. The teaching of the moralists of the Catholic Church on abortion is particularly rich in interaction between specifically supernatural themes — for example, the Nativity of the Lord and the Immaculate Conception of Mary — and principles of a general ethical applicability. In its full extent, the teaching depends on the self-sacrificing example of the Lord — to the Greeks, foolishness. In its basic assumption of the equality of human lives, it depends on a stoic, democratic contention which any man might embrace and Western humanism has hitherto embraced. In its reliance on ecclesiastical authority to draw a line, it withdraws from the sphere of debate with all men of goodwill; in its casuistic examination of principle, it offers instances where the common tools of moral analysis may be observed industriously employed. The teaching in its totality cannot be detached from the religious tradition which has borne it. The teaching in its fundamental questions about the meaning of love and humanity cannot be disregarded by those who would meet the needs of man humanly.

I. THE CONTEXT

In the Mediterranean world in which Christianity appeared, abortion was a familiar art. The most learned of Greco-Roman gynecologists, Soranos of Ephesus (c. A.D. 98–138), discussed abortion in terms of two main genres of abortifacients, *phthorion*, "which destroys what has been conceived," and *ekbolion*, "which expels what has been conceived." He then listed the following ways of achieving the destruction of the embryo: purging the abdomen with clysters; walking about vigorously; carrying things beyond one's strength; bathing in sweet water which is not too hot; bathing in decoctions of linseed, mallow, and wormwood; applying poultices of the same decoctions; injecting warm and sweet olive oil; being bled and then shaken after softening by suppositories.[1] He is opposed to the use of sharp instruments which may injure the mother. In addition he lists a number of contraceptives (*atokia*) which will also operate as abortifacients, in particular drugs composed of plant mixtures. These drugs will apparently operate at an early stage of the pregnancy if they have failed to prevent contraception; the abortifacients proper are intended for later stages of fetal life. As to the effectiveness of the means proposed, Soranos notes that contraception is surer and therefore to be preferred, but it would seem that some if not all of the abortifacient methods he proposes would have achieved the desired effect.

The reasons for abortion were as various as the means. Soranos notes three: to conceal the consequences of adultery; to maintain feminine beauty; to avoid danger to the mother when her uterus is too small to accommodate the full embryo. Plato and Aristotle thought of abortion as a way of preventing excess population.[2] St. Ambrose was familiar with propertied families who practiced it in order not to divide their patrimony among too many children.[3]

The morality of practicing abortion was debated by physicians, philosophers, and religious teachers. The Hippocratic Oath was well known with its pledge "not to give a deadly drug [*pharmakon*] to anyone if asked for it, nor to suggest it. Similarly, I will not give to a woman an abortifacient pessary. In purity and holiness

---

1. SORANOS, *Gynecology*, ed. J. Ilberg, in 4 *Corpus Medicorum Graecorum* 1.19.60 (London and Berlin, 1927). I follow the translation of technical terms made by L. Edelstein and O. Temkin in their English translation of the *Gynecology* (Baltimore, 1956).
2. PLATO, *The Republic* 5.461ᶜ; ARISTOTLE, *Politics* 7.16, 1335ᵇ.
3. *Hexameron* 5.18.58, *Corpus Scriptorum Ecclesiasticorum Latinorum* (hereafter *CSEL*) 32.11.184.

I will guard my life and my art." [4] Influenced by the authority attributed to the oath as the work of Hippocrates, some physicians of the first century A.D. refused to prescribe abortifacients for anyone. They also had in mind that "it is the task of medicine to maintain and save what nature has engendered." [5] Others, like Soranos himself, prescribed abortion only where completion of the pregnancy would endanger the mother. Another writing also ascribed to Hippocrates was cited where he himself told a girl how to accomplish an abortion by jumping.[6] In the ideal commonwealth sketched by Socrates in Plato's *Republic* abortion was proposed as a solution to prevent endangering the optimum population of the state; it is impossible to say with what seriousness Plato endorsed this suggestion.[7] Aristotle also proposed abortion if a couple had too many children for the good of the state, but he did so with remarkable caution, saying it is to be done before there is "sensation and life," and "what is right depends on the question of sensation and life," a restriction which in his biology might have permitted only contraception.[8]

4. LUDWIG EDELSTEIN, *The Hippocratic Oath: Text, Translation, and Interpretation* 3 (Baltimore, 1943). The commentators have generally taken the first part of the oath as a pledge not to give a poison or, as in Edelstein, not to participate in euthanasia (*ibid.*, p. 10.) It seems to me that one reading of the oath is to see the "deadly drug" as one type of abortifacient which is rejected along with the pessary. This reading would accord with the paraphrase furnished by Soranos, who, at 1.19.60, says it forbids the furnishing of "an abortifacient" (*phthorion*).

5. SORANOS, at 1.19.60.

6. HIPPOCRATES, *The Nature of the Child*, in *Oeuvres*, ed. E. Littré, 7:409 (Paris, 1834–1861). Although this work may not belong to the Hippocratic corpus, it was accepted by Soranos as written by Hippocrates.

7. *The Republic* 5.461^c. Sometimes Plato is cited as favoring abortion; but the reference in *The Laws*, 5, 740^d, is entirely a vague and general one to methods of restraining excessive fertility in an ideal city, and colonization is suggested as the last resort for population excess.

8. *Politics* 7.16, 1335^b. As Aristotle himself leaves it a question, one can only suggest what the elements of the solution would have been for him. When an abortion occurs, distinct parts are found in an embryo if it is male and forty days old, or after ninety days if it is female (*History of Animals* 7.3.583^b). This belief as to the time of formation of the fetus would suggest that there is no sensation before the fortieth day. Moreover, referring to growth in the early stages of the gestation of an animal, Aristotle speaks of its "nutritive soul," a soul which would be like that of a plant (*The Generation of Animals* 2.5.714^a); and the original state of animals is not sleep, but something resembling sleep, a state which plants are in (5.1). On the other hand, this nutritive soul has the capacity for using heat and cold as its "instruments" (*ibid.*). Where male and female are sentient, what the male contributes to generation is a "sentient soul" (2.5.741^b). The animal "first and foremost lives because it can feel" (*The Soul*

The Old Testament has nothing to say on abortion, but the Hellenic Jews of the diaspora developed an opinion. The Septuagint translation of Exod. 21:22 provided an opportunity. Where the Hebrew had said that when a man accidentally causes an abortion "life is given for life" only if the mother dies, the Greek read "life is given for life" if the embryo is "formed," so that an express penalty was provided for the abortion. In his first-century commentary Philo noted that by implication intentional as well as accidental abortion was thereby condemned. Philo himself associated abortion with infanticide and the abandonment of children, practices of inhumanity which he now found regarded "with complacence" by many nations.[9]

Abortion, indeed, according to contemporary observers, was practiced very generally in the Greco-Roman world. The divided opinions of a few sages scarcely checked the powerful personal motives which made it attractive. The law of the empire punished abortion committed without the father's consent.[10] It also punished the giving of drugs for abortion,[11] but it is unlikely that the law was enforced unless the recipient died. The object of the law was not to protect the embryo as a human person, for it was regarded as part of the mother.[12] The purpose was to restrain "bad example," that is, the bad example of giving magical potions which could cause death to the recipient.[13] As pagan observations and Christian complaints indicated, parents' freedom to dispose of their young offspring was taken for granted by the empire.[14] That the Jews should

---

2.2.431[b]). Can it be said that what is generated by the copulation of two animals is a plant? All that can be said with certainty is that Aristotle distinguished the first seven days from the later period of life, and considered that if an "effusion" of seed occurred then, it was not the same as abortion of an embryo (*History of Animals* 7.3.583[a-b]).

9. *The Special Laws* 3.20.110.

10. *Digest*, ed. Theodore Mommsen, 1 *Corpus juris civilis* (Berlin, 1893) 47.11. 4. According to Plutarch, Romulus in his original laws for Rome permitted a husband to divorce his wife for "*pharmakeia*" toward the children. Plutarch, *Romulus* 22. Probably the use of contraceptive or abortifacient drugs to prevent children is meant.

11. *Digest* 48.19.38.5; cf. *Digest* 48.8.8.

12. *Id.* at 24.4.1.1; 35.2.9.1.

13. The "bad example" rationale for the law is given by the jurist Paul, *Digest* 48.19.38.5, without explanation. As it also applies to the giving of aphrodisiac potions, I take it that the bad example relates to the character of the potion, not to the effect on the birth rate.

14. On the acceptance of abandonment of children by their parents, see SUETONIUS, *Gaius Caligula* 5; on the acceptance of infanticide, see SENECA, *De ira*

have children born after their fathers' wills had been made, when heirs were no longer desired by the parents, was a cause for wonder to Tacitus.[15] The Roman upper classes diminished during the empire; the decline was probably due, in good part, to the practice of contraception and abortion.[16]

It was in this culture generally distinguished by its indifference to fetal and early life that the Christian teaching developed; it was in opposition and conflict with the values reflected in popular behavior that the Christian word was enunciated. Where some wise men had raised voices in defense of early life so that the question was in the air and yet not authoritatively decided, where even the wisest presented hesitant and divided counsel, where other authorities defended abortion, the Christians proposed a rule which was certain, comprehensive, and absolute.

II. THE ABSOLUTE VALUATION, A.D. 50–450

The New Testament and the Early Community

The specific Christian teaching on abortion developed in a theological context in which the commands of the Old Testament to love God with all your heart (Deut. 6:5) and to love your neighbor as yourself (Lev. 19:18) were singled out as the two great commandments on which depended "the whole law and the prophets" (Matt. 22:40). The standard for fulfillment of these commandments was set in terms of the sacrifice of man's life for another (John 15:13) and embodied in the self-sacrifice of Jesus. Jesus told the disciples, "This is my commandment, that you love one another as I have loved you" (John 15:32). In terms of his example, the commandment was "a new commandment" (John 13:34). The Christian valuation of life was made in view of this commandment of love.

1.15; cf. his praise of his own mother for not having had an abortion, unlike so many, *Ad Helviam* 16.1. For references where abortion is taken for granted by contemporary pagans, see PLAUTUS, *Truculentus* 1.2.99; OVID, *De amoribus* 1.2.13; JUVENAL, *Satira* 2.6; AULUS GELLIUS, *Noctes atticae* 12.1. For Christian criticisms of the prevalence of abortion see the texts cited at notes *infra*, 20–36. On the frequency of abortion see also J. H. Waszink, "Abtreibung," in *Reallexicon für Antike und Christentum* 57, ed. Theodor Klauser (Stuttgart, 1950).

15. *Historiae* 5.5.
16. JOHN T. NOONAN, JR. *Contraception: A History of Its Treatment by the Catholic Theologians and Canonists* 18–29 (Cambridge, Mass., 1965).

John T. Noonan, Jr.

The place of children in the Christian community was broadly established in the words of the Lord, "Suffer little children [*paidia*] and do not prevent them from coming to me" (Matt. 19:14; Mark 10:14; Luke 18:16). In Luke 18:15, the children the Lord welcomed were expressly described as "newborn babies" (*brephe*). The ethos of the infancy narratives reflected a high interest in infant and fetal life. The infanticide practiced by Herod and its violent threat to the life of Jesus formed the introduction to the life of the Messiah (Matt. 2:1–18). Mary was described as having in her womb what was "from the Holy Spirit" (Matt. 1:18). In Luke she was greeted in pregnancy by Elizabeth "as the mother of my Lord," and the "fruit" of her womb was then described as "blessed" (Luke 1:42). The infant (*brephos*) in Elizabeth's womb "leaps" when Elizabeth is greeted by Mary (Luke 1:40). The interest in the behavior of this holy but not miraculous child of Elizabeth and the interest in the life in Mary's womb reflected the valuations of a community sensitive to the living character of the embryo, and the Gospel accounts must in turn have enhanced that sensitivity. What was unspoken was in its way as important as what was said in reflecting community valuations, attitudes, expectations. It was not necessary in this community to say that a man who protected the state by killing infants was not a good man. It was necessary to say that the first reaction of Joseph to Mary's unexplained pregnancy was "to put her away" (Matt. 2:19); it was not necessary to say that his first thought was not to procure an abortion.

At the level of specific moral rule, the Apostle Paul denounced the foolish carnality of the Christian community in Galatia (Gal. 3:1–6), reminded them that there was a law which was fulfilled in one word, "Love your neighbor as yourself" (5:14), and set out specific types of behavior which violated this law of love (5:19–21). The works of the flesh included not only "lecheries" and "wraths" but *pharmakeia* (5:20). *Pharmakeia* is a term best translated as "medicine" in the sense in which a North American Indian medicine man makes medicine.[17] It is the employment of drugs with occult properties for a variety of purposes, including, in par-

17. See CLYDE PHARR, "The Interdiction of Magic in Roman Law," 63 *Transactions and Proceedings of the American Philological Association* 272–73 (1932). The word is regularly mistranslated as "sorcery" or "witchcraft" in English Bibles.

ticular, contraception or abortion.[18] Paul's usage here cannot be restricted to abortion, but the term he chose is comprehensive enough to include the use of abortifacient drugs. The association of these drugs with sins of lechery and wrath was indeed a constant aspect of the Christian approach to *pharmakeia* (the practice of "medicine") and *pharmaka* (the drugs employed).

The same association and same comprehensive use of the term appeared in the *Apocalypse*. The sinners who were not saved "did not repent of their homicides nor their medicine [*pharmaka*] nor their fornications nor their thefts" (9:21). The *pharmakai*, the medicine men, were condemned by the Lord with the homicides and the fornicators (21:8). Those outside the heavenly city were "the dogs and the medicine-men and the fornicators and the homicides and the idolaters and everyone who loves and practices falsehood" (22:15).[19]

That abortion could have been specifically in the mind of the authors of *Galatians* and the *Apocalypse*, and that it was specifically dealt with by the early Christian communities, is established by several contemporary writings. The most important is the *Didache*, or *Teaching of the Twelve Apostles*. This ancient and authoritative statement of Christian principles in Syria was composed no later than A.D. 100 and may well have been written much earlier.[20] Here a list of precepts was given for the instruction of the Christian: "You shall not kill. You shall not commit adultery. You shall not corrupt boys. You shall not fornicate. You shall not steal. You shall not make magic. You shall not practice medicine (*pharmakeia*). You shall not slay the child by abortions (*phthora*). You shall not kill what is generated. You shall not desire your neighbor's wife" (*Didache* 2.2). In this list of related sins, one sentence expressly prohibited abortifacients. The commands on either side of this sentence dealt with other aspects of the same sin, as the com-

---

18. PLUTARCH, *Romulus* 22, in *Parallel Lives*, trans. B. Perrin (New York, 1914–1926).

19. "Dogs" may mean simply "heathen," but it was also applied to the sodomitic priests who served Astarte. See R. H. CHARLES, 2 *A Critical Commentary and Exegesis of Revelations* 178 (1920).

20. The later date is preferred by THEODORE CAMELOT, "Didache," 3 *Lexikon für Theologie und Kirche* 369 (1959). An early date, connecting the work with an apostolic mission at Antioch, is preferred by the author of a recent detailed study, JEAN-PAUL AUDET, *La Didachè: Instructions des Apôtres* 197 (Paris, 1958).

mandments on sexual sins complemented each other. Abortion was ranked as a principal sin included with those sins expressly named by the Ten Commandments.

In the kernal of the *Didache*, which is probably its oldest part, the Two Ways, the Way of Life was contrasted with the Way of Death. The latter way was followed by sinners who included those who practice "medicine" and those who are "killers of the child, who abort the mold [*plasma*] of God." Again there was a complementary character to the acts denounced: *pharmakeia*, killing of the child, and abortion. The offense of abortion was seen as an offense against God because it attacked what He had made. It was associated with the sinful use of drugs to prevent birth and with the slaying of the child. It may be that both abortion of the mold and killing of the child were mentioned so that any distinction between formed and unformed fetuses would not provide an escape.

The somewhat later *Epistle of Barnabas* was based on the *Didache* and provided a commentary by its paraphrases and additions. It put the commandment on abortion in the *Didache* 2.2 in this framework: "You shall love your neighbor more than your own life. You shall not slay the child by abortions. You shall not kill what is generated" (*Barnabas* 19.5). The proscription was thus related to the love of neighbor. The killing of the fetus to save one's own life was implicitly rejected.

A third writing is of special relevance to the teaching of the canonical Apocalypse. This is the *Apocalypse of Peter*, a species of apocalyptic literature which "ranked next in popularity and probably in date to the canonical Apocalypse of St. John." [21] Here there was a pit of torment for sinners, among them women "who have caused their children to be born untimely and have corrupted the work of God who created them." The phrasing was close to the "abort the mold of God" of the Way of Death in the *Didache*. Some of these women had conceived the children in fornication; others had husbands who were punished with them because "they forsook the commandments of God and slew their children." [22] The

21. MONTAGUE RHODES JAMES, *The Apocryphal New Testament* 505 (Oxford, rev. ed. 1953).

22. *Id.* at 510 (James's translation from the Ethiopic text). In the same style the much later *Apocalypse of Paul* condemns women who "defiled the creation of God when they brought forth children from the womb," i.e., by abortion (*id.* at 545).

offense described was killing what God had made, an offense heightened because it was mothers who had killed their own offspring.

The Fathers

Later in the second century the writing of the "most learned" of the Fathers, Clement of Alexandria, also contained a statement on abortion. In the *Pedagogus* Clement, the founder of the first school of Christian theology, sought to present Christ as the supreme educator for Christians and to provide teaching on Christian morality to the turbulent Christian community at Alexandria. He declared that Christians do not, in order to hide their fornication, "take away human nature, which is generated from the providence of God, by hastening abortions and applying abortifacient drugs [*phthoriois pharmakois*] to destroy utterly the embryo and, with it, the love of man." [23] Here there is the same nexus of ideas found in the first century. Drugs to destroy offspring are associated with lechery. Their use is condemned not merely because they furnish an aid to sexual sin or incorporate magic, but because they offend God in destroying what He has shaped and because they violate the love of neighbor in destroying the fetus.

The foregoing documents were all addressed to Christian communities containing converts and were directed to impressing the new Christian morality upon them. Other evidence of Christian belief is furnished by the Christian claims addressed to the pagans. The contention was made that Christians are "homicides or devourers of men." The second-century philosopher and Christian convert Athenagoras answered this charge in his apologia for Christianity to the emperor: "How can we kill a man when we are those who say that all who use abortifacients are homicides and will account to God for their abortions as for the killing of men. For the fetus in the womb is not an animal, and it is God's providence that he exist." [24] The dedicated Christian defense of life at the embryonic stage seemed to Athenagoras the surest proof of the Christian reverence for life.

In a similar vein the lawyer Minucius Felix repelled the charge of infanticide in his apologia (c. 190–200): Who would believe that

23. *Pedagogus* 2.10.96.1, *Die grieschen christlichen Schriftsteller der ersten drei Jahrhundert* (hereafter *GCS*).
24. *Embassy for the Christians, Patrologia graeca* 6.919 (hereafter *PG*).

the tender bodies of infants would be destroyed? "No one would believe it unless he dared it." In charging this crime the pagans reveal their own conduct. They expose their unwanted children to wild beasts and birds or strangle them. "By drinks of drugs they extinguish in their viscera the beginning of a man-to-be and, before they bear, commit parricide." These things are derived from their gods, for Saturn devoured his own children.[25] The use of the term *parricidium* is especially striking here. Roman law had no generic term for the "killing of a man," and so Minucius used the closest legal term in use, "parricide," the killing of a near relation, designating a crime punished with great severity by the law. It conveyed the idea of heinous killing at the same time that Minucius expanded its meaning far beyond its recognized legal meaning to encompass abortion.[26] In describing the pagans' practice, he expressed his own judgment that it was wrong. At the same time he made the suggestion, of much psychological interest, that the Greek myth of a god devouring his children was related to abortion.

In a parallel passage Tertullian in his apologia to the pagans dismissed the charge of infanticide practiced by Christians and asserted: "For us, indeed, as homicide is forbidden, it is not lawful to destroy what is conceived in the womb while the blood is still being formed into a man. To prevent being born is to accelerate homicide, nor does it make a difference whether you snatch away a soul which is born or destroy one being born. He who is man-to-be is man, as all fruit is now in the seed." [27] The substance is the same as the Two Ways: the mold in the womb may not be destroyed. The offense is expressed as the killing of a potential human, an act which seems forbidden by the commandment, "You shall not kill."

In his treatise on ensoulment Tertullian appealed to a mother's

25. *Octavius, CSEL* 2.43.
26. On the meaning of *parricidium* see T. Mommsen, *Römisches Strafrecht* 613 (1899).
27. *Apologeticum ad nationes* 1.15. The relation of Tertullian to Minucius is discussed in Marti Sordi, "L'apologia del martire romano Apollonio come fonte dell' Apologeticum di Tertulliano e i rapporti fra Tertulliano e Minucio," 18 *Rivesta di storia della Chiesa in Italia* 169–188 (1964). Another example of apologetical criticism of pagan inhumanity toward children is provided by Lactantius, *Divinarum institutionum* 6. His strong terms seem principally aimed at infanticide and the abandonment of children to beasts, but may include abortion and reflect the teaching of the *Didache* when he says that "with wicked hands they corrupt the works of God." The central thought is, "It is always wrong to kill a man; this animal God willed to be sacred," *Patrologia latina* 6.707–708 (hereafter *PL*).

experience of the being within her to establish that a living and therefore ensouled being existed in pregnancy: "In this matter, there is no more fitting teacher, judge, witness, than one of this sex. Reply, you mothers, you bearers of children, let the sterile and the masculine be silent, the truth of your nature is sought." He continued the argument by noting that dead embryos were extracted from a womb and asked,

How are they dead unless they were first alive? But still in the womb an infant by necessary cruelty is killed when lying twisted at the womb's mouth he prevents birth and is a matricide unless he dies. Therefore there is among the arms of physicians an instrument by which with a rotary movement the genital parts are first opened, then with a cervical instrument the interior members are slaughtered with careful judgment by a blunt barb, so that the whole criminal deed is extracted with a violent delivery. There is also the bronze needle by which the throat-cutting is carried out by a robbery in the dark; this instrument is called an embryo-knife from its function of infanticide, as it is deadly for the living infant. This Hippocrates taught, and Asclepiades, and Erasistratus and Herophilus, the dissecter of adults, and the milder Soranos himself, — all of them certain that a living being had been conceived and so deploring the most unhappy infancy of one of this kind who had first to be killed lest a live woman be rent apart. Of this necessity of crime, Hicesius, I believe, did not doubt, as he added souls to those being born from blows of cold air, because the word itself for "soul" among the Greek relates to such cooling.[28]

Tertullian is here not making direct moral judgments, as he is focusing on the argument that even this kind of fetus has been alive. But the suggestion of Franz Dölger that this passage accepts therapeutic abortion is clearly wrong.[29] What the physicians find necessary Tertullian finds a crime, and he uses the strongest terms of vituperation to stigmatize it — "slaughtered" (*caeduntur*), "victim of a crime" (*facinus*), "throat-cutting" (*iugulatio*, a fierce, vulgar term), "infanticide" (*infanticidium*), "crime" (*scelus*). His harsh and sarcastic rhetoric deliberately contrasts the "careful judgment" of the physician with the "violent delivery" effected like "a robbery in the dark."

In addition to its expression in formal moral teaching and apolo-

28. *De anima*, ed. J. H. Waszink, 25.5–6 (1947). I have adopted Waszink's learned and helpful suggestions on translation.
29. Franz Dölger, *Antike und Christentum*, vol. 4, at 46. See the extended refutation of Dölger by Constancio Palomo Gonzalez, *El aborto en San Augustino* at 221–228 (Salamanca, 1959).

gias to the gentiles, the Christian belief was expressed in the course of controversy within the Church. Abortion was a serious charge in ecclesiastical disputes. When the ex-slave Calixtus, bishop of Rome, permitted Christian women to marry their slaves though the marriages were unrecognized by Roman law, some women did not want to draw attention to their union, and used drugs to produce sterility or "bound themselves tightly to expel a fetus already engendered." According to Calixtus' critic and bitter rival, Hippolytus, this conduct was homicide, and Calixtus was responsible for encouraging it.[30] When Novatian broke from Rome because its bishop accepted the repentance of apostates, his foe Cyprian wrote of him that he was himself guilty of serious sin: he had struck his pregnant wife to cause an abortion. He has "committed parricide"; "he has killed a son who was being born."[31] A lawyer like Minucius, Cyprian used the legal term "parricide." The charge of a crime inexpiable in life was no doubt especially effective against a man who denied others an opportunity to repent.

As the Church emerged as a legal religion and a social force in the fourth century, the sentiments on abortion so uniformly expressed in the first two centuries of Christian life took the form of legislation. There already existed a rule excluding from the Church for life women who conceived in fornication and committed an abortion. The Council of Ancyra in 314, a gathering of a dozen Eastern bishops representing Syria and Asia Minor, denounced such women, who "slay what is generated and work to destroy it with abortifacients"; but "more humanely" the Council reduced their penance to ten years.[32] The Council retained the life penance for voluntary homicide, so that the reduction marked a recognition of mitigating circumstances in the character of the crime, while its gravity was indicated by the still severe penalty imposed. In the West, in some contrast, the movement was toward greater sanctions. At Elvira on the Iberian peninsula, a council held in 305 excommunicated women committing abortion after adultery and declared that they were not to be readmitted even at the point of death.[33]

30. HIPPOLYTUS, *Elenchos* 9.12.25, *GCS* 26.250.
31. CYPRIAN, *Epistle* 52, *CSEL* 3².619.
32. Council of Ancyra, canon 21, J. D. MANSI, *Sacrorum conciliorum nova et amplissima collectio* (hereafter MANSI) 2.5.19.
33. Council of Elvira, canon 53, MANSI 2.16.

These laws, like the earlier condemnations, made no distinction between the formed and unformed fetus. In the course of the fourth century this distinction, based for Christians on the Septuagint translation of Exod. 21:22, became a focus for analysis. In the East the *Apostolic Constitutions,* an apocryphal set of apostolic canons from Syria, condemned the killing of a "formed fetus." [34] In the West, St. Jerome explained to a female correspondent, Algasia, that "seeds are gradually formed in the uterus, and it is not reputed homicide until the scattered elements received their appearance and members." [35] Augustine, commenting on a Latin translation from the Septuagint, observed that at Exod. 21 the question of ensoulment was usually raised, and "because the great question about the soul is not to be hastily decided by unargued and rash judgment, the law does not provide that the act pertains to homicide, for there cannot yet be said to be a live soul in a body that lacks sensation when it is not formed in flesh and so not yet endowed with sense." [36] This was a distinction accepted out of a cautious agnosticism on ensoulment; both Jerome and Augustine affirmed that, in fact, man did not know when the rational soul was given by God.[37]

As far as Jerome and Augustine were concerned, the theoretical distinction led to no difference in moral disapprobation. They simply adopted language broad enough to condemn both contraceptive acts and acts destroying the fetus after conception. Jerome wrote to his star pupil Eustochium on how to preserve her virginity among the temptations to adolescents in Rome. He denounced those Christian girls who, saying "all things are pure to the pure," had affairs and sought to prevent or conceal pregnancy. Some "will drink sterility and kill a man not yet born." Others will use potions to commit abortions. These are parricides, and as sometimes the abortifacients are fatal to them, too, they go to judgment thrice condemned as adulteresses, killers of their children, and killers of them-

---

34. *Didiscalia et constitutiones apostolorum* 7.3.2, ed. Francis X. Funk (Paderborn, 1905).

35. *Epistles* 121.4, *CSEL* 56.16.

36. *On Exodus* 21.80, *CSEL* 28².147. The old Latin text spoke of "aborting an immature one," A. E. BROOKE and NORMAN McLEAN, *The Old Testament in Greek* (1909).

37. AUGUSTINE, *De origine animae* 4.4 (PL 44.527); JEROME, *On Ecclesiastes* 2.5.

selves.[38] Here, in the language of Minucius, abortion became parricide, and the age of the fetus was unmentioned.

Augustine in his anti-Pelagian work, *Marriage and Concupiscence*, analyzed abortion with his usual attention to psychology. Using terms that seem to anticipate modern analyses of sadism, he described it as the work of minds characterized by "lustful cruelty" or "cruel lust." Speaking of the married who avoided offspring, he declared, "Sometimes [*Aliquando*] this lustful cruelty or cruel lust comes to this that they even procure poisons of sterility, and if these do not work, they extinguish and destroy the fetus in some way in the womb, preferring that their offspring die before it lives, or if it was already alive in the womb, to kill it before it was born. Assuredly if both husband and wife are like this, they are not married, and if they were like this from the beginning, they come together not joined in matrimony but seduction. If both are not like this, I dare to say that either the wife is in a fashion the harlot of her husband, or he is an adulter with his own wife." [39] Augustine thus condemned three kinds of act: contraception, the killing of the fetus before it is formed or "lives," and the killing of the live fetus. The analysis was a new approach in treating each of these acts as a sin against marriage.[40]

38. JEROME, *Epistle* 22, *To Eustochium* 13, CSEL 54.160–61.
39. AUGUSTINE, *De nuptiis et concupiscentia* 1.15.17, CSEL 42.229–30.
40. In his *El aborto en San Augustino*, Constancio Palomo Gonzalez states that Augustine considered abortion to be homicide and entitles one section of his book "Abortion, A Grave Sin of Homicide According to St. Augustine." However, he cites no text where Augustine so teaches. True, Augustine holds every killing of a man to be homicide, as Gonzalez argues at 217. True, Augustine speaks of the infusion of the soul in the uterus by God. True, for Augustine the distinction between formed and unformed, which he accepted from the Septuagint, was not the same as a distinction between souled and soulless (Gonzalez at 141–142). Speaking of embryos "dead" in the womb, which had to be extracted to prevent the death of the mother, Augustine said he did not dare deny that they had lived (*Enchiridion* c. 86, PL 40.272). In *The City of God*, Augustine declared he found nothing relevant to the resurrection of the dead which did not relate to "those of all kinds who have died in their mothers' wombs" (*De civitate Dei* 22.13). This statement, Gonzalez well notes, supposes the belief that the fetus was ensouled at all stages. But while it may be argued from this belief that Augustine should have called abortion homicide, he did not do so, and his reservation can only reflect his uncertainty about the time of ensoulment.
Stronger language is found in Augustine's old teacher, St. Ambrose, who had denounced the use of a "parricidal potion" of married mothers "to take away life before it is transmitted," *Hexameron* 5.18.58, CSEL 32¹.184. Ambrose, while speaking thus of parricide, had emphasized in particular the cruelty of mothers in destroying their children and invoked the "piety" of birds to their young to rebuke them.

The preservation of life within the womb also became a reason for restricting what St. Paul in the First Epistle to the Corinthians had set out in terms of justice, the right to intercourse within marriage (1 Cor. 7:3–5). Led by Stoic thought to restrict intercourse to procreative purpose alone, many Christian writers prohibited the necessarily nonprocreative intercourse of the pregnant. But an additional reason for the prohibition was found in the danger to the embryo that such intercourse was believed to create. Commenting on the pregnancy of Elizabeth in the Gospel of Luke, Ambrose stated the belief that intercourse in pregnancy "contaminated" the offspring.[41] Even more forcefully, Jerome incorporated a quotation from Seneca vigorously attacking intercourse from "affection," not "judgment," and urging restraint at least in pregnancy, so as not to "destroy the offspring." [42] Thus the risk of abortion became a reason for limiting what St. Paul had described as a duty.

The principal texts quoted from Jerome and Augustine were to be the *loci classici* on abortion in the West. In the East, St. John Chrysostom preached against abortion as encouraged by married men engaged in intercourse with prostitutes: "You do not let a harlot remain only a harlot but make her a murderess as well." [43] In the most definitive statement by a leader of the Greek Christian community, St. Basil of Cappadocia set out in a letter to Amphilocius the standards of the Church as he knew them in the late fourth century. The distinction founded on the Septuagint was rejected: "The hair-splitting difference between formed and unformed makes no difference to us." "Whoever deliberately commit abortion are subject to the penalty for homicide." [44] The penance, however, was that set by Ancyra: ten years. Unlike Ancyra, Basil did not restrict his condemnation to women who conceived in fornication. Like Jerome he noted that often the potions killed the mothers, too. Like the *Didache*, he made his condemnation repetitiously: In general, sodomists, homicides, medicine men (*pharmakoi*), adulterers, and idolaters were condemned together;[45] specifically, those were classed as homicides who "gave abortifacient drugs" (*amblōthridia*

41. *Expositio evangelii secundum Lucam* 1.43–45, CSEL 32⁴.38–39.
42. *Contra Jovinianum* 1.49, in *Seneca: Fragmenta* n. 84, ed. F. G. Haase (Leipzig, 1897). In its original context in Seneca, the injunction not to destroy the offspring could be taken as a warning against abortion of any kind.
43. *Homily 24 on the Epistle to the Romans*, PG 60.626.27.
44. *Letters* 188, PG 32.672.
45. *Id.* at 674.

pharmaka) and those who "receive what entraps the embryo." [46]
Basil's comprehensive summing up on abortion in a document later
characterized as "The Canonical Letter" was to constitute the
fundamental norm on this behavior for the Greek Church.[47]

By 450 the teaching on abortion East and West had been set out
for four centuries with clarity and substantial consistency. There
was a distinction accepted by some as to the unformed embryo,
some consequent variation in the analysis of the sin, and local differences in the penance necessary to expiate it. The sin itself was often
associated with lechery, sometimes with marriage. The usual
method of accomplishing abortion was by drugs, sometimes associated with magic, sometimes with danger to the user. The motive
animating it was seen variously as shame, as avarice, as lust. Although therapeutic and social reasons for abortion were known
from the best of doctors and philosophers, these reasons were never
mentioned as justification. All the writers agreed that abortion was
a violation of the love owed to one's neighbor. Some saw it as a special failure of maternal love. Many saw it also as a failure to have
reverence for the work of God the creator. The culture had accepted abortion. The Christians, men of this Greco-Roman world
and the Gospel, condemned it. Ancient authorities and contemporary moralists had approved, hesitated, made exceptions; the
Christian rule was certain.

III. TRANSMISSION, 450–1450

In the period from 450 to 1100, when monks and bishops were
the chief transmitters of Christian moral ideas, the teaching on abortion was reiterated. It was conveyed by enactments against abortion
by local synods.[48] It was conveyed by collections which contained
the canons of Elvira or the canons of the more prestigious council
of Ancyra. By the eighth century Ancyra was the law of the
Frankish kingdom of Charlemagne.[49] It was conveyed by collec-

46. *Id.* at 678.
47. On the authority of "The Canonical Letter," see J. Gribomont, Introduction
to *PG* 32 (rev. 1960).
48. See ROGER JOHN HUSER, *The Crime of Abortion in Canon Law* 33–39
(Washington, 1942).
49. *Id.* at 21.

tions which contained St. Jerome on homicide by abortifacients.[50] The penitentials developed by the monks for use in hearing confession regularly prescribed specific penances for abortion, ranging from one to ten years for the killing of an embryo.[51] When interrogatories for use in questioning penitents were devised in the tenth century, questions on abortion were included.[52] The early Christian and patristic attitudes were faithfully preserved in the various channels communicating the teaching of past authority and instilling its observance.

Liturgy and Canons

Interest in the conception of the Lord was fostered by popular reflection on the Gospel stories, and the liturgical embodiment of this reflection also played a part in the development of reverence for life in the womb. The December 25th feast of the Nativity of the Lord was established by the late fourth century. By the seventh century in the East a feast was established marking the Annunciation to Mary or "the Conception of Christ." [53] This feast was established on March 25, with the implication that nine months had elapsed between conception and birth, and with the further implication that what had come from the Holy Spirit to Mary had been holy from the moment of conception. The feast of the Conception of Christ, it may be supposed, served, beyond its primary meaning, as a symbol of the sacredness of any conception. In the late sixth century there also came into existence in the East the feast of the Nativity of Mary, fixed on September 8.[54] A century later the feast

50. E.g., in the eighth century, "Simulated Virgins and Their Morals," in *Womanly Questions, Die irische Kanonsammlung*, ed. F. W. H. Wasserscheben (Leipzig, 1885).

51. See NOONAN, *Contraception supra* n. 16, at 164. Some penitentials have lesser penalities for the destruction of what is less than an embryo — apparently a reflection of the old distinction between the formed and the unformed.

52. BURCHARD OF WORMS, "Interrogatory," *Decretum* 19.4, PL 140.972.

53. P. TOSCHI, "Annunziazione," 1 *Enciclopedeia Catholica* 1384. It has been argued that March 25 was fixed first as both the date of conception and the death of Christ. The coincidence of birth and death date on this day was asserted by AUGUSTINE, *De trinitate* 4.5, PL 42.894. However, the better opinion appears to be that Christmas was set on December 25 because that was the winter solstice. See C. SMITH, "Christmas and Its Cycle," 3 *New Catholic Encyclopedia* 656. Accordingly, March 25 would have been set in view of the previously established date for the nativity.

54. FRANCIS DVORNIK, "The Byzantine Church and the Immaculate Conception," in *The Dogma of the Immaculate Conception* 90, ed. E. O. O'Connor (1958).

of Mary's conception by St. Anne was established on December 9 with an elaborate vigil on December 8.[55] The prayers in the office of the day rejected the belief that Mary had been "born after seven months,"[56] an apparent repudiation of the view that her soul was infused after her conception. The feast in honor of Christ's conception could be explained as a feast for a conception of a divine man; but the conception of Mary was believed to be the conception of a human being by the intercourse of humans. The recognition that she deserved honor at conception had specific implication for the humanity of all men.

In the great formative period of Western canon law between 1140 and 1240, and in the course of the contemporary conflict with the Cathars, who opposed all procreation, Augustine on abortion was incorporated in the basic collection of canons made by Gratian. There, in a section devoted to marriage, appeared the Augustinian denunciation of the lustful cruelty of the married who procured abortions. It was now the canon *Aliquando*.[57] Until the new Code of Canon Law in 1917 this text was to instruct all students of the canon law. It was supplemented by Gratian's answer to a question he himself proposed, "Are those who procure an abortion homicides or not?" The answer was supplied by Jerome to Algasia and Augustine on Exodus, quoted earlier, plus a spurious quotation from Augustine which taught expressly that there was "no soul before the form."[58] Clearly, in Gratian, abortion was homicide only when the fetus was formed.

The distinction was reaffirmed in slightly different language by Innocent III. A priest incurred "irregularity," that is, he was suspended from his functions, if he committed homicide. The case was put of a Carthusian monk who in playing had accidentally caused his mistress to abort. Was he irregular? Innocent III held that he was, if the fetus was "vivified." The decretal entered the universal law of the Church in the decretal collection of Gregory IX as the canon *Sicut ex* in the comprehensive section entitled, "Voluntary and Chance Homicide."[59] "Vivified" was treated as the equivalent

55. CORNELIUS A. BOWMAN, "The Immaculate Conception in the Liturgy," *id.* at 115.
56. *Id.* at 117.
57. GRATIAN, *Decretum* 2.32.2.7, in *Corpus juris canonici*, ed. E. Friedberg (Leipzig 1879–1881).
58. *Id.* at 2.32.2.8-10.
59. GREGORY IX, *Decretales* 5.12.20, in *Corpus juris canonici*.

of "ensouled," and the decretal was seen as implying that homicide occurred only after ensoulment had taken place according to the texts furnished by Gratian.[60]

At the same time the decretals of Gregory IX provided a new canon, *Si aliquis*, derived from a tenth-century penitential of Regino of Prüm. *Si aliquis* declared: "If anyone for the sake of fulfilling lust or in meditated hatred does something to a man or a woman, or gives them to drink, so that he cannot generate, or she conceive, or offspring be born, let it be held as homicide." [61] The canon thus applied the penalty for homicide to contraception and to abortion at any stage of fetal life. How was it reconcilable with *Sicut ex?* The usual answer was that *Si aliquis* merely stated that the acts it condemned were to be punished "as homicide." It set the law for all persons. *Sicut ex* added the extra penalty of irregularity for clerics only in the case of true homicide.[62] Thus the ordinary law of *Si aliquis* went beyond what was held to be speculatively true by declaring that, for practical purposes of penance, abortion of any fetus must be put on a par with the killing of a man.

The concern with the sanctions for abortion was not a mere academic exercise. A wide variety of techniques for abortion was provided to medieval physicians and students by the *Canon of Medicine* of Avicenna, translated from Arabic to Latin by Gerard of Cremona about 1150 and thereafter until the middle of the seventeenth century the standard text of European medical schools.[63] Avicenna taught that abortion might sometimes be necessary where birth would endanger the life of the mother. For such cases he set out a list of measures. They included exercise, the carrying of heavy weights, the evacuation of the humors, the insertion by instrument in the matrix of drugs to kill the fetus, and the drinking of various drugs in potions.[64] Baths, excessive exercise, and violent jumping were also observed to be causes of abortion.[65] Abortion

60. *Glossa ordinaria* at 5.12.20.
61. *Decretales* 5.12.5.
62. The explanation of the compiler of the decretals, St. Raymond, in *Summa confessariorum* 2.1.4.
63. CHARLES SINGER and E. ASHWORTH UNDERWOOD, *A Short History of Medicine* 76 (Oxford, 2nd ed. 1962).
64. AVICENNA, "De regimine abortus," book 3, Fen 21, tract 2, c. 12 of *Canon Medicine,* trans. Gerard of Cremona (Venice, 1608). The index of this edition lists drugs which "produce an abortion." The operation producing evacuation of the humors is *phlebotomia,* defined 1.4.20.
65. *Id.* at c. 8, "De abortu."

John T. Noonan, Jr.

was said to be most likely at the beginning and near the approach of birth.[66] A number of the means described were doubtless effective to accomplish their objective. The information about them was communicated by the wide distribution of the *Canon of Medicine* itself and by books deriving their information from it. St. Albert the Great, for example, in his encyclopedic work on plants described the abortifacient properties of several vegetables; writing on animals he told how to accomplish an abortion.[67] His principal source was Avicenna.

The analysis and treatment given by the canon law dominated both canonical and theological treatment of what was not an unknown sin. Many writers, influenced by *Si aliquis*, followed the suggestion of Hostiensis that the use of "poisons of sterility" was "interpretively homicide" in both contraception and early abortion.[68] Among those classifying abortion as a form of homicide were the great lay canonist Joannes Andreae, the Franciscan summists Monaldus and Astesanus, the English canonist William of Pagula, and the German Dominican John Nider.[69] In the same way Chaucer's Parson classified the destruction of the fetus among the sins of wrath.[70]

Theological Analysis

For those who gave more weight to the express canonical texts on ensoulment a different approach to early abortion was necessary. In the standard book of the schools, the *Sentences* of Peter Lombard, the texts chosen by Gratian were repeated. As in Gratian's framework, *Aliquando* formed a central passage in the analysis of the purposes of marriage.[71] The pseudo-Augustinian citation on ensoulment in Gratian was confidently repeated to show that the soul

66. *Id.* at c. 8.
67. ALBERT, *De vegetabilibus et plantis*, in 10 *Opera omnia*, ed. A. Borgnet (Paris 1890–1899), 6.1.16, "Colloquintida"; 6.1.26, "Myrrha"; 6.24, "Coriandrum"; 6.2.17 "Scamonea." *De animalibus*, 11 *Opera omnia* 10.2.2.
68. HOSTIENSIS, *Summa aurea* (Lyons, 1542) 5, "Homicidium" 1.
69. JOANNES ANDREAE, *Novella commentaria in libros decretalium* (Venice, 1581) 5.12; MONALDUS, *Summa perutilis* (Lyons, 1516) f.135 r.; ASTESANUS, *Summa de casibus conscientiae* (Ratisbon, 1780) 8.9. WILLIAM OF PAGULA, *Summa summarum* (Huntington Library, MS 1638), at "Homicidium voluntarium"; JOHN NIDER, *De lepra morali* (Paris, 1490) 2.7.2.
70. *The Canterbury Tales* (ed. F. N. Robinson, 1957), "The Parson's Tale," lines 570–80.
71. PETER LOMBARD, *Libri IV Sententiarum* (Quarrachi, 1916) 4.31.

was not inserted until the body was formed.[72] Peter Lombard him-self observed, "From this it appears that they are homicides who procure an abortion when the fetus is ensouled." [73] The implication left by the *Sentences* from the use of *Aliquando* was that before ensoulment abortion was a sin against marriage. This judgment was explicitly made by St. Albert speaking of use of "the poisons of sterility," the generic term for both contraceptives and abortifa-cients.[74] In his youthful commentary on the *Sentences*, St. Thomas Aquinas treated the use of these drugs as a sin "against nature be-cause even the beasts look for offspring." [75] He did not repeat this analysis again, and it was not in harmony with his later treatment of sins against nature as sins preventing insemination in inter-course.[76] He was clear that there was actual homicide when an en-souled embryo was killed.[77] He was equally clear that ensoulment did not take place at conception.[78] There was sin, but not the sin of destroying a man in destroying the conceptus in its early stage, for "seed and what is not seed is determined by sensation and move-ment"; this phrase seems to mean that, at the early stage, seed is being destroyed, not man.[79] The result was that there was a period of fetal existence where Thomas' later writing did not specify the offense involved in fetal destruction yet where, according to his clear opposition to contraception, he believed a sin was being com-mitted. It was, however, according to both Albert and Thomas, mortal sin to have intercourse in pregnancy with the risk of abor-tion. Moreover, both accepted Avicenna's opinion that such risk was especially acute at the beginning.[80] Hence, even in the early

72. *Id.* at 4.31; 2.18.
73. *Id.* at 4.31.
74. *In Libros IV sententiarum* in *Opera*, vol. xxx, 4.31.18.
75. *In Libros IV sententiarum* ed. Vives (Paris, 1871), 4.31.2.3, "Expositio textus."
76. *Summa theologica* (Leonine ed. Rome, 1882) 2.2.154.11 and 12.
77. *Id.* at 2.2.64.8, reply to objection 2. The topic was "whether one who kills a man by chance incurs the guilt of homicide?" Like the Septuagint version of Exodus, Thomas held that striking a pregnant woman was an illicit deed, and if the death of either the woman or an ensouled fetus followed, it was homicide.
78. That a being does not have a rational soul at conception formed a principal objection for him to the doctrine of the Immaculate Conception of Mary, which he denied, *In libros IV sententiarum* 3.1.1.: she was "sanctified" in the womb, but "when it definitely was, is uncertain."
79. The passage occurs in explaining why Aristotle accepted a lesser evil in accepting abortion, *In octo libros Politicorum* 7.12.
80. ALBERT, *In libros IV sententiarum* 4.31.22; THOMAS, *In libros IV sententiarum* 4.31.2.3, "Expositio textus."

state of pregnancy, they held the life of the fetus more valuable than the obligation of the marital debt.

As for deliberate abortion, Thomas considered only one case where justification was alleged, but it was the case with the greatest appeal in a theologically-oriented society: the case of abortion for the child's own good, abortion to baptize the child. In medieval society this case had the appeal of abortion of a defective child in a modern society. In the medieval case it would have been to prevent the child from suffering eternal loss of happiness, as in the modern case it would be to prevent the child from suffering the loss of secular happiness. Why not "split the mother" and extract the fetus, so that, baptized, he "may be freed from eternal death"? To this appeal Thomas replied, "Evils are not to be done that good may come from them, Romans 3; and therefore a man ought rather to let the infant perish than that he himself perish, committing the criminal sin of homicide in the mother." [81] The text cited from St. Paul was in itself not decisive; the reference was to a rejection by Paul of his opponents' charge that "we do evil that good may come" (Rom. 3:8). What was decisive was the perception that God's providence could not be anticipated by a paternalism which would have permitted man to act as God in determining human life and assuring its salvation.

The case of abortion for the child's own good was rejected. What of abortion to save the mother? Thomas did not face the case expressly, but he posed broader principles of relevance; and, as the case itself was known as a medical problem from Avicenna, it cannot be supposed that he was unaware of the relation of the principles to therapeutic abortion. [82] The question was put, "Is it lawful for someone to kill someone in defending himself?" The case posed was not, as many later interpreters would have it, a case of unjust aggression. When Thomas wanted to characterize the one being killed he used the terms "sinner" and "innocent." [83] Here the one killed was merely "someone." His answer to the question was, "If

81. *In libros IV sententiarum* 1.1.3 ad 4.

82. A leading teacher at Paris in the late twelfth century, Peter Cantor, had condemned the opinion of some that a woman could "procure a poison of sterility" to prevent conception when childbirth would be fatal to her. Peter said simply, "This is prohibited in every case" (*Summa de sacramentis* 350, ed. Jean-A. Dugauquier, Louvain, 1965, III² 463–64). He doubtless had in mind the controlling canons, *Aliquando* and *Si aliquis*.

83. *Summa theologica* 2-2.64. 2. and 6.

someone kills someone in defense of his own life, he will not be guilty of homicide." [84] The conclusion was based on the principle that "nothing prevents there being two effects of a single act." One effect could be "in intention," the other "beyond intention;" and by intention Thomas meant the mental state of the person killing, for the act itself had as *finis operis* the double end of preservation of life and the killing of another. The act was lawful, because "what was intended was the preservation of one's own life." This intention was not sinful, for it is "natural to everyone to preserve himself as far as he can." The justification was necessity. Fornication, for example, was a lesser sin, but was always mortal, for "it is not ordered to the preservation of one's own life from necessity like the act from which homicide sometimes follows." [85] Put another way, every lie is a sin, and homicide is a worse sin than lying; yet, unlike lying, homicide can sometimes be lawfully done "as when a judge kills a thief." Hence one can say, "Homicide imports not the killing of a man;" it imports "the undue killing of a man." You can then conclude, "Homicide is never lawful, although it is sometimes lawful to kill a man." [86]

From these principles, that all killing is not forbidden, that one may lawfully act to preserve one's own life, and that an indifferent act may be justified by a good intention, an argument could be made to justify abortion to save the life of the mother. Much would depend on how absolutely Thomas meant his declaration in other contexts that "in no way is it lawful to kill the innocent." [87] If the statement held literally, it would seem to preclude capital punishment for a repentant thief, who has become innocent, as most men become innocent, by repentance; yet Thomas justified capital punishment. Applying the principle absolutely, he would have held sinful many acts in warfare such as the killing of enemy soldiers who were in good faith or the killing of infants in attacking a fortress. It cannot be said definitively how Thomas would have

84. *Id.* at 2–2.64.7.
85. *Id.* at ad 4.
86. Thomas, *Quodlibeta* 8.14.
87. *Summa theologica* 2.2.64.6. The thrust of this article is the distinction between "sinners" who may be killed by public authority and the "innocent" who may not. In *De malo* he stated, "to kill the innocent imports a determination of evil, and this can never be well done" (*De malo* 13.4 at 11). The remark occurred in a discussion of the intrinsic evil of usury, and it would probably be unwise to read it as applying definitely to every case of killing from necessity.

answered in these cases or in the case of therapeutic abortion to save the mother's life.

In summary, the monks had transmitted the apostolic and patristic prohibition of abortion. The canon law set it out as a universal requirement of Christian behavior. The theologians explored the relation of the law to the theory of ensoulment, but on one basis or another condemned abortion at any point in the existence of the fetus. The prohibition was still absolute. But the basis for weighing the life of the embryo against other values had been laid, and in the next period of development a balance was to be sought.

IV. THE BALANCE OF THE CASUISTS, 1450–1750

Therapeutic Abortion

The work of St. Antoninus of Florence may be taken to mark the beginning of a new era of thought on abortion, for he brought into the main line of moral theology an opinion of an obscure thirteenth-century theologian in favor of abortion to save the mother. His author is another Dominican from Thomas' country, John of Naples, in 1315 teacher at Paris, later holder of a chair of theology at Naples.[88] John based his position on the distinction between the ensouled and unensouled fetus in addressing himself to the duty of the physician. A doctor sinned in giving medicine to cause an abortion "to preserve a pregnant woman" when the fetus was ensouled, for, when "one cannot help one without hurting the other, it is more appropriate to help neither." But if the fetus was not ensouled, then the physician "ought to give such medicine," because "although he impedes the ensoulment of a future fetus, he will not be the cause of death of any man." [89]

It cannot be said that Antoninus adopted this opinion as his own. He quoted it in his treatise on the sins of the different professions and added the remark that, if there was a doubt as to the ensoulment, the physician sinned mortally "because he exposes himself to the risk of mortal sin, that is, to homicide." [90] He had earlier spoken

88. H: HURTER, *Nomenclator literarius theologiae catholicae* (Innsbruck, 1906) 2.537.
89. JOHN OF NAPLES, *Quodlibeta*, as quoted in SILVESTER DA PRIERAS, *Summa summarum quae sylvestrina dicitur* (1518) at "Medicus," 4.
90. *Summa sacrae theologiae* (Venice, 1581) 3.7.2, "The Various Vices of Physicians."

as though all abortion were homicide, though only the killing of the formed embryo was so held by the law.[91] In reciting the opinion of John of Naples he did not withdraw his earlier views, but must have considered that John of Naples' opinion was also probable.

Sixty years later a less important but influential Dominican, Sylvester da Prieras, followed Antoninus' example. He quoted John of Naples with the same caution as to where there was doubt of ensoulment.[92] The leading Dominican moralists, Cajetan and Soto, made no comment of any kind. Then the opinion was formally embraced by Martin Azplicueta, "the doctor of Navarre," the guide in moral questions of three popes, and the leading canonist of the sixteenth century.[93] Where the physician "believed with probability" that the fetus was not ensouled, he was not the cause of death of another.[94] Azplicueta was under Gregory XIII a principal consultor of the Sacred Penitentiary, the Roman tribunal for deciding cases of conscience submitted to confessors, and he noted elsewhere that the rule of the Penitentiary was to treat a fetus over forty days as ensouled.[95] Hence therapeutic abortion was accepted in the case of a fetus under this age.

To this point no one had attempted to set out a complete theoretical defense of therapeutic abortion or to distinguish it from contraception for medical reasons. Defense and distinctions were the work of the great Spanish specialist on marriage, the Jesuit Tomás Sanchez (1550–1610). His theory was highly dependent on his new analysis of the malice of contraception. It was always evil, he argued, to ejaculate semen and prevent it reaching the vagina, because man could not be trusted with "the administration of the seed," for the pleasure experienced was too great to make him a responsible administrator; he might seek this pleasure as his "sovereign good." [96] There was, therefore, an absolute prohibition of acts preventing insemination in intercourse even if the acts were

91. *Id.* at 2.7.8, dealing with abortion by women who had conceived in fornication, adultery, or incest. It is "homicide," but "it is not reputed homicide." In his earlier manual for confessors, he had provided interrogations on abortion.
92. *Summa summarum supra* n. 89.
93. Hurter, *Nomenclator supra* n. 88, at 3.344–347.
94. Navarrus, *Enchiridion seu manuale confessariorium et poenitentiarum*, 3 *Opera* (Lyons, 1594) c. 25, nn. 60–64, "The Sins of Physicians and Surgeons," 4. The printed gloss in this edition added, "John of Naples, St. Antoninus, Sylvester, and commonly."
95. Navarrus, *Consilia*, 5.22, in 4 *Opera* (Rome, 1591).
96. *De sancto matrimonii sacramento* (Venice, 1737) 9.17.15.

necessary for health. The sole exception was in the case of rape. Here the semen emitted was not in possession. To expel it lawfully the victim must act at once. If she did so, she acted as properly as a property owner who was entitled to pursue and strike a thief until he had reached a safe place.[97] In this case, apparently, Sanchez believed there was no risk of abuse of conceding human beings power to dispose of the seed.

With these distinctions made, Sanchez could argue that while the prohibition of contraception was general, the prohibition of abortion had exceptions. The conceptus, in the intermediate state between being semen and being an ensouled human, was open to attack. *Si aliquis* applied only if the abortion was to hide sin or further lust. Where the mother would otherwise die, and the fetus was not ensouled, its killing, "more probably," was lawful.[98] In this case, "the fetus invades, and, as it were, attacks." The fetus was described not as unjust, but as dangerous. Unlike contraception, there was no administration of the seed, no danger of "too great delight." Moreover, where contraception was urged for health, there was no present attacker, and the alternative of abstinence was available. Here, by hypothesis, destruction of the attacker alone could meet the danger.[99]

Having set up the strongest case, Sanchez considered three more difficult extensions. Suppose the girl had conceived in unlawful coitus and her relatives would probably kill her if they discovered that she was pregnant. Might she kill the fetus to save her life? Again Sanchez thought it more probable that she could. Suppose she was betrothed to one other than the man who had impregnated her, could not without scandal terminate the engagement, and ran the risk of bearing another's child to her husband. Could she avert the danger by destruction of the embryo? Sanchez believed she could.[100] There was, too, no mortal sin in intercourse just after conception, where the medical biology of the day indicated that the risk of abortion was high. The intercourse itself was lawful; the loss of "the unformed matter" was not "such a great loss" as to be mortal sin.[101] In contrast, if an abortion were merely to protect a

97. *Id.* at 2.22.17.
98. Sanchez, *De sancto matrimonii sacramento* at 9.20.9.
99. *Id.* at 9.20.8, 11-12.
100. *De sancto matrimonii sacramento* at 9.20.11.
101. *Id.* at 9.22. On this point Sanchez followed his Dominican contemporary PEDRO DE LEDESMA, *De magno matrimoniae sacramento* (Venice, 1595) 64.1.4.

girl's reputation, the peril was too remote, the fetus not an attacker, and abortion would be unjustified.[102] It was apparent that once other values were allowed to be weighed against the embryo's life, fine scales indeed were necessary to make a just balance.

The subhuman character of the unensouled fetus authorized man to prefer other values to its existence. What of the ensouled fetus where medicines necessary for the mother's health would endanger it? Sanchez made a distinction. If the means "tended directly" to killing the embryo, as would its wounding or beating or the use of poisonous drugs directed to its death, they were not lawful. Nor were they lawful if there were a doubt as to the ensoulment of the fetus, for "it is intrinsically evil to procure the death of the innocent or to expose oneself to the risk of doing so." [103] But other means which endangered the embryo also served the health of the mother. These included the opening of her veins, the cleansing of the uterus, baths — all listed by Avicenna as abortifacient. Sanchez held that they were lawful even if they were equally directed to the killing of the fetus and the salvation of the mother, for she "principally intends her own life." She was not bound under pain of sin to prefer the embryo's physical life to her own. Charity did require that she sacrifice herself only if the child could be born and baptized and so assured of spiritual life; but that the infant could be born if the mother died "is very rare and morally impossible."

To justify his conclusion Sanchez invoked the passage from St. Thomas on the double effect of an act of killing which saved one's life. There was, it would seem, a failure to take this passage as far as it logically might have carried, for by itself it implied the rightfulness of any abortion necessary to save life. As necessarily must often happen in moral reasoning, Sanchez checked this logical implication by assigning a higher value to innocent life where the means used were such as only to harm it. The distinction he made was not logical, but the point at which he struck a balance. By his statement on means which equally served the mother and killed the fetus, he made the intention of the mother, not the *finis operis*, decisive.

Sanchez buttressed this application of Thomistic principle by analogy drawn from the scholastic theory of the just war. In a just

102. *De sancto matrimonii sacramento* at 9.20.9.
103. *Id.* at 9.20.7, 13.

war, "when a city is burnt in which it is established that there are many innocent such as infants," the burning is lawful, "as experience teaches and as all state in the treatise on war." In the case proposed, "just war is waged against lethal humors by applying medicine." The argument was confirmed by commonsense analogy: If a pregnant woman were attacked by a bull, she could run though running caused an abortion; so here she could use the means necessary to save her life.[104]

These illustrations, like Thomas Aquinas' original example, each involved an act where one end or intention of the act itself was the killing of an innocent human being. Another example of the same sort, approved by the acute Belgian Jesuit, Leonard Lessius, was the killing of an infant in escaping from an enemy threatening one's life. It was, Lessius taught, lawful to step on and kill an infant who was in the route of escape. He quoted Cajetan commenting on Thomas, "to kill the innocent *per accidens*, by doing a lawful and necessary act is not against a natural, divine, or human law." [105] With this principle generally accepted, it was not a serious restriction on therapeutic abortion for Lessius to take a different path from Sanchez on the killing of the unensouled fetus. Not "condemning" the opinion of "our Sanchez," Lessius reached a different formal result in that case, because he did not accept the explanation Sanchez gave why contraception was prohibited. The common opinion of moralists was that contraception was wrong because it was "against the nature of generation." Accepting this approach, Lessius concluded that abortion was even more "against the nature of generation." Consequently, one could not deliberately act for this purpose.[106] But the practical result was the same as Sanchez's, for Lessius simply extended to all therapeutic abortion what Sanchez had reserved for the ensouled embryo. For a mother to take medicine to save her life was lawful, provided the killing of the fetus was "beyond her intention." Indeed Lessius explicitly recognized that he thus reached the same result as Antoninus and Sylvester; what they meant, he said, was that the killing was lawful as long as there was no "direct intention" to kill. From the exam-

104. *De sancto matrimonii sacramento* at 9.20.13–17.
105. LEONARD LESSIUS, *De iustitia et iure* (Lyons, 1653) 2.9.2.58. The quotation from Cajetan was taken from CAJETAN, *In summam theologicam S. Thomas Aquinatis* 2.2.76.2.
106. LESSIUS, 2.9.10.61.

ples given, it was evident that "direct intention" was distinguished from "indirect intention" or killing "per accidens," not by the physical acts which were done, but by the dominant purpose of the mother; the intent to kill was indirect if the dominant purpose was to save her own life.

Almost a century and a half later, when St. Alfonso de' Liguori made his masterly summation of the work of the casuists, he reached the conclusion of Lessius. Under the general heading, "Is it sometimes licit to kill the innocent?" and under the specific heading, "Is it sometimes lawful to procure an abortion?" he held that Sanchez's opinion permitting the intentional killing of the unformed fetus to save the mother was a probable opinion. But the "more common opinion" held that as it was never licit to expel the seed, even in rape, "so much less is it lawful to expel the fetus which is closer to human life." The more common opinion was "safer" and therefore to be followed.[107] Moreover, there was no point to the first opinion because, "as our Father Busenbaum says, 'Why take a drug directly to expel the fetus when one can—and it suffices — expel it indirectly?' " The reference to Busenbaum was to the German Jesuit whose treatise on moral theology was the text taken by Liguori for his own exposition of doctrine. Busenbaum, quoted by Liguori, had further taught that if it is judged that the mother of an ensouled embryo will die unless she takes medicine fatal to the fetus, "it is lawful to take it, and, according to some she is bound to take it, intending directly only her own health, although indirectly and consequently the fetus is destroyed." [108]

In principle, then, lawfulness turned on the mother's intention. But the logic of one principle never rules the solution of a complex moral problem. Like Sanchez, Liguori introduced the distinction of means "tending directly" to kill the fetus, such as blows and wounding, and held those illicit while allowing the cutting of the mother's veins, purging of her body, and baths. Moreover, the threat to the mother's life had to be immediate. The danger of death in childbirth was "far distant," the fetus was not a "present aggressor," and abortion was not justified to avert the danger; a fortiori, the danger of being killed by relatives was not justification

107. LIGUORI, *Theologia moralis*, in *Opera omnia*, ed. L. Gaudé (Rome, 1905), book 3, n. 394.
108. *Id.*

31

for the mother. With these reservations stated, therapeutic abortion to save the mother from immediate danger was permitted; the intention to save her own life must predominate; only some means were permitted. The balance struck by the casuists and now set out by St. Alfonso treated the embryo's life as less than absolute, but only the value of the mother's life was given greater weight.

Papal Legislation

The tendency of casuistic examination of abortion had been to question the absolute prohibition. An opposite tendency, to reinforce the prohibition, may be discerned in the legislative activity of the papacy. The difference between legislation and speculation was at least as old as the *Decretals* of Gregory IX, where *Si aliquis* took a far stronger stand on abortion of the unformed fetus than the majority of contemporary theorists did. The same split may be observed in the nineteenth and twentieth centuries between legislative severity and theoretical hesitancy. The difference does not lie in the difference between canonists and theologians; instances of canonists on the softer speculative side and theologians on the harder legislative side are not rare.[109] The difference seems to lie in the work being done. The tendency of the legislator has been prudential or paternalistic, seeking to safeguard as strongly, certainly, and absolutely as possible the rights of the embryo unable to defend itself.

In the period of the great casuists there were two bursts of this legislative prudence. One occurred in the reforming reign of Sixtus V and reflected not so much a prudential concern for the embryo as a split of judgment as old as Ancyra and Elvira. Although *Si aliquis* had been canon law for over three hundred years, the Sacred Penitentiary by the time of Gregory XIII did not treat as homicide the killing of an embryo under 40 days. Even where the embryo over 40 days was sinfully destroyed, the Penitentiary made less difficulty about dispensations than when an adult human was killed. The reason was not that the older embryo was regarded as subhuman, but the influence of the canon *Sicut ex* and the observation that an embryo was rarely killed in hatred. The cases

---

109. See, for example, *supra*, sec. III, the split on interpretation of *Si aliquis*. For later example note that the theologians of the Holy Office were taking a hard legislative line, while moralists were taking a soft speculative one, *infra*, sec. V.

regularly involved women who had conceived in fornication and killed to protect their reputations and men who counselled them to do so to save their own. Like Ancyra, the Penitentiary saw the motive of protecting reputation as extenuation.[110]

Sixtus V had another view, the view of Elvira, that abortion as an adjunct to fornication intensified the evil. In the course of a campaign largely aimed at prostitution in Rome, on October 29, 1588, he issued the bull *Effraenatam*. The pope invoked *Aliquando* and asked rhetorically, "Who would not punish such cruel lust with the most severe punishments?" The bull went on to provide that all the penalties of both canon and secular law against homicide were to apply to those producing an abortion, whatever the age of the fetus, and to those practicing contraception by drug. The old exception on irregularity of *Sicut ex* was wiped out. No exception was mentioned for therapeutic abortion. Persons guilty of the crime were excommunicated, and absolution from the excommunication was reserved to the Holy See alone.[111]

Effraenatam was not an unqualified success. The reservation of absolution to the Holy See created administrative difficulties. The bull clashed with the practice of the Penitentiary and the theory of the canonists and theologians. Sixtus V had not been dead long when, in 1591, Gregory XIV restricted the bull. Noting suavely that "the hoped-for fruit" had not resulted, the new pope repealed all its penalties except those applying to a fetus which had been ensouled.[112] The bull was not cited in the controversy on therapeutic abortion. The legislative incursion into the field had not changed the theologians' balance.

Almost a century later the papacy acted again in the area. Its intervention this time was the fruit of the efforts of conservative theologians centered at Louvain to check what they deplored as "laxism" in moral theology.[113] After a theological and a cardinalatial commission had examined one hundred propositions taken from a variety of theological treatises and delated to Rome by

110. Navarrus, *Consilia supra* n. 95, at 5.22.
111. *Effraenatam, Codicis iuris fontes,* ed. P. Gasparri (Rome, 1927) vol. 1, p. 308. On the bull's relation to prostitution, see NOONAN, *Contraception supra* n. 16, at 362–63.
112. *Sedes apostolica, Codicis iuris fontes* I, 330–331.
113. On the history of the Louvain efforts, see FRANCIS DEININGER, *Joannes Sinnich: der Kampf der Louvener Universität gegen den Laxismus* 53 (Düsseldorf, 1938).

Louvain, the Holy Office under Innocent XI issued a condemnation on March 2, 1679. Sixty-five propositions were condemned, of which two related to abortion:

> 34. It is lawful to procure abortion before ensoulment of the fetus lest a girl, detected as pregnant, be killed or defamed.
> 35. It seems probable that the fetus (as long as it is in the uterus) lacks a rational soul and begins first to have one when it is born; and consequently it must be said that no abortion is homicide.

The 65 propositions were globally designated by the Holy Office as "at least scandalous and in practice dangerous." [114] The censure, therefore, at the minimum bore on the prudence of teaching the propositions, not on their abstract truth. What were rejected was Sanchez' opinion that danger of death from relatives was ground for abortion and the opinion of "the prince of laxists," Juan Caramuel y Lobkowicz, on the time of ensoulment. [115] The main line of casuistic thought on therapeutic abortion was unmentioned and unaffected. Outer limits of permissible teaching were, however, established in practice by the decree.

Opinion on Ensoulment

A stream of thought distinct from papal authority also began in the seventeenth century, without immediate effect but with ultimate significance for the view of abortion. It came from medical doctors versed in philosophy. The title of the first work of the new approach summarizes its content: *A Book on the Formation of the Fetus in which It Is Shown that the Rational Soul Is Infused on the Third Day.* It was written by a physician at Louvain, Thomas Fienus, and appeared in 1620. [116] A year later there was an even more influential treatise, *Medico-Legal Questions*, by a Roman physician, Paolo Zacchia. In his learned treatise on medical aspects of the canon and civil laws Zacchia attacked the prevailing interpretation of Aristotle which envisioned the fetus progressing by

---

114. *Enchiridion symbolorum definitionum et declarationum re rebus fidei et morum*, ed. H. Denzinger, rev. Adolf Schönmetzer (Barcelona, 1963). Hereafter Denzinger.

115. CARAMUEL Y LOBKOWICZ, *Theologia moralis fundamentalis libri* (Lyons, 1675).

116. See (Anonymous) "De animatione foetus," 11 *Nouvelle revue théologique* 182 (1879).

stages from vegetable ensoulment to animal ensoulment to rational ensoulment. This "metamorphosis of souls," he declared, was "an imaginary thing." [117] Belief that the rational soul was in fact instilled after forty days rested on no evidence that the rational soul was then in operation; nor could the movement of the fetus have any significance in showing the presence of a rational soul. Those who argued that there was a rational soul at some time in the embryo, but at some time after conception, were thus entangled in "absurdities" in trying to show the basis of their conviction. On the contrary, a true Thomistic view of the unity of man required that there be a single human soul from the beginning of the existence of a new fetus.[118] The rational soul, Zacchia argued, must be "infused in the first moment of conception." [119]

Zacchia's thesis on ensoulment was well received, and he himself in 1644 received from Innocent X the grand title of "General Proto-Physician of the Whole Roman Ecclesiastical State." In 1658 Geronimo Florentinio of the Congregation of the Mother of God brought out a work entitled *Baptisms of Doubtful Men,* in which he argued that a fetus should be baptized if it was taken from the mother's womb before forty days. In the next thirty years the thesis of Florentinio was found unobjectionable by the theological faculties of Paris, Vienna, Prague, and Rheims. Delated to the Roman tribunal of the Index of Prohibited Books, the treatise was declared blameless if Florentinio added that no one was bound under pain of mortal sin to baptize a fetus under forty days.[120]

The theory of Zacchia had no immediate impact on the theologians dealing with abortion. He himself in answering objections to his novel proposition agreed that the "milder" opinion of the canons could be followed as to punishment for abortion of a fetus under forty days; a "greater injury" was done in killing an older embryo.[121] The theologians themselves were slow to respond to the new arguments. By the eighteenth century Constantino Roncaglia of the Congregation of the Mother of God contended in analyzing the sin of abortion that it was "most probable" that the fetus was ensouled at the instant of conception or "at least from the third or

117. *Quaestiones medico-legales* (Lyons, 1701) 9.1.
118. *Id.* at 9.5.
119. *Id.* at 9.1.
120. "De animatione foetus" *supra* n. 116, at 182.
121. ZACCHIA, *Quaestiones supra* n. 117, at 9.5.

seventh day." [122] But the leading moralist of the day, St. Alfonso, declared that "some say badly" that the soul is infused at conception.[123] He preferred to rely on the Septuagint translation of Exodus, which Zacchia had dismissed as "a commentary" which was not Scripture, and to hold it "certain" that the there was not immediate ensoulment.

Another trend with long-run, rather than immediate, implications was the growing cult of the Immaculate Conception of Mary and the increase in theological and papal support for this doctrine. Zacchia used the argument from its liturgical celebration in favor of his contention. The Catholic Church, he said, celebrated the conception of Mary, who was conceived according to the flesh; it did not celebrate the coming into existence of what was "brute, corruptible, and mortal." [124] When, in 1701, Clement XI made the Immaculate Conception a feast of universal obligation in the Church, belief in immediate ensoulment of all human beings received indirect support and encouragement.

The three strands of thought — the pastoral-legislative interest in a sure and certain protection of the embryo, the medical-philosophical rejection of a "metamorphosis of souls" in the stages of fetal development, the popular liturgical devotion to the Immaculate Conception — all represented powerful impulses destined to affect the conclusions drawn by the casuists from their abstract and narrow consideration of cases of therapeutic abortion. As of 1750, however, it was the balance struck by the casuists which dominated the teaching on abortion.

V. CARE FROM CONCEPTION, 1750–1965

In the course of the next two centuries the teaching of the Church developed to an almost absolute prohibition of abortion. This development represented a substantial return to the patristic prohibition without the glosses and exceptions written in by

122. *Universale moralis theologia ad usum confessariorum* (Lucca, 1834) 11.1.2.3.

123. LIGUORI, *Theologia moralis* 6.394. Elsewhere, on baptism, he said that an aborted fetus was also to be baptized conditionally, "especially since today there flourishes the opinion, received not without approbation from experts, that the fetus from the beginning of conception, or at least after several days, is informed by a soul," 6.121.

124. *Quaestiones supra* n. 117, at 9.5.

casuistry; but it was not a naïve invocation of the past; it was a conscious rejection of some solutions which had once been appealing. Hence, it was development — a testing of principles by human experience in the light of the Gospel and a reformulation of doctrine after this testing. Like other developed Christian teaching on slavery, on the rights of labor, on war, it embodied a sensitivity to certain values affirmed in the Gospel but not made effective in Roman, medieval, or post-Reformation culture.

In the formation of teaching, the pastoral interest of the papacy played a strong part; and it was the central authority of the Church, far more prestigious in moral matters in the period 1880–1950 than ever before in its history, which dominated the development. The moral theologians and canonists bent to the papal leadership which, while reflecting the view of moral theologians, incorporated a broader sense of situation and likely trends and dangers. In 1588 Sixtus V, the most energetic of popes, could do nothing to change the views of the dominant moralists; beginning with the papacy of Leo XIII the moralists, in this area of thought, followed the papal lead.

Sensitivity to Life

The pastoral concern to protect the embryo was particularly animated by the spread of abortion in Western Europe. As early as 1795, the Marquis de Sade had attacked restrictions on abortion as the result of religious superstition and had exulted in the delight of destroying an embryo.[125] His book, the first in Western Europe to praise abortion, carried a revolutionary destructiveness to the ultimate, and his special temper was not universal; but in a similar spirit of freedom from religious bonds, many Frenchmen practiced birth control during the last quarter of the eighteenth century, and the French birth rate declined precipitously.[126] While contraception by coitus interruptus probably accomplished much of the reduction, it was the opinion of observers that abortion often supplemented ineffective contraception.[127] By the twentieth century, the number

125. ALPHONSE DE SADE, *La philosophie dans le boudoir* c. 2. De Sade, in passing, contended that France was overpopulated and that the "Chinese" practice of abandoning infants was desirable; but these themes were subordinated to his general celebration of unrestrained lust and cruelty as rational.

126. CHARLES H. POUTHAS, *La Population française pendant la première moitié du 19e siècle* 21 (Paris, 1956).

127. JACQUES BERTILLON, *La Dépopulation de la France* 240-244 (Paris, 1911).

of abortions, though hard to establish because of their criminal and therefore secret character, was believed to be large in such nominally Christian countries as France, Switzerland, and Italy.[128]

Against the current in favor of abortion, the Church reacted. In part, its position became sharper and stronger because of a development of the teaching on ensoulment. The Aristotelian interpretation of gestation, which supposed a transformation from vegetable soul to rational soul occurring in the embryo, had become obsolete. Even in the eighteenth century medical opinion had rejected it.[129] In the nineteenth century the theologians, who had been slow to surrender a theory with so many famous supporters, inclined now to the idea of Zacchia. Both theological and biological developments affected their confidence in the old forty-day–eighty-day formula. In 1854 Pius IX proclaimed as a dogma of the Catholic Church that Mary was free from sin "in the first instant of her conception." [130] The new dogma dealt the old formula a glancing if not fatal blow. Meanwhile, educated European opinion could not accept Aristotelian biology in the light of the new discoveries in biology. Karl Ernest von Baer in 1827 had discovered the ovum in the human female; by 1875 the joint action of spermatozoon and ovum in generation had been determined. A change in organism was seen to occur at the moment of fertilization which distinguished the resultant from the components. It was easier to mark this new organism off from the living elements which had preceded it than it was to mark it off from some later stage of its organic growth in the uterus. If a moment had to be chosen for ensoulment, no convincing argument now appeared to support Aristotle or to put ensoulment at a late stage of fetal life.

The slowly changing attitude can be seen in the standard works. The most popular manual for seminary instruction in the nineteenth century was the *Compendium of Moral Theology* of the French Jesuit Jean Gury. The book was largely a succinct presentation of St. Alfonso de' Liguori, and in mid-nineteenth century Gury said, "The fetus, although not ensouled, is directed to the forming of

128. See, e.g., ROBERT TALMY, *Histoire du mouvement familial en France 1896–1939*, at 106, 210–212 (Aubenas, 1962); FEDERICO MARCONCINI, *Culle vuote* 210–211 (Alba, 1945); Bishops of Switzerland, "Le Droit à la vie," 55 *Documentation catholique* 205 (1958).
129. See "De animatione foetus" *supra* n. 116, at 184.
130. *Ineffabilis Deus*, Denzinger at 1641.

man; therefore its ejection is anticipated homicide." [131] In 1869, in the constitution *Apostolicace sedis*, Pius IX dropped the reference to the "ensouled fetus" in the excommunication for abortion, so that the excommunication now seemed to include the abortion of any embryo. An implicit acceptance of immediate ensoulment was found in the action: "otherwise it would be making an old law more onerous, which is contrary to the intent of the constitution." [132] Thereafter, Thomas Gousset in his work for the practical instruction of confessors treated immediate ensoulment as the opinion to be followed, so that all abortions were homicides. [133] Augustine Lehmkuhl, the German Jesuit who was perhaps the ablest of the nineteenth-century moralists, taught that abortion is "true homicide," "as follows from what is today the more common opinion that teaches that every fetus is ensouled with a rational soul." [134]

In the twentieth century vigorous champions of the old theory could still be found. The most influential was Arthur Vermeersch, the Belgian Jesuit who was to be the principal draftsman of *Casti connubii*. No "solid arguments," he maintained, proved the immediate infusion of the soul. [135] However, a more modern writer and the most persuasive of moral theologians of postwar Europe, Bernard Häring, taught that the teaching of Aristotle had but "slight probability" and that, consequently, "every abortion is murder." In keeping with this approach, Häring condemned as abortion the use of intrauterine devices if their use was to prevent nidation of the fertilized ovum. As long as contraception was not accepted by the Church, the time of ensoulment did not determine whether a sin was committed. If some form of contraception were to be accepted by the Church, the line between contraception and abortion would be highly important to draw. The tendency, reflected by Häring's work, was to draw the line at conception. [136]

131. *Compendium theologia moralis* (1864 ed.), "De praeceptis decalogi," n. 402.

132. "De animatione foetus" *supra* n. 116, at 186. A commentary on *Apostolicae Sedis* in the same magazine (p. 331), however, contended that the old distinction stood.

133. *Théologie morale à l'usage des curés et des confesseurs* n. 621 (Paris, 1874 ed.).

134. 1 *Theologia moralis* n. 840 (Freiburg i. Br., 5th ed., 1888).

135. 2 *Theologia moralis* n. 622 (Bruges, 1924).

136. BERNARD HÄRING, 3 *The Law of Christ* 206, trans. by Edward Kaiser from the 7th German ed. (New York, 1966).

John T. Noonan, Jr.

Catholic theologians had defended the right to kill in defense of property of great importance to the owner.[137] By analogy, would it be right to kill a fetus endangering some substantial economic good? There were two difficulties in applying the analogy. First, a mother stood in a fiduciary relation to her child. To kill the child in defense of the mother's interests was to be faithless to a trust. Second, the child in the womb was peculiarly helpless in a way that distinguished him from all older aggressors against property; he had no way of escape if death was to be inflicted for his aggression. For these reasons, the analogy with the defense of property was not developed to justify the killing of the fetal aggressor against some good less than life.[138]

The changed view of ensoulment could be seen as part of a broader humanistic movement of the nineteenth and twentieth centuries to be more sensitive to the value of life. This sensitivity, indeed, was heightened as more terrible ways of destroying life were perfected. In the twentieth century much of the old casuistry on killing appeared obsolete because of its narrow focus on a few facts of a case and its insensitivity to life. In particular, the Catholic teaching on the just war which had provided a substantial analogy for abortion began to be questioned. By 1965 the Second Vatican Council could call for an "examination of war with an entirely new mind" and could declare the indiscriminate bombing of cities (which had been a usual act in World War II) to be "a crime against God and man." [139] In the very long run, the slowly shifting approach to what was lawful in the killing of adults would presumably have a reinforcing effect on the Church's desire to protect embryonic life.

Papal Rulings

To speak of this twentieth-century trend is to anticipate. In the period between 1850 and 1965, the pastoral activity of the papacy carried the main burden of protective measures. It acted through the canon law, through the rulings of the Holy Office, and through public teaching. The 1869 extension of excommunication, the final sanction of the Church, has been noted. The new Code of Canon

137. Liguori, *Theologia moralis* 3.383.
138. Compare Häring, *Law of Christ supra* n. 136 with Charles E. Curran, *A New Look at Christian Morality* 242 (Notre Dame, 1968).
139. SECOND VATICAN COUNCIL, *Gaudium et spes* 80.

40

Law in 1917 made a further extension. Because of the special phrasing of the original bull of excommunication. *Effraenatam* of Sixtus V, it had been argued that the excommunication did not apply to the mother herself who sought or consented to an abortion, although it did to the doctor and other principals in abortion.[140] In 1917 the new Code of Canon Law specifically included "mothers" in those excommunicated for procuring an abortion.[141]

A hardening position on the medical cases was initiated with a series of responses from the Holy Office running from 1884 to 1902. The old casuistry on therapeutic abortion had existed in the teeth of *Effraenatam* which, by its terms, made no exceptions. In the midst of keen debate in Roman theological circles, the Holy Office began to eliminate the exceptions. After consideration of the case for several years, it declared in 1889 that it was not "safe" to teach in Catholic schools that a craniotomy necessary to save the mother's life was lawful, although without it both mother and child would die.[142] It extended this ruling to any operation "directly killing the fetus." [143] In 1895 it dealt not with the "safeness" of teaching but the moral "safeness" of an actual operation. The question asked of the Holy Office concerned a doctor who, to save a mother from "certain and imminent death," used means which do not "per se and directly tend to the killing of the fetus in the maternal breast but act only so that the fetus will, if possible, be extracted alive, although it will soon die as it is entirely immature." The Holy Office declared that the operation might not safely be performed; on July 25, 1895, this answer was personally approved by Leo XIII.[144]

In 1898 the Holy Office declared that if birth was not possible

140. The prevailing view was that *Effraenatam* intended to apply to the mother, but that as the opposite interpretation was "probable," the benign view had to be observed in practice. "Avortement," 1 *Dictionnaire de théologie catholique* 2651.

141. *Codex juris canonici*, c.2350. Canon 985 suspends any priests procuring abortion of a "human fetus."

142. To the Archbishop of Lyons, May 31, 1889. Denzinger, n. 1889. As recently as November 28, 1872, the Sacred Penitentiary, when asked if a craniotomy could be actually performed, had answered, "Consult approved authors, old and new, and act prudently." Old approved authors like Sanchez probably could have been interpreted to authorize the operation to save the mother's life.

143. To the Archbishop of Cambrai, August 19, 1889. Denzinger, n. 1890. The questions, submitted in 1886, are printed in full in T. LINCOLN BOUSCAREN, *Ethics of Ectopic Operations* 183–186 (Chicago, 1933).

144. To the Archbishop of Cambrai, July 24, 1895. Denzinger, n. 1890a.

because of the mother's "tightness," it was not licit to provoke an abortion. Where there was an extrauterine pregnancy, a laparotomy was lawful "to extract the ectopic conceptus from the breast of the mother, provided that, to the extent possible, serious and appropriate provision is made for the life of the fetus and mother." [145] Was it lawful, the theologians of Montreal asked, to extract an ectopic fetus under six months? In 1902 the Holy Office answered, "No, according to the decree of May 4, 1898, by force of which the life of the fetus, to the extent possible, must be seriously and appropriately provided for." It added that both decrees meant that the operation could not be performed except at a time and by means according to whose "ordinary results" both lives would be provided for.[146] If this decree were taken literally, even the ectopic exception to the abortion rule was eliminated.[147] Read together, the Holy Office decrees turned back even the most appealing exceptions to the inviolability and independent integrity of the embryo.

The answers of the Holy Office, in the first instance, instructed bishops and theologians, and only through them the priests and people; considerable caution was urged by the theologians on confessors in disturbing the good faith belief of doctors performing therapeutic abortions that they were acting rightly.[148] A split developed between the teaching of the theologians and the medical schools. In 1924 the leading Catholic moralist, Vermeersch, recognized this conflict and wished for "perspicuous statements of authority by

145. To the Archbishop of Sinaloa, Mexico, May 4, 1898. Denzinger, n. 1890b.
146. To the Dean of the Faculty of Theology of the University of Montreal, March 5, 1902. Denzinger, n. 1890c.
147. The morality of aborting an ectopic pregnancy had been presented by three of the six questions raised by the Archbishop of Cambrai in 1886. The general, negative response by the Holy Office in 1886 had made no distinction between abortion in this case and other cases of therapeutic abortion. In 1892, however, the morality of the ectopic case was debated as a "new" question in the *Ecclesiastical Review.* Joseph Aertyns denied that abortion was lawful here, *Ecclesiastical Review* 10.62; Thomas Sabetti argued that the ectopic fetus could be treated as a "materially unjust aggressor" and destroyed, *ibid.* 9.347; Lehmkuhl defended the practice as "indirect" abortion, *ibid.* 10.62. The controversy continued in Rome with A. Eschbach, rector of the French Seminary in Rome, attacking Lehmkuhl for not accepting the Holy Office decisions of 1884, 1886, and 1889, "Casu de ectopicus seu extra-uterinus conceptus," 2 *Analecta Ecclesiastica* 88 (1894). Lehmkuhl vigorously defended himself, *id.* at 220 and 321. When the 1895 decree appeared, the editors of *Analecta Ecclesiastica* asserted that the question had been decisively determined against Lehmkuhl, *ibid.* 3.482. The question, however, was not explicitly answered until 1902, and the 1902 decree did seem to foreclose all discussion. But, as will be seen, this was not the last word.
148. See LEHMKUHL, 1 *Theologia moralis supra* n. 134, at n. 1002.

which the consciences of Catholics could be firmly directed." [149] This supposed need to speak forcefully to Catholic doctors formed part of the pressure for a papal statement, which was in fact made in 1930. There were also general reasons for a public statement to a wide audience. Advocates were now appearing for the right of women to dispose of the fetus as part of her body; abortion was seen by some as a liberty of the modern woman. [150] In revolutionary Russia abortion had been legalized; other countries were considering permissive legislation. To dissipate the doubts of Catholic doctors, to answer the champions of abortion, to speak to the legislators, to reach the widest possible audience, it seemed necessary for the pope to speak. The opportunity was presented when, specifically responding to the new Anglican teaching on contraception, Vermeersch and Franz Hürth prepared an encyclical on Christian marriage. This small summa on Christian marriage, a synthesis of many basic theses of Christian teaching on human sexuality, was issued by Pius XI on December 31, 1930. It contained sharp condemnation of abortion in general and of abortion as practiced by three specific kinds of people.

The encyclical spoke of "that most grave crime by which the offspring hidden in the maternal breast is attacked." Speaking first of those who justified it by medical and therapeutic indications, the pope asked, "What cause can ever avail to excuse in any way the direct killing of the innocent? For it is a question of that. Whether it is inflicted on mother or on offspring, it is against the commandment of God and the voice of nature, 'You shall not kill. The life of each is sacred'." The argument that the state could authorize the taking of life did not apply; the state had power only over criminals. The argument that the mother could treat the fetus as an unjust aggressor did not apply, "for who will call an innocent little one an unjust aggressor?" As for what had been the usual defense in writers such as Sanchez, the encyclical, without adverting to contrary authority, simply denied that "there is a law of extreme necessity which can lead to the direct killing of the innocent." [151]

Then there were those who practiced abortion in marriage to prevent offspring. They were described as "wicked." Against them

---

149. VERMEERSCH, 2 *Theologia moralis supra* n. 135, at n. 630.
150. HAVELOCK ELLIS, 6 *Studies in the Psychology of Sex* 607 (1924).
151. PIUS XI, *Casti connubii, Acta apostolicae sedis* 22.562 (1930).

Pius XI invoked the ancient words of *Aliquando* and upbraided them for their "lustful cruelty" or "cruel lust." [152]

Finally, there were the advocates of abortion on social and eugenic grounds. Their arguments were analyzed as saying that some persons could be involuntarily sacrificed for the good of others. The "killing of the innocent" for such reasons was "contrary to the divine commandment promulgated also by the words of the Apostle, 'Evils are not to be done in order that good comes from them'." Like St. Thomas on the "salvific abortion" of a fetus to baptize it, Pius XI invoked Rom. 3:8, which was now given the status of a divine command. The independent destiny of the fetus, not to be destroyed for its own good or the good of others, was thus asserted.

The encyclical showed considerable concern with the actions of public authority. German law could be interpreted to make a doctor liable if he did not save the mother by a therapeutic abortion.[153] Not referring to this by name the pope observed that public authority could not confer a right to dispose of innocent life. Rather, the legislators had a serious obligation to defend the innocent by "laws and sanctions." They were prophetically reminded that if they permitted embryos to be killed by doctors or others, "God is judge and avenger of the innocent blood which cries from earth to heaven." [154]

In this compact and sweeping statement, the tones of early Christianity were heard: embryonic life was sacred; God and man were grievously offended by its destruction; there was no exception. The strongest and most comprehensive denunciation of abortion made by papal authority, it did not constitute infallible teaching; but, addressed to the bishops of the whole Church and authoritatively proclaiming the moral law, it was of controlling force for Catholics.

The central teaching authority found one occasion to reaffirm its stand. Twenty years later, legalized abortion had swept Japan, while the advocates of legalized abortion were beginning to resume their work in postwar Europe. At the same time the Church was opening its stand on contraception by permitting the syste-

152. *Id.* at 563.
153. Vermeersch had remarked on the law in 2 *Theologia moralis* n. 630.
154. Pius XI, *Casti connubii supra* n. 151, at 564.

matic avoidance of conception by the use of rhythm. In the first papal address to approve definitively this system, the difference between it and both contraception and abortion was emphasized. In the allocution, addressed to the Italian Catholic Society of Midwives on October 29, 1951, Pius XII taught: "The baby in the maternal breast has the right to life immediately from God. — Hence there is no man, no human authority, no science, no medical, eugenic, social, economic or moral 'indication' which can establish or grant a valid juridical ground for a direct deliberate disposition of an innocent human life, that is a disposition which looks to its destruction either as an end or as a means to another end perhaps in itself not illicit. — The baby, still not born, is a man in the same degree and for the same reason as the mother." [155] A more succinct and complete assertion of the rights of the embryo had not been made.

The Second Vatican Council had reason to consider abortion specifically in relation to family planning. In its pastoral constitution, *Joy and Hope*, on the Church in the modern world, the Council had affirmed the duty of responsible procreation, of conscientious decision-making by spouses as to how many children they should have. The Council had also affirmed that conjugal love was "perfected" in conjugal intercourse. It then had recognized that there might well be a conflict between the expression of love and responsible parenthood.[156] The Council, carefully refraining from a decision on contraception, did not attempt to solve the conflict. It did observe, however, "There are those who presume to offer to these problems indecent solutions; indeed they do not shrink from killing." In response to such solutions, the Council declared, "Life from its conception is to be guarded with the greatest care. Abortion and infanticide are horrible crimes." [157]

In this declaration the Council made several doctrinal advances.

155. Pius XII, *Address to the Italian Catholic Society of Midwives*, Acta apostolicae sedis 43:838–39 (1951). The draftsmen of this statement were the German Jesuits Franz Hürth and Robert Leiber, according to an interview I have had with Father Leiber.

The most recent condemnation of even therapeutic abortion is Paul VI, *Humanae vitae*, Acta apostolicae sedis 60:481–503 (1968), an encyclical whose concern to protect human life led to comprehensive rule-making against a variety of means interrupting the process of generation.

156. Second Vatican Council, *De ecclesia in mundo huius temporis* (*Gaudium et spes*), secs. 47–50.

157. *Id.* at sec. 51.

John T. Noonan, Jr.

For the first time contraception was treated differently from abortion. A line was drawn, with contraception on one side, abortion and infanticide on the other. Certain commands on contraception were specified as being for "children of the Church." The teaching on abortion, in contrast, was in a document otherwise addressed to "all men of good will." Abortion was condemned; no final judgment was made on all forms of contraception. Beyond these distinctions, an amendment, specifically made and adopted, added the words "from its conception." [158] In this way the Council sharply marked off the status of the conceptus from the status of spermatozoa and ova. Finally, the declaration was the first statement ever made by a general council of the Church on abortion; its judgment, promulgated by Paul VI on December 5, 1965, represented a commitment by the Catholic bishops of the world to care from conception.

Exceptions

In three successive stages then — decision by Roman congregations, teaching by popes, affirmation by pope and general council — authority had intensified the opposition of the Church to abortion. Exceptions, however, still survived, and it is essential to understand these exceptions to understand the balance now struck. Their survival may perhaps be best followed in the changing use of "direct" and "indirect." Lehmkuhl used "direct" in the sense in which Thomas had used it in justifying an act of killing in self-defense. As late as 1886 he taught that to procure an abortion to save the mother's life was "scarcely a direct abortion in a theological sense, any more than yielding a plank in a shipwreck to a friend is direct killing of oneself." [159] In this sense "direct" was equated with what was intended by the person acting. Yet, like Liguori, Lehmkuhl found some means objectionable whatever the person's intention. He restricted permissible direct abortion to the removal of the immature fetus from the embryo, but condemned craniotomy en-

158. Second Vatican Council, *Schema constitutionis pastoralis, De ecclesia in mundo huius temporis: Expensio modorum* pt. 2, p. 36, n. 101 (1965). The words "in utero" were struck because of the objection that "the fertilized ovum, although not yet in the uterus is sacred." In striking this language, the drafting committee said, "the time of animation is not touched on."
The distinction made by the Second Vatican Council between contraception and abortion was again blurred by the encyclical *Humanae vitae supra*, n. 155.
159. LEHMKUHL, 1 *Theologia moralis supra* n. 134, at 841.

tirely. As in Liguori, the basis for the distinction between means was not clear, because to consider means in some way meant to judge the act of killing on the basis of the *finis operis*, rather than by the intention of the person performing the act. Lehmkuhl attempted to distinguish by saying that where the fetus was removed there was an act with a double effect — on the one hand, the good effect of removing a danger to the mother with the additional benefit of opportunity to baptize the fetus; on the other hand, the bad effect of "acceleration of the death of the fetus." The good, he contended, outweighed the bad, and the bad effect was not a means of achieving a good end. In contrast, in craniotomy the fetus was killed at once, and the good effect, the removal of danger to the mother, followed from the act of killing. It is apparent that this analysis rested on a distinction without foundation in the example from St. Thomas where the act of killing was the means of self-defense in the same way that the craniotomy simultaneously saved the mother and removed the fetus.

Lehmkuhl's opinion permitting therapeutic abortion as indirect was rejected by the Holy Office in the decree approved July 25, 1895. As late as 1930, however, the meaning of "direct" which he had used was invoked by Ernesto Pestalozzi, director of the Obstetrical-Gynecological Clinic of the University of Rome. Writing in the Vatican newspaper, *Osservatore Romano*, three weeks after *Casti connubii*, he contended that Pius XI had not condemned the usual practice of Italian physicians in procuring an abortion "to save the mother from very serious danger." Such a procedure, where the doctor's intention was to save the mother, was not a "direct killing of the innocent" condemned by the encyclical. Pestalozzi's effort was treated by the theologians as a gross misinterpretation of *Casti connubii*.[160] "Direct" was now applied to any means used to abort a normal fetus, with whatever intention it was done.

There were two cases, however, which received special consideration. One was the case of an ectopic pregnancy, the other of a cancerous uterus. Despite the Holy Office decree of 1902, Lehmkuhl refused to accept defeat on the moral propriety of terminating an ectopic pregnancy. He now argued that it was lawful to remove

160. The substance of Pestalozzi's article, and theological reaction to it, are set out in Agostino Gemelli, "De l'avortement indirect,' 60 *Nouvelle revue théologique* 509 (1933).

the tumor which "sometimes appears in various organs of the mother" as a result of the ovum being outside the uterus. He did not make clear whether the tumor was "the swelling of the tube quite independent of the pregnancy or whether the mass growing in the tube was the result of the pregnancy itself." [161] He argued that the removal of the tumor was an indirect, permissible abortion. Like his distinction between craniotomy and removal of a normal fetus, Lehmkuhl's distinction appeared to attach the term "indirect" to a means which brought about fetal death gradually; that he could still use this distinction after the Holy Office decrees and win supporters for it from the moral theologians reflected a willingness to treat the ectopic pregnancy differently. In the 1920s and into the 1930s, the moralists continued to be divided.[162] No one supposed, however, that Casti connubii had decided the case. The distinction which won more support than Lehmkuhl's was argued by T. Lincoln Bouscaren as follows: In the case of an ectopic pregnancy in the Fallopian tube, the tube became pathological. An operation to remove the tube was lawful like other surgery. The fetus was not the direct object of the operation; its indirect killing was justified whenever there was "a notably greater probability of saving the mother's life." [163] In this usage "direct" was applied to the intention of the physician to remove the pathological condition. As to the physical act of removal, it had the good effect of removing the pathological tube, the bad effect of killing the fetus. Neither effect considered in itself was more "direct" than the other; but the intention of the physician was said to be directed only to the good end.

An analogous solution had been proposed by Lehmkuhl and unchallenged by the Holy Office in the case of the cancerous uterus. The removal of the uterus was said to be a moral act to remove a pathological condition; the death of the fetus it contained was indirectly accomplished.[164] This analysis was seriously questioned after Casti connubii by Agostino Gemelli, the Franciscan biologist who was rector of the Catholic University of the Sacred Heart in

---

161. This is the critical description of Lehmkuhl's presentation given by BOUSCAREN, *Ectopic Operations supra* n. 143, at 33.

162. The manuals of Noldin-Schmitt (2.341) and Sabetti-Barrett (273) decided the operation to be lawful. Vermeersch hesitated in his 1924 edition, but decided in favor of the operation in his 1928 edition (*Theologia moralis* n. 628). See BOUSCAREN at 31–32.

163. BOUSCAREN, *Ectopic Operations supra* n. 143, at 167.

164. LEHMKULH (1910 ed.), 1 *Theologia moralis supra* n. 134, at n. 1010.

Milan. Vermeersch defended Lehmkuhl's position, arguing that it was a standard case of double effect: removal of the fetus and removal of the cancer with the good effect outweighing the bad.[165] He was pressed by Gemelli to deny that the bad means, the death of the fetus, was not the means used to the good end of the mother's health, and so forbidden by the principle that evil might not be done to achieve good. Surely, Gemelli contended, who wills the means wills the consequences even though he might prefer one of the consequences might not occur.[166] Vermeersch replied with a new criterion of means to an end: Could a similar act be done without killing a fetus? The cancerous uterus, he argued, could be morally removed if it were empty; the operation did not become immoral by the presence of a fetus in the uterus, because the operation, not the death of the fetus, was the means to the end.[167] Gemelli attacked this reasoning as too abstract. Concretely, when a hysterectomy was performed on a pregnant uterus, the fetus was killed; concretely, the death of the fetus was a means used to achieve health for the mother. It was, therefore, a direct killing, condemned by the encyclical.[168]

The vigorous debate between Gemelli and Vermeersch illustrated the ambiguity and question-begging involved in arguing about what was "direct"; and not surprisingly, neither moralist convinced the other. If an act whose *finis operis* was to kill a fetus was always wrong, Gemelli was right, and the killing was to be condemned. On the contrary, if such an act was sometimes lawful for the purpose of saving the mother's life, Vermeersch was right; but to show that he was right it was necessary to admit that there were cases where the balance of values was in favor of abortion. Vermeersch was unwilling to make this admission in so many words. In fact, even after the severe condemnation of *Casti connubii*, Vermeersch and other leading Catholic moral theologians admitted the lawfulness of killing the fetus in the two special situations of ectopic pregnancy and a cancerous uterus. Their position

---

165. VERMEERSCH, "Avortement direct ou indirect," 60 *Nouvelle revue théologique* 600 (1933).

166. GEMELLI, "Avortement indirect" *supra* n. 160, at 520–27.

167. VERMEERSCH, "Une courte conclusion," 60 *Nouvelle revue théologique* 695 (1933).

168. GEMELLI, "Encore l'avortement indirect," 60 *Nouvelle revue théologique* 693 (1933).

was puzzling and irritating to their critics because they used terminology inadequate to convey what they were doing.

What the theologians were doing was drawing a line. Line-drawing is the ordinary business of moralists and lawmakers. It says that up to a certain point such-and-such a value will be preserved, but after that point another value will have play. Line-drawing brings charges of inconsistency of principle only from a critic who believes that one value should not have any limits. The proper criticism of line-drawing, however, is not that it is inconsistent but that the line is drawn at the wrong place; usually, indeed, charges of "logical inconsistency" are simply disguises for real objections to where the line has been fixed.[169] In the case of abortion Catholic moralists wanted to draw a line so tightly fixed in favor of the fetus that abortion could be rarely justified — justified indeed only when there was an unusual, extra circumstance added such as a cancerous uterus or an ectopic pregnancy. The permission of these two exceptions was consistent with the desire to establish a general rule of inviolability for the fetus; they were inconsistent only with an absolute valuation of fetal life.

As exceptions were admitted, why not more exceptions? The reason was fear that the exceptions would eat up the protection of the embryo. Vermeersch discussing the ectopic pregnancy observed sadly, "It is not without soulful solicitude that we weigh cases where, whether you embrace the benign or severe solution, what must be said is often at least indirectly dangerous to human lives." [170] The consciousness that all but the most special exceptions would be pushed further weighed heavily. With one excusing cause, men would be led to seek others; insist on preserving both mother and child and maximum efforts would be made to save both.[171] Trying to reach a point where maximum protection was afforded the fetus, the decision was made to except only the two unusual cases.[172]

169. E.g., "Catholic reasoning on the subject of therapeutic abortion is inconsistent with its own principles." GLANVILLE WILLIAMS, *The Sanctity of Life and the Criminal Law* 704 (1957).

170. VERMEERSCH, 2 *Theologia moralis supra* n. 135, at n. 630.

171. *Id.* at n. 623.

172. Bouscaren cited figures showing that roughly 1% of observed pregnancies in the 1920s were ectopic pregnancies. BOUSCAREN, *Ectopic Operations supra* n. 143, at 102.

VI. CONCLUSION

The most fundamental question involved in the long history of thought on abortion is: How do you determine the humanity of a being? To phrase the question that way is to put in comprehensive humanistic terms what the theologians either dealt with as an explicitly theological question under the heading of "ensoulment" or dealt with implicitly in their treatment of abortion. The Christian position as it originated did not depend on a narrow theological or philosophical concept. It had no relation to theories of infant baptism.[173] It appealed to no special theory of instantaneous ensoulment. It took the world's view on ensoulment as that view changed from Aristotle to Zacchia. There was, indeed, theological influence affecting the theory of ensoulment finally adopted, and, of course, ensoulment itself was a theological concept, so that the position was always explained in theological terms. But the theological notion of ensoulment could easily be translated into humanistic language by substituting "human" for "rational soul"; the problem of knowing when a man is a man is common to theology and humanism.

If one steps outside the specific categories used by the theologians, the answer they gave can be analyzed as a refusal to discriminate among human beings on the basis of their varying potentialities. Once conceived, the being was recognized as man because he had man's potential. The criterion for humanity, thus, was simple and all-embracing: if you are conceived by human parents, you are human.

The strength of this position may be tested by a review of some of the other distinctions offered in the contemporary controversy over legalizing abortion. Perhaps the most popular distinction is in terms of viability. Before an age of so many months, the fetus is not viable, that is, it cannot be removed from the mother's womb

173. According to Glanville Williams (*The Sanctity of Human Life supra* n. 169, at 193), "The historical reason for the Catholic objection to abortion is the same as for the Christian Church's historical opposition to infanticide: the horror of bringing about the death of an unbaptized child." This statement is made without any citation of evidence. As has been seen, desire to administer baptism could, in the Middle Ages, even be urged as a reason for procuring an abortion. It is highly regrettable that the American Law Institute was apparently misled by Williams' account and repeated after him the same baseless statement. See American Law Institute, *Model Penal Code: Tentative Draft No. 9* (1959), p. 148, n. 12.

. and live apart from her. To that extent, the life of the fetus is absolutely dependent on the life of the mother. This dependence is made the basis of denying recognition to its humanity.

There are difficulties with this distinction. One is that the perfection of artificial incubation may make the fetus viable at any time: it may be removed and artificially sustained. Experiments with animals already show that such a procedure is possible.[174] This hypothetical extreme case relates to an actual difficulty: there is considerable elasticity to the idea of viability. Mere length of life is not an exact measure. The viability of the fetus depends on the extent of its anatomical and functional development.[175] The weight and length of the fetus are better guides to the state of its development than age, but weight and length vary.[176] Moreover, different racial groups have different ages at which their fetuses are viable. Some evidence, for example, suggests that Negro fetuses mature more quickly than white fetuses.[177] If viability is the norm, the standard would vary with race and with many individual circumstances.

The most important objection to this approach is that dependence is not ended by viability. The fetus is still absolutely dependent on someone's care in order to continue existence; indeed a child of one or three or even five years of age is absolutely dependent on another's care for existence; uncared for, the older fetus or the younger child will die as surely as the early fetus detached from the mother. The unsubstantial lessening in dependence at viability does not seem to signify any special acquisition of humanity.

A second distinction has been attempted in terms of experience. A being who has had experience, has lived and suffered, who possesses memories, is more human than one who has not. Humanity depends on formation by experience. The fetus is thus "unformed" in the most basic human sense.[178]

174. E.g., R. L. BRINSTER and J. L. THOMSON, "Development of Eight-Cell Mouse Embryos in Vitro," 42 *Experimental Cell Research* 308 (1966).
175. J. EDGAR MORISON, *Fetal and Neonatal Pathology* 99–100 (1963).
176. PETER GRUENWALD, "Growth of the Human Fetus," 94 *American Journal of Obstetrics and Gynecology* 1112 (1966).
177. MORISON, *Fetal and Neonatal Pathology supra* n. 175, at 101.
178. This line of thought was advanced by some participants at the International Conference on Abortion sponsored by the Harvard Divinity School in cooperation with the Joseph P. Kennedy, Jr., Foundation in Washington, D.C., Sept. 8–10, 1967.

This distinction is not serviceable for the embryo which is already experiencing and reacting. The embryo is responsive to touch after eight weeks[179] and at least at that point is experiencing. At an earlier stage the zygote is certainly alive and responding to its environment.[180] The distinction may also be challenged by the rare case where aphasia has erased adult memory: has it erased humanity? More fundamentally, this distinction leaves even the older fetus or the younger child to be treated as an unformed inhuman thing. Finally, it is not clear why experience as such confers humanity. It could be argued that certain central experiences such as loving or learning are necessary to make a man human. But then human beings who have failed to love or to learn might be excluded from the class called man.

A third distinction is made by appeal to the sentiments of adults. If a fetus dies, the grief of the parents is not the grief they would have for a living child. The fetus is an unnamed "it" till birth, and is not perceived as personality until at least the fourth month of existence when movements in the womb manifest a vigorous presence demanding joyful recognition by the parents.

Yet feeling is notoriously an unsure guide to the humanity of others. Many groups of humans have had difficulty in feeling that persons of another tongue, color, religion, sex, are as human as they. Apart from reactions to alien groups, we mourn the loss of a ten-year-old boy more than the loss of his one-day-old brother or his 90-year-old grandfather. The difference felt and the grief expressed vary with the potentialities extinguished, or the experience wiped out; they do not seem to point to any substantial difference in the humanity of baby, boy, or grandfather.

Distinctions are also made in terms of sensation by the parents. The embryo is felt within the womb only after about the fourth month.[181] The embryo is seen only at birth. What can be neither seen nor felt is different from what is tangible. If the fetus cannot be seen or touched at all, it cannot be perceived as man.

Yet experience shows that sight is even more untrustworthy than feeling in determining humanity. By sight, color became an appropriate index for saying who was a man, and the evil of racial dis-

---

179. FRANK D. ALLAN, *Essentials of Human Embryology* 165 (1960).
180. FREDERICK J. GOTTLEIB, *Developmental Genetics* 28 (1966).
181. ALLAN, *Essentials of Human Embryology supra* n. 179, at 165.

crimination was given foundation. Nor can touch provide the test; a being confined by sickness, "out of touch" with others, does not thereby seem to lose his humanity. To the extent that touch still has appeal as a criterion, it appears to be a survival of the old English idea of "quickening" — a possible mistranslation of the Latin *animatus* used in the canon law.[182] To that extent touch as a criterion seems to be dependent on the Aristotelian notion of ensoulment, and to fall when this notion is discarded.

Finally, a distinction is sought in social visibility. The fetus is not socially perceived as human. It cannot communicate with others. Thus, both subjectively and objectively, it is not a member of society. As moral rules are rules for the behavior of members of society to each other, they cannot be made for behavior toward what is not yet a member. Excluded from the society of men, the fetus is excluded from the humanity of men.[183]

By force of the argument from the consequences, this distinction is to be rejected. It is more subtle than that founded on an appeal to physical sensation, but it is equally dangerous in its implications. If humanity depends on social recognition, individuals or whole groups may be dehumanized by being denied any status in their society. Such a fate is fictionally portrayed in *1984* and has actually been the lot of many men in many societies. In the Roman empire, for example, condemnation to slavery meant the practical denial of most human rights; in the Chinese Communist world, landlords have been classified as enemies of the people and so treated as nonpersons by the state. Humanity does not depend on social recognition, though often the failure of society to recognize the prisoner, the alien, the heterodox as human has led to the destruction of human beings. Anyone conceived by a man and a woman is human. Recognition of this condition by society follows a real event in the objective order, however imperfect and halting the recognition. Any attempt to limit humanity to exclude some group runs the risk of furnishing authority and precedent for excluding other groups

182. See DAVID W. LOUISELL and JOHN T. NOONAN, JR., "Constitutional Balance," *infra.*

183. Another line of thought advanced at the Conference mentioned in n. 178. Thomas Aquinas gave an analogous reason against baptizing a fetus in the womb: "As long as it exists in the womb of the mother, it cannot be subject to the operation of the ministers of the Church as it is not known to men" (*In sententias Petri Lombardi* 4.6 1.1.2).

in the name of the consciousness or perception of the controlling group in the society.

A philosopher may reject the appeal to the humanity of the fetus because he views "humanity" as a secular view of the soul and because he doubts the existence of anything real and objective which can be identified as humanity.[184] One answer to such a philosopher is to ask how he reasons about moral questions without supposing that there is a sense in which he and the others of whom he speaks are human. Whatever group is taken as the society which determines who may be killed is thereby taken as human. A second answer is to ask if he does not believe that there is a right and wrong way of deciding moral questions. If there is such a difference, experience may be appealed to: to decide who is human on the basis of the sentiment of a given society has led to consequences which rational men would characterize as monstrous.[185]

The rejection of the attempted distinctions based on viability and visibility, experience and feeling, may be buttressed by the following considerations: Moral judgments often rest on distinctions, but if the distinctions are not to appear arbitrary fiat, they should relate to some real difference in probabilities. There is a kind of continuity in all life, but the earlier stages of the elements of human life possess tiny probabilities of development. Consider for example, the spermatozoa in any normal ejaculate: There are about 200,000,000 in any single ejaculate, of which one has a chance of developing into a zygote.[186] Consider the oocytes which may become ova: there are 100,000 to 1,000,000 oocytes in a female infant, of which a maximum of 390 are ovulated.[187] But once spermatozoon and ovum meet and the conceptus is formed, such studies as have

---

184. Compare John O'Connor, "Humanity and Abortion," 12 *Natural Law Forum* 128–130 (1968), with John T. Noonan, Jr. "Deciding Who Is Human," 12 *Natural Law Forum* 134–138.

185. A famous passage of Montesquieu reads:

"Ceux dont il s'agit sont noirs depuis les pieds jusqu'à la tête; et ils ont le nez si écrasé qu'il est presque impossible de les plaindre.

"On ne peut se mettre dans l'esprit que Dieu qui est un être très-sage, ait mis une âme, surtout une âme bonne, dans un corps tout noir.

"Il est si naturel de penser que c'est la couleur qui constitue l'essence de l'humanité, que les peuples d'Asie, qui font des eunuques, privent toujours les noirs du rapport qu'ils ont avec nous d'une façon plus marquée." *Montesquieu, De l'esprit des lois*, in *Oeuvres Complètes* book 15, chap. 5 (Paris, 1843).

186. J. S. Baxter, *Frazer's Manual of Embryology* 5 (1963).

187. Gregory Pincus, *The Control of Fertility* 197 (1965).

John T. Noonan, Jr.

been made show that roughly in only 20 percent of the cases will spontaneous abortion occur.[188] In other words, the chances are about 4 out of 5 that this new being will develop. At this stage in the life of the being there is a sharp shift in probabilities, an immense jump in potentialities. To make a distinction between the rights of spermatozoa and the rights of the fertilized ovum is to respond to an enormous shift in possibilities. For about twenty days after conception the egg may split to form twins or combine with another egg to form a chimera, but the probability of either event happening is very small.

It may be asked, What does a change in biological probabilities have to do with establishing humanity? The argument from probabilities is not aimed at establishing humanity but at establishing an objective discontinuity which may be taken into account in moral discourse. As life itself is a matter of probabilities, as most moral reasoning is an estimate of probabilities, so it seems in accord with the structure of reality and the nature of moral thought to found a moral judgment on the change in probabilities at conception. The appeal to probabilities is the most commensensical of arguments, to a greater or smaller degree all of us base our actions on probabilities, and in morals, as in law, prudence and negligence are often measured by the account one has taken of the probabilities. If the chance is 200,000,000 to 1 that the movement in the bushes into which you shoot is a man's, I doubt if many persons would hold you careless in shooting; but if the chances are 4 out of 5 that the movement is a human being's, few would acquit you of blame. Would the argument be different if only one out of ten children conceived came to term? Of course this argument would be different. This argument is an appeal to probabilities that actually exist, not to any and all states of affairs which may be imagined.

The probabilities as they do exist do not show the humanity of the embryo in the sense of a demonstration in logic any more than the probabilities of the movement in the bush being a man demonstrate beyond all doubt that the being is a man. The appeal is a "buttressing" consideration, showing the plausibility of the standard adopted. The argument focuses on the decisional factor in any moral judgment and assumes that part of the business of a moralist is drawing lines. One evidence of the nonarbitrary char-

188. *Idem.* Apparently there is some small variation by region.

acter of the line drawn is the difference of probabilities on either side of it. If a spermatozoon is destroyed, one destroys a being which had a chance of far less than 1 in 200 million of developing into a reasoning being, possessed of the genetic code, a heart and other organs, and capable of pain. If a fetus is destroyed, one destroys a being already possessed of the genetic code, organs, and sensitivity to pain, and one which had an 80 percent chance of developing further into a baby outside the womb who, in time, would reason.

The positive argument for conception as the decisive moment of humanization is that at conception the new being receives the genetic code.[189] It is this genetic information which determines his characteristics, which is the biological carrier of the possibility of human wisdom, which makes him a self-evolving being. A being with a human genetic code is man.

This review of current controversy over the humanity of the fetus emphasizes what a fundamental question the theologians resolved in asserting the inviolability of the fetus. To regard the fetus as possessed of equal rights with other humans was not, however, to decide every case where abortion might be employed. It did decide the case where the argument was that the fetus should be aborted for its own good. To say a being was human was to say it had a destiny to decide for itself which could not be taken from it by another man's decision. But human beings with equal rights often come in conflict with each other, and some decision must be made as whose claims are to prevail. Cases of conflict involving the fetus are different only in two respects: the total inability of the fetus to speak for itself and the fact that the right of the fetus regularly at stake is the right to life itself.

The approach taken by the theologians to these conflicts was articulated in terms of "direct" and "indirect." Again, to look at what they were doing from outside their categories, they may be said to have been drawing lines or "balancing values." "Direct" and "indirect" are spatial metaphors; "line-drawing" is another. "To weigh" or "to balance" values is a metaphor of a more complicated mathematical sort hinting at the process which goes on in moral judgments. All the metaphors suggest that, in the moral judgments made, comparisons were necessary, that no value com-

189. GOTTLEIB, *Developmental Genetics supra* n. 180, at 17.

pletely controlled. The principle of double effect was no doctrine fallen from heaven, but a method of analysis appropriate where two relative values were being compared. In Catholic moral theology, as it developed, life even of the innocent was not taken as an absolute. Judgments on acts affecting life issued from a process of weighing. In the weighing, the fetus was always given a value greater than zero, always a value separate and independent from its parents. This valuation was crucial and fundamental in all Christian thought on the subject and marked it off from any approach which considered that only the parents' interests needed to be considered.

Even with the fetus weighed as human, one interest could be weighed as equal or superior: that of the mother in her own life. The casuists between 1450 and 1895 were willing to weigh this interest as superior. Since 1895, that interest was given decisive weight only in the two special cases of the cancerous uterus and the ectopic pregnancy. In both of these cases the fetus itself had little chance of survival even if the abortion were not performed. As the balance was once struck in favor of the mother whenever her life was endangered, it could be so struck again. The balance reached between 1895 and 1930 attempted prudentially and pastorally to forestall a multitude of exceptions for interests less than life.

The perception of the humanity of the fetus and the weighing of fetal rights against other human rights constituted the work of the moral analysts. But what spirit animated their abstract judgments? For the Christian community it was the injunction of Scripture to love your neighbor as yourself. The fetus as human was a neighbor; his life had parity with one's own. The commandment gave life to what otherwise would have been only rational calculation.

The commandment could be put in humanistic as well as theological terms: Do not injure your fellow man without reason. In these terms, once the humanity of the fetus is perceived, abortion is never right except in self-defense. When life must be taken to save life, reason alone cannot say that a mother must prefer a child's life to her own. With this exception, now of great rarity, abortion violates the rational humanist tenet of the equality of human lives.

For Christians the commandment to love had received a special imprint in that the exemplar proposed of love was the love of the Lord for his disciples. In the light given by this example, self-sacrifice carried to the point of death seemed in the extreme situations not without meaning. In the less extreme cases, preference for one's own interests to the life of another seemed to express cruelty or selfishness irreconcilable with the demands of love.

PAUL RAMSEY

Reference Points in Deciding about Abortion

I. THE RELIGIOUSNESS OF ETHICAL COMMITMENTS

My first point is a plea for greater sanity in the debate over abortion laws — a plea directed against the credence currently given the contention that anyone who opposes any of the proposed legal reforms must illicitly be seeking to impose his religious opinions on the rest of us. Although persons who hold religious opinions are regarded as free to subscribe to them, it is alleged that in the matter of legislation every identifiably religious belief should be excluded from any bearing at all upon public policy.

One way to overcome any such narrow-mindedness concerning the terms of reference that are legitimately a part of public debate over abortion legislation (or any other matter in which religion, morality, and public policy are intertwined) would be to reflect for a brief moment upon what counts as a conscientious "religious" opinion in our present society. Here appeal can be made to no less a theological authority than the Supreme Court of the United States. In 1961, in *Torcaso*[1] the Court pronounced as dictum that "Secular Humanism" is a religion, despite the absence of any belief in God. Dicta of the Supreme Court have a tendency to become doctrine if they are in accord with the trends of the age. So it was that in 1965, in *Seeger*[2] the Court recognized in a conscientious objector a belief in a "lower case" supreme being which the Congress, being composed of reasonable men, must have meant by the 1948 requirement of a belief in a "higher case" Supreme

1. *Torcaso v. Watkins*, 397 U.S. 488 (1961) at 495, n. 11.
2. *United States v. Seeger*, 380 U.S. 193 (1965).

Being. In the same spirit, the Court of Appeals for the Ninth Circuit recognized man's conscientious belief in "man thinking his highest, feeling his deepest and living his best" to be a religious belief.[3] In another case the same court accepted as religious a man's belief in "godness" or — if that be too traditional language — "livingness" at the heart of all the objects in the world.[4]

The test established by *Seeger* of whether or not a belief is to be regarded as religious is "whether a given belief that is sincere and meaningful occupies a place in the life of the possessor parallel to that filled by orthodox belief in God." True, the Court was interpreting the Selective Service Act and engaging in "strenuous statutory construction."[5] But in this process the Court was driven to an anatomization of "conscience" in order to find in the hearts of most men some crux, some organizing principle, some supremacy of moral claims which is the equivalent of duties arising from a relation to the Supreme Being.

This development in our law is a mirror of what we as a people really believe as a people. We believe that a deeply felt, conscientious belief in or outlook on some public question is really the same, at least in the public forum, as any belief traditionally called religious. This is the reason the Court's decision in these cases received such widespread acceptance. The conclusion that a conscientious conviction may be *functionally equivalent* to a religious belief appeared to Americans as a proper elevation of conscientious ethical beliefs. The Court judically endowed such convictions with the sanctity that was formerly reserved for denominationally religious beliefs. Its interpretation in these cases gained credence among us for reasons that go far beyond the particular statutes to which the Court's decision was limited.

A well-founded conclusion from this trend of American opinion is that any of the positions taken on controversial public questions having profound moral and human or value implications hold for us the functional sanctity of religious belief. The question concerning nonreligious positions is whether they any longer exist. The question is whether proponents of one or another public

3. *Peter v. United States*, 324 F.2d 173 (9th Cir. 1963).
4. *Macmurray v. United States*, 330 F.2d 928 (9th Cir. 1964).
5. John H. Mansfield, "Conscientious Objection — 1964 Term," *Religion and the Public Order*, ed. Donald Giannella (Chicago, Ill.: University of Chicago Press, 1965), p. 6.

policy must not all be deemed religious whether they agree with this designation or not. In this ecumenical age there must be dialogue between orthodox religions and contemporary atheism and secular humanism. The latter is America's fourth religion; it is indeed our prevailing religion — even the operational religion of many churchmen and clergymen. Unless secular humanism and the religious communities wish to join forces to roll back the Court's interpretation of the religious or transcendent element in conscience, then in the debate over abortion and public policy we should hear no more charges that one party or another is trying to legislate for the whole of society a particular religious opinion. To paraphrase *Seeger*, on the question of abortion, each disputant has a religious faith in an ethical creed.

Any fundamental "outlook" productive of an "onlook" on abortion enters the public forum with the same credentials as one or another of our traditional religious teachings concerning morality and the common life. There are some who seem to *reduce* the discussion of abortion law reform to nonmoral terms, or to judgment in terms of their own moral ultimates, by shouting silence in a loud voice to members of religious communities or to anyone who holds any relic of the position once uniformly held by these communities. This simply will not do. Nor will more sophisticated attempts to reduce the terms of reference in the debate to the meanings some science might supply. "An 'onlook which rejects onlooks,'" Donald Evans writes, "is perhaps what some people have called 'the scientific attitude.'" [6] That may be a perfectly proper determination of the methods of science. But it is still an "outlook" not to be found among the contents of any science or demonstrated by any science to be the only perspective proper to take toward every question. As a proposal in the public forum for the resolution of legal and social problems, it is on all fours with any other "onlook" concerning the individual and the common good.

II. SIN AND CRIME

There is, however, a certain "self-denying ordinance" that needs to be imposed on all ethical outlooks in a pluralistic society as a precondition of good public debate. A distinction must be made

6. *The Language of Self Involvement*, London: S.C.M. Press, 1963, p. 254.

between what would be for us a "sin" and what would be for us a "crime." Norman St. John-Stevas, although himself adhering to generally Catholic distinctions between right and wrong, affirms that "all contraventions of natural [moral] law are not fit subjects for legislation." [7] He proposes three tests for telling when wrong practices become a fit subject for legislation: (1) the practice injures the common good substantially, (2) the law can be enforced equitably in its incidence, and (3) its enforcement does not cause greater evils than those it represses. These criteria would exert a salutary restraint upon the propensity of at least every moralist to conclude that "there ought to be a law." They would give us pause in passing from sin or wrong to crime.

Like the lawyer's explanation that something is "contrary to public policy" or his invocation of "a reasonable man" as a norm, the assertion that something is "substantially contrary to the common good" would be the beginning and not the end of argument. This test only points us in the direction of unlimited and continuing self-government. Discussion may then lead to provisional agreement as to the meaning of the common good and of substantial injury to it. Yet a person's understanding of morality will in good measure shape his understanding of the common good; and people will disagree about action which contributes to or injures the common good as deeply as they disagree about the features of actions that are "sin."

Those among us who believe that morally abortion is, or sometimes is, a species of the sin of murder should be able to distinguish this belief from any conclusion to the question whether such abortion ought to be defined as a crime in the penal code. A weaker version of this same distinction between sin or wrong and *crime* would be operative in the minds of anyone who was willing to say that not every act of abortion that he believes to be morally wrong should be prohibited by law. In the stronger version, it might be possible for a Catholic who morally would forbid all direct abortion and who himself believes this teaching to belong

7. *Life, Death and the Law* (Bloomington: Indiana University Press, 1961), p. 94. Thomas Aquinas is frequently cited (*ibid.*, p. 20, n. 6) in support of this distinction, widely accepted among Catholics today: "Human law does not prescribe concerning all the acts of every virtue: but only in regard to those that are ordainable to the common good," *Summa theologica* I-II, Q. XVI, arts. 2 and 3.

to the meaning of general human justice still, for purposes of jurisprudence, to treat the morality of abortion as if it were for him within the sphere of moral theology, a science based on revelation and the teaching authority of the Church, rather than on natural justice.[8]

Suppose someone believes that abortion is morally a matter of taking a human life which is small and weak and wholly dependent upon others for protection. Could that person put his conscientious belief aside and refuse to allow this moral judgment decisively to shape his verdict on the effect on the common good of permitting abortion? Suppose someone who, confronting the plight of women in our urban slums or families on the very edge of collapse from the burdens of child-rearing, is convinced that it is utterly shameful and a "sin" against God for the values of conscious lives to be wasted and sacrificed by antiquated laws that seek to protect mere globs of unformed tissue, or for women to be forced by our present laws to go to back-alley abortionists. Could such a person for purposes of jurisprudence suspend that conscience enough to open his mind to the greater desirability, instead, of other possible solutions that should be admitted to the public debate? *Ought* each of these persons do this? That is a question which bears equally on both.

III. IMPLANTATION, SEGMENTATION, AND THE GENOTYPE

If we are to ask when a new life first has a sanctity that claims protection, and if scientific findings have anything to do with the answer to that question, we must ponder four different possibilities of such a beginning: the moment of origin of the genotype, the time of implantation, the time of segmentation, and the development of the fetus in the first 4–8 weeks. Compared to any one of these determinations, the difference made by capacities later discernible in the fetus, by its quickening or by birth, would seem

8. This paraphrases Norman St. John-Stevas' recommendation (*Life, Death and the Law*, p. 30) to his fellow Catholics in regard to artificial contraception —a recommendation made *before* many Catholics began to declare publicly their disagreement with the Church's teaching to date on the inherent moral evil, for Catholics and non-Catholics alike, of acts of artificial intervention frustrating the natural procreative purposes of conjugal acts while performing such acts. His recommendation, therefore, accepted the intrinsic grave immorality of the very matter he placed in brackets.

to be lesser disjunctions in the total course of the transmission of life disclosed to us by modern knowledge. These latter, common-sense tests are as crude or gross determinations, even if not as speculative, as the Mediterranean world's old measure of forty and eighty days.

One could say that human life begins with the implantation of the fertilized egg in the uterus seven or eight days after ovulation. Such a definition is a questionable apology for the "morning after" pill now being experimentally developed. Embracing this view, Gregory Pincus, who with John Rock developed the antiovulant pill, declared that "the new pill is not an abortifacient." [9] The basis for the theoretical assertion that life begins with implantation is the merely practical consideration that the "union of sperm and ovum cannot be detected clinically unless implantation occurs." If this is the case, one might correctly draw the conclusion that a scientist's clinical knowledge that life has started begins with implantation. We could say that *pregnancy* begins with implantation, if to say this is not a redundancy. However, to declare categorically that new life begins with implantation is to make oneself by definition ignorant of the first six or seven days. This proposal can only be set down as self-serving. As a layman, I can only express surprise if it is a statement of scientific fact that fertilized ova before implantation have not been "clinically detected." [10] Such a working definition of the origin of life can only mean: our knowledge that implanted life has begun can only begin with implantation.

The segmentation of the sphere of developing cells in the case of identical twins (who have the same genotype) is entitatively distinct from implantation as a process, though this is completed at about the same time as implantation. A "primitive streak" across the hollow cluster of developing cells (the blastocyst) signals the separation of the same genotype into identical twins. This occurs by about the time of implantation, that is, on the seventh or eighth

9. Lawrence Lader, "Three Men Who Made A Revolution," in the *New York Times Magazine*, April 10, 1966, p. 8, at p. 55. On this Dr. Rock disagrees with his colleague.

10. Dr. John Rock's report of the experiments carried out at the Free Hospital for Women in Brookline, Mass., from 1938 to 1954 seems plainly to assert that fertilized ova were secured from "a two-day, two-cell egg to a 17-day ovum already implanted in the uterus" (*The Time Has Come*, New York: Alfred A. Knopf, 1963, pp. 184–185).

day after ovulation. It might be asserted that it is at the time of segmentation, not earlier, that life comes to be the individual human being it is ever thereafter to be. The religious word for that process would be to say that then germinating matter becomes "animate," or is informed by, or constituted, a unique human "soul."

There is a species of biological life close to us in evolution, though not in gross physical form, whose reproduction takes place in every case by, so to speak, quadruple identical "twins." Each individual of the species armadillo has the same genotype with three others arising from segmentation. Let us imagine that, similarly, every case of human reproduction resulted in identical twins. Then I suggest that, upon acquiring our modern knowledge of segmentation explaining this phenomenon, the minds of men would be strongly drawn to locate at that point, and not earlier or later, the first origins of nascent individual human life that places upon us the claims we may acknowledge to be due to any individual of our kind. If there is a moment in the development of these nascent lives of ours subsequent to fertilization and prior to birth (or graduation from college) at which it would be reasonable to believe that an individual human life begins and therefore begins to be inviolate, that moment is arguably at the stage when segmentation may or may not take place.

The argument from genotype is, to say the least, a remarkable one. The unique, never-to-be-repeated individual human being comes into existence first as a minute informational speck, and this speck has been drawn at random from still more minute informational specks his parents possessed out of the common human gene pool. Arguably, he began to be at the moment of impregnation. There was a virtually unimaginable number of combinations of the specks on his paternal and maternal chromosomes that did not come to be when these were refused and he began his life. No one else (with the single exception of an identical twin if segmentation happens seven days later) in the entire history of the human race has ever had or ever will have exactly the same genotype. Thus it might be said that in all essential respects the individual is whoever he is going to become from the moment of impregnation. He already is this while not knowing this or anything else. Thereafter, his subsequent development cannot be described as his becoming someone he now is not. It can only be described as a process of achieving, a process of becoming the one he already is. Genetics teaches that we were from the beginning what we essentially still are in every cell and in every generally human attribute and in every individual attribute. There are formal principles constituting us from the beginning. Thus genetics seems to have provided an approximation to the religious belief that there is a soul animating and forming a man's bodily being from the very beginning. That far, theological speculation never dared to go with theoretical certainty.

What is this but to say that we are all fellow fetuses? From impregnation to the tomb ours is a nascent and a dying life; we are bound together as congeners from our Mendelian beginnings. Any unique sanctity or dignity we may have cannot be because we are any larger than the period at the end of a sentence. Although we know only in the light of our particular span of conscious existence, this light and that darkness from which we came and toward which we go are both alike to the One who laid his hand upon us, covered us in the womb, and by whom we were fearfully and wonderfully made. We will never be anything more or anything other than the beings we always were in every cell and attribute.

In a remarkable way, modern genetics seems to teach — with greater precision and assurance than theology could ever muster — that there are "formal causes," immanent principles or constitutive elements long before there is any shape or motion of discernible size or subjective consciousness or rationality in a human being — not merely potency for these things that later supervene, but in some sense the present, operative actuality of these powers and characteristics. These minute formal elements are already determining the organic life to be not only generally "human" but also *the* unique *individual* human being it is to be. It is now not unreasonable to assert, for the first time in the history of scientific speculation upon this question, that who one is and is ever going to be came about at the moment an ovum was impregnated.

The teachings of genetics here is about as close as science is likely to come to the doctrine of creation ex nihilo. This doctrine affirms the radical contingency of the whole created world; the world need not have been or might have been wholly otherwise.

Such also, genetics seems to tell us, is the nature of that lottery by which any human creature comes to be. There were no compelling reasons, no substance simply emanating or drawn forth by necessary laws from generation to generation, no causal predetermination requiring or even making for the conception of this particular individual and not one of a myriad other possibilities. It is true, of course, that once a unique combination of informational specks comes to be science can then give an account of him as an understandable resultant of the genes of his maternal and paternal chromosomes. Genetic clinics can unfold the pre-existent factors in laws of probability; but none of these factors reaches the individual who is actualized. There can never be an account of why *he* had to be the who and what he is rather than some other individual being. In this sense, *he* was procreated "out of nothing."

So generally with the doctrine of creation ex nihilo. Any creature or the whole creation might have been quite otherwise, or might not have been and some other creation have been instead. The creation did not emanate from the divine substance, nor can we ask what necessity the recalcitrance of pre-existing matter imposed on the Creator. If either of these world views were tenable, it would be theoretically possible to forecast the nature of the creature. To the contrary, creation ex nihilo means that if one wants to know who or what the creature is, one must look to see. This doctrine was a main source of the empiricism of science in the western world; it placed upon man's way of knowing a requirement stemming from the radical contingency of the entire creation, from the fact that nothing about creation could be deduced from anything.

So with regard to the individual human being. He cannot be predictably "traduced" out from the being of his mother and father. There is no necessity, rational or nonrational, why as a particular individual he should be; nor is there any prior propensity toward his emanation from among myriad possibilities. *That* he is may be explained scientifically or romantically, but not why he is this particular one and not one of those many, many others who might have been. Once he, that is, his genotype, *is* and once his individual "determiners" *are* in the land of the living, a sort of explanation can be proffered by specifying the genes. Still there is no explaining why he who has these characteristics and not someone else having another set of characteristics came to be. There is no explaining why he who was conceived on the particular occasion has these characteristics and not others that might just as well have been. This is the nature of our strange passage from being only a gleam in one father's eye or only an informational genetic possibility; from this nonbeing we became the actuality of the genotype each of us is for the entirety of nascent and conscious life. Some call this process the genetic "lottery." Others call it *pro*creation, the transmission of life by a mechanism that serves as the occasion upon which from things that are not God calls into being the things that are.

IV. IMPLANTATION AND THE DEVELOPMENT OF THE FETUS

Given our present knowledge of reproductive biology, there is also some evidence to support us if we take the development of the fetus, as distinct from the activity of implantation, to be the span of time in which there comes to be a human being in the womb. The signal stages in the development of the fetus take place, as we shall see, quite early. Development of the fetus is entitatively distinct from the blastocyst's activity in implanting itself in the wall of the uterus. Both lines of development, both capacities — to implant and to grow into the fetus — were contained, it can reasonably be argued, in the mere "outline" of the person or the "formal principles" contained in the genotype and in the sphere or spheres of cells. A moral "argument" based on the signal importance of the early development of the fetus, is, therefore, a kind of rebuttal of the arguments from genotype or from the time of identical twinning which we have reviewed.

This is a strong argument precisely because of the separation between the activity of implantation and the activity of development of the fetus, both of which are activities of the new life (of the blastocyst) and not of the mother-to-be. After six or seven days of cell division in the tube, if all goes well the sphere of cells enters the uterus. The blastocyst buries itself in the wall of the uterus like a parasite. More now begins to take place than the cells' single-minded self-reproduction and differentiation into the organic life to come. A "beachhead" must first be secured in this new environment. That now is crucial. The uterus alone is no place to live; and, without the preparation of a separate "system" within which the new life can live for the next nine months, the self-reproductive power of the cells and their destiny to become the differentiated organs of a human being could not proceed. If the activity of both poles of the sphere of cells proceed simultaneously, one of these — implantation — is now fundamental to the success of the other: further embryonic development. It has to be stressed that it is the sphere of cells that accomplishes both tasks, not the mother. The original "outline" contained a determination toward the execution of the task of implantation, the growth of the placental system and amniotic sac, and not solely a determination toward the human being (the fetus) in the womb and beyond.

One pole of the sphere of cells, called the trophoblast, burrows its way into the lining of the uterus.[11] This pole is later to become the placenta, which, it is important to emphasize, is a fetal and not a maternal system for sustaining the life of the fetus. The opposite pole becomes the embryo, then the fetus. In other words, the sphere of cells (the blastocyst that has grown by division of cells having the same, original genotype) now devotes some of its fore-ordained cellular powers to throwing out a lifeline by which it can be attached to the life of the mother. Having made the catch, the system in which the fetus is to live must then be developed in a remarkable way. This activity of implantation and development of the placenta, it can reasonably be argued, and not only the development of the fetus, was contained in the directions the original cells contained. Thus it could be argued that "the person in the womb" (I would prefer to say, the human being in the womb, who later becomes personal) comes to be with the early development of the fetus following or entitatively distinct from the blastocyst's activity in implantation. In terms of development, the fetus is more than genotype or blastocyst. Yet in a sense it is less, because implantation and placenta sprang also from the original cells.

The sphere of cells can throw out its lifeline, in rare cases, in

11. For the following account of fetal development, except for footnoted references and for some of the references, I draw upon a paper by Dr. André Hellegers, "Fetal Development," prepared for the Conference on Abortion sponsored by the Harvard Divinity School in cooperation with the Joseph P. Kennedy, Jr., Foundation at the Washington Hilton Hotel, Washington, D.C., Sept. 5–8, 1967. Dr. Hellegers' paper has also been published in *Theological Studies* (March 1970).

the tubes or, in rarer cases, in the abdominal cavity. The mother's uterus is simply the appropriate place for its activity of nidation or "nesting," where the fetal blood system can be connected with that of the mother and there is room for 9 months' fetal growth. The placental system and amniotic sac are *not* to be compared with the rope that links two mountain climbers together. The rope "belongs" to both those lives. But the placental system and amniotic bag "belongs" to the unborn child. This, I suppose, is the reason that the procedure of amniocentesis, that is, taking a sample from the amniotic sac, discloses to a medical investigator information about the genetic make-up or chromosomal difficulties of the unborn child, rather than those of the mother.

At the time one side of the sphere "nests" or implants, it may have become a hollow mass of several hundred cells. The decision whether there is to be one or two or more individuals (segmentation) may still be somewhat uncertain. In any case, shelter and supply lines come first. The trophoblast burrows into the lining of the upper wall of the uterus, creating for itself a small nutritive bath of blood and broken cells for its immediately future needs. The part of the sphere of cells later to become the placenta also produces hormones. These hormones enter the mother's blood system and serve the critical function of preventing menstruation. The time interval from ovulation to menstruation is approximately 14 days, and the developing cells have already been alive 7 days in the tubes. Therefore, the implanting trophoblast has only about 7 days to produce enough hormones to stop the mother from menstruating. Otherwise, the new life will be flushed out. (These hormones are also the basis for chemical tests determining pregnancy.)

The patch of cells buried in the uterine wall has work to do which it is difficult to follow. There apparently takes place a branching, fingerlike process growing larger and more numerous, to create the whole mechanism of support and sustenance (the placenta, a rather large organ) that will take care of the nutritional and chemical needs of embryo and fetus by drawing upon the mother "until birth do them part." The placenta "acts aggressively toward the tissues of the mother, takes what it needs and on the whole only what it needs, and passes out to the mother's system whatever products of its own that can be considered waste." [12] Thus the navel which is supposed to be an external mark of the dependence of everyone since Adam and Eve is actually a sign of an independent and entitatively distinct activity of the germinating cells. Such also is the barrier between the mother's blood and nutritional system and the fetal blood system which the original implanting patch of cells has created around the developing embryo. "These appurtenances," whose design came from the cells everyone was from conception, to be discarded later as the afterbirth, are "as truly a part of each of us as were our milk teeth." [13]

Meantime, back at the patch of cells at the opposite pole from the burrowing, hormone-producing, placenta-forming trophoblast, another line of development takes place. At the end of the second week, the patch of cells that protrudes into the uterine cavity is no longer spherical; it has stretched along one axis and has ends and sides. This aspect of the blastocyst or original sphere is now called the "embryonic plate."

At the end of the third or fourth week following fertilization (or the second or third week after implantation), when the woman begins to wonder whether she is pregnant, the *embryo* is said to be present. This is an exceedingly crucial stage in development. While the embryo is only an elongated mass about one-third of an inch long, scientists can recognize more. "All the most important decisions and events have been made by the end of the first month." [14] There is a head, rudimentary eyes, ears and brain, a body with digestive tract, heart and bloodstream, simple kidneys and liver, two pairs of bulges where future arms and legs will grow. The differentiation is sufficient for heart pumping to occur,[15] although the human heart reaches its final four-chamber configuration later on.

Certainly by the end of six weeks all the internal organs are present in rudimentary formation. At the end of seven weeks the fetus will flex its neck if tickled on the nose. After eight weeks the embryo ceases to be called an embryo and becomes known as a

12. N. J. Berrill, *The Person in the Womb* (New York: Dodd, Mead & Co., 1968), pp. 42, 43.
13. *Ibid.*, p. 44.
14. Berrill, *The Person in the Womb*, p. 45.
15. J. W. C. Johnson, "Cardio-Respiratory Systems," *Intrauterine Development*, ed. A. C. Barnes (Philadelphia: Lea and Febiger, 1968).

fetus, to emphasize the completion of an important phase of its existence. After the end of eight weeks there is growth, not crucial development, yet to take place, although the fetus is only one inch in length. Here at eight weeks there is readable electrical activity coming from the fetal brain.[16] Fingers and toes are now recognizable. "By the end of the second month, therefore, we can say with some assurance that the person in the womb is present, with all the basic equipment and some sensitivity, although with a long, long way to go to be fully human." [17]

By the end of the ninth or tenth week the child has local reflexes such as swallowing, squinting, and movement of the tongue. By the tenth week he is capable of spontaneous movement, without any outside stimulation. By the eleventh week thumb sucking has been observed. After twelve weeks brain structure is complete, although the fetus is only 3½ inches long, and growth of structure and organs (including the brain) will continue. By twelve weeks, also, a fetal heartbeat has been monitored by modern electrocardiographic techniques, via the mother.

Between the 12th and 16th weeks, "quickening" will occur. This means that fetal movements are felt by the mother — an event long considered important in human sentiment and in law. "Quickening," however, "is a phenomenon of maternal perception rather than a fetal achievement." [18] The child quickens or is the source of its own motion two weeks or more earlier, at ten weeks.

Between the 18th and 20th week it is possible to hear the fetal heart by simple stethoscope, not by refined ECG.

A delivery before the 20th week is called an *abortion;* after this date it will be called a *premature delivery* in medical terminology, since a fetus one pound or more in weight and from 20 to 28 weeks of gestational life has 10 percent chance of survival. The dividing line in former days was 28 weeks. However, *current* possible "viability" determines for medical practice (though often not for the law) the distinction between an abortus and a premature infant. Later on, we shall return to the significance for the morality of abortion of the fact that "viability" is bound in the

16. D. Goldblatt, "Nervous System and Sensory Organs, *Intrauterine Development*, ed. A. C. Barnes (Philadelphia: Lea and Febiger, 1968).

17. Berrill, *The Person in the Womb*, pp. 45–46. "We are all there in every important way" (p. 51).

18. Hellegers, "Fetal Development."

Paul Ramsey

future to be pushed further back in the development of the fetus which we have sketched. The difference between an abortus and a premature infant is a phenomenon of medical achievement and not of medicine's perception of the fetus' actual development. The law also lags behind medicine in that a certificate of death is required for an abortus or a miscarriage only at 20 weeks and after; before that the abortus can be treated as a pathological specimen. Since 10 percent viability now begins at this point, this could mean the erasure of a class of *infants* born dead or quite nonviable. At the same time, this lag may account for a pedagogy in the law toward justifying abortion as late at 20 weeks, that is, on the border of viability, because before that the fetus is only a pathological specimen.

Albert Rosenfeld, science writer for *Life* magazine, reports that "Many readers of *Life* who saw Lennart Nilsson's marvelous photographs of fetuses in their sacs, especially in the later stages of development, wrote in to say that they could never again think of their *babies* as disposable *things*. Such sentiment might well increase as fetuses become visible from the outset. And if the day of conception were to become a person's official birth date, then the act of aborting a fetus would be ending a baby of a given age." [19] Good morality, however, ought not to depend on "visual aids." Ethical judgments are not constructed out of sentiment or emotions or feelings of identification stimulated by pictures. The latter, of course, and a sympathetic imagination grasping the facts of fetal development which we have reviewed, help to sustain in us an appropriate respect for human life hitherto hidden from view. Doubtless it is our fellow-feeling and identification with children that accounts for the fact that people generally tend to *perceive* that human life begins at birth.

Ethics, however, is based on the nature of things and not on heightened imagination or feelings, however important these may be in strengthening moral behavior. Medical science knows the babies to be present in all essential respects earlier in fetal development than the women who wrote in to *Life* magazine perceived

19. *The Second Genesis: The Coming Control of Life* (Englewood Cliffs, N.J.: Prentice-Hall, 1969), pp. 125–126. Nilsson's photographs were published in *Life*, April 30, 1965; and are reprinted in *The Terrible Choice: The Abortion Dilemma* (Bantam Books, 1968).

them in the pictures. It is the rational account of the nature of fetal development that matters most.

We have, then, three stages at which it is reasonable to believe that human life begins: conception, when the unique genotype originates; segmentation, or when it is irreversibly settled whether there will be one, two, or more individuals; and the early development of the fetus when the "outline" the cells contained is actualized in all essential respects, with only growth to come. By comparison, with the achievements already made by the unborn life, quickening refers to no change and birth to less significant change in the human life that is present in the womb. By "When does human life begin?" we, of course, mean to ask and possibly to answer this question in the medical-ethical context and not in the evolutionary context of the continuity of three billion years. We mean to ask and possibly to answer the question, When is there human life deserving respect and protection like any other? The fact that nascent life is minute and vulnerable and "incapable of independent existence" does not matter in determining its worth. Certainly, a religious ethics will have special regard for the near-neighbor beneath a woman's heart and the distant-neighbor in foreign lands, for the alien resident or sojourner in the womb no less than for the alien resident or sojourner in the land of Israel — for we know the heart of the stranger, the weak and the vulnerable, and God's special redemptive care for every one of us in like circumstances. As Professor Ralph Potter of the Harvard Divinity School has written, "The fetus symbolizes you and me and our tenuous hold upon a future here at the mercy of our fellow men." [20]

Anyone who seeks a clearer or better place to light upon in answering the question, When in nascent life is there a right of life in exercise? than genotype (conception), segmentation, or the early stages of fetal development will have to wait for the development of personal self-consciousness. That would be at about age one in an infant's life, when it begins to exercise the power of speech; before that, an infant is likely only potentially human by the standard of self-awareness or incipient rationality. Indeed,

20. "The Abortion Debate," *The Religious Situation 1968*, ed. Dwight Culver (Boston: Beacon Press, 1968), p. 157.

there is scientific confirmation of such a choice, in the fact that at about this time *full* cortical brain activity is achieved, as evidenced by the appearance of *rhythmical* markings on an electroencephalogram. Otherwise, brain and heart activity as signs of life have been evident long before birth.

These and other indices of life (except for autonomous breathing) are all present in the morphologically human, the organically complete and interrelatedly functioning fetus in its early development. Only the growth of what the individual already is, plus breathing on its own, locomotion by crawling and by walking upright, and the final completion of cortical brain activity (at about age one) are yet to come. Every one of these achievements, indeed, may be described better as further growth, not as additional stages in development.

One may remark in passing upon the oddity of an age in which we are elevating the importance of evidences of brain activity and rejecting the singular significance of heart or lung activity when we are dealing with men in the last of life, while we seem willing to settle every question of their moral claims upon our common humanity in the continuum of life's first beginnings by reference solely to the start of spontaneous respiration which a physician evoked from every one of us (or inflicted upon us) in the birthroom, taking little or no account of the early evidence of heartbeat and brain activity in the unborn child.[21] The "breath of life" is today taken to be the sole evidence that a woman has a child or that a man and a woman have become parents, while the "breath of life" is more and more minimized among the tests for whether that same child grown-up and now terminal is still alive. A proper comment upon this must be that we can indulge in many a sophisticated inconsistency if we too quickly address ourselves to the solution of the serious social problem of abortion, without an adequate concept of what the life is that claims respect and protection that can cohere with our notion of what the death is that brings these claims to an end.

21. In an article by Dr. Hannibal Hamlin of Boston, notably entitled "Life or Death by EEG," one finds the following significant description of the EEG of an unborn child: "The intra-uterine fetal brain responds to biochemical changes associated with oxygen deprivation by abnormal EEG activity similar to that produced in the adult brain. Thus at an early prenatal stage of life, the EEG reflects *a distinctly individual pattern that soon becomes truly personalized.*

To conclude this section, the time table for the important stages in fetal development, given above, should be compared with the time limits suggested in the Model Abortion Law Reform Bill, and with the time limits in the legislation that has been passed by several of the states and proposed in many others. At most it may be said that the Model Penal Code proposed by the draftsmen of the American Law Institute "suggested" a time limit, by the mention of *twenty-six weeks* in its definition of "unjustified abortion" in sec. 230.3(1): "A person who purposely and unjustifiably terminates the pregnancy of another otherwise than by a live birth commits a felony of the third degree or, where the pregnancy has continued beyond the twenty-sixth week, a felony of the second degree." When the Commissioners came to the definition of "justifiable abortion," however, nothing was said about the time abortion could rightfully be performed. Only the "indications" were specified, in sec. 230.3(2): "A licenced physician is justified in terminating a pregnancy if he believes there is substantial risk that continuation of the pregnancy would gravely impair the physical and mental health of the mother or that the child would be born with grave physical or mental defect, or that the pregnancy resulted from rape, incest, or other felonious intercourse." On one interpretation, the Commissioners may have wanted abortion upon these approved indications to be open-ended as to time.

On another interpretation, however, they may have meant to leave it to the state legislatures to determine the time limits upon the abortions to be justified for these reasons. In fact this is what has happened. The California law, for example, stipulates a sliding scale of acceptability, by stating that the abortions must be performed in the first 12 weeks, by requiring that between 12 and 20 weeks an abortion must receive the *unanimous* approval of a committee of at least three doctors, and that no abortion can be legally done after 20 weeks. Of several bills Assemblyman Albert H. Blumenthal has introduced in New York, the first required that no more than 24 weeks have passed since conception; to meet criticism this was lowered to 20 weeks; then raised again to 24.

At this point the reader may compare these times with the account of fetal development given above. There we saw that heart pumping starts by the end of 4 weeks; there is readable electrical activity in the fetal brain at 8 weeks and all essential organic formations; the fetus is capable of spontaneous movement at 10 weeks; heart beat can be monitored via the mother at 12 weeks; "quickening" may occur to the mother's perception between the 12th and 16th week; and the heart beat can be heard by stethoscope between the 16th and the 20th.

Fetal development might lend some support to limiting permissible abortion to 8 weeks — at most, perhaps 10 weeks — of gestational life. No such laws have been proposed.[22] Why?

Searching for an explanation of this strange discrepancy, we must simply conclude that the proposed liberalization of abortion law is in no way based rationally on concern for the fetus and the nature of its development. The proposed laws are rather statements about the mother, or based upon the assumed safety of the operation upon her.

Some scientists may have an interest in obtaining later abortuses for research purposes. Some medical practitioners may have an interest in doing abortion for the sake of the fetus if its impairment is discoverable only late in pregnancy. Still the earlier time limits are the ones realistically to consider. The time limits that are being enacted have, as we have seen, no basis in the nature of fetal development nor in the current alternative methods of performing an abortion. These limits are based on the danger to the woman of one method only — curettage — and, of course, on the general psychological and emotional desirability of early abortion, if this is to be done.

Finally, the time limits being enacted are quite unenforceable. On the most optimistic expectation, one more month of fetal development must be added to them. A physician may easily mistake by one month the length of the pregnancy. In statistically improbable numbers doctors record that women report that they last menstruated on the fifteenth of the month. In about 20 percent of women, bleeding occurs prior to the 20th week of pregnancy; and this bleeding may be mistaken for the last menstrual period although the woman was pregnant before the bleeding episode. Where a physician errs by one month in estimating the age of the

22. *The Christian Science Monitor* reported on July 22, 1969, a poll of 5,000 British doctors showed that nearly two-thirds of them wanted the Abortion Law modified or repealed. The modifications would allow *no abortions after 12 weeks' gestation,* and provide that the "social grounds" — certainly not a medical matter — be assessed by local committees or authorities.

fetus, the baby is exceedingly likely to die of pulmonary insufficiency if born prematurely.

Therefore, the reader may want to compare the time limits upon legalized abortion in any statute or proposed legislation *plus one month* with the timetable of important stages in fetal development, given above.[23] This he will do if he believes that morality should be rationally based on the nature of things and if he believes that morality has anything to do with the laws he should favor in the matter of abortion.

V. FETICIDE AND INFANTICIDE

There is need for a rational moral argument for feticide that is not also logically an argument for infanticide. A rational analysis of moral arguments can show this to be a need made increasingly clear by the practice of fetal medicine, erasing the significance of "birth" as the line to be drawn in either saving life or destroying it. The need for an argument for abortion that does not also justify infanticide can be shown by the following examples that fail this test.

Robert M. Byrn in a letter to the editor of the *New York Times* championing the moral and legal rights of the fetus quoted the following passage from Ashley Montagu's book *Life Before Birth*: "In spite of his newness and his appearance, he [a two-week old fetus] is a living striving human being from the very beginning." [24] Byrn was promptly answered by Ashley Montagu who reaffirmed his statement, saying he meant by it that "from the moment of conception the organism thus brought into being possesses all the potentialities for humanity in its genes, *and for that reason must be considered human.*" [25] Professor Montagu then went on to say that nevertheless he supported the legalization of abortion because the embryo, fetus, and *newborn* of the human species, in point of fact, do not really become functionally human until humanized in the human socialization process. "Humanity is an achievement not an endowment." He believed that it was a "crime against humanity" to bring a child into the world himself

23. As to the laws being enacted, see David W. Louisell and John T. Noonan, Jr., "Constitutional Balance," sec. III, *infra*.
24. The *New York Times*, Feb. 22, 1967.
25. The *New York Times*, March 9, 1967.

Paul Ramsey

"menaced" or "who itself menaces the life of the mother *or the quality of the society into which it is born*" (all italics added). It is evident that the structure of that argument would warrant infanticide under certain conditions as readily as abortion. It does so in so many words, only no one could rightly suppose Professor Montagu was advocating infanticide. He was only giving telling support for abortion law reform — telling because congruent with many modern men's views of man and society and "humanization."

Christianity and Crisis published an article entitled "Abortion and Promise-Keeping" in which the author, Ronald M. Green, took a fresh and profound approach to the moral question of abortion. He rejected the " 'tissue' school of opinion," and yet he sought to "bypass the fruitless controversy whether the fetus is a human being." [26] Green's approach was this: he understood the moral bond between the woman and potential life in such a way as to give great moral weight to the claims of nascent life and at the same time to take the state out of the prohibition of abortion. "Not life itself but a promise to life is the real issue." He found an obligation of "faithkeeping or promise keeping occasioned by the sexual act." If one is aware of the nature of human sexual intercourse as a potentially life-giving act of love-making, there is "an implicit promise to life made in the sexual act." Intercourse freely engaged in means that a "promise-making situation exists, realized or not." The promise made is not to the fetus as such but to the future person that is begun.

This line of reasoning is worth serious consideration, although the author brings this argument to bear too exclusively upon the woman for the purpose of emancipating her. In common with many writings on this subject, including the writings of some women, a male-centered point of view goes to work reforming allegedly male-centered laws and moral formulations.[27]

26. May 15, 1967. For discussion of other issues in Green's article, see *Christianity and Crisis*, Aug. 7, 1967, pp. 195–196.
27. It seems not to have occurred to Marya Mannes, in reference to the figures she gives showing that 80 to 90 percent of all abortions are performed on married women with several children, to suggest that voluntary sterilization before the unwanted pregnancy, performed upon the husband, would be less grave than abortion after the event. This ommission was in an article that suggested that for too long society has been pitching upon women for whom abortion itself is pain enough ("On the Casting of Stones," The *New York*

One of the "indications" which, Green concludes, can morally justify abortion is what he calls the " 'fetal' indication," that is, if the child may have some serious mental or physical defect or injury. Passing over the fact that the author's language assumes that the lives nascent in mothers who have had German measles or have taken thalidomide *"would* be miserably deformed" (and not that there is a calculable likelihood they would and a calculable likelihood they would not be injured in some unspecified degree) Green's contention is that "when the mother conceived, her obligation bound her to fashion for the child a normal start in life." If the child in its prenatal state has been injured or is gravely defective, her promise-keeping is then "rendered actually destructive to the recipient of that promise . . . The obligation ceases to have binding power."

This argument reflects a sensitive understanding of the moral bond between conscious and nascent life. The structure of the argument, however, is capable of producing a moral justification for infanticide for the same reasons. Indeed, it would seem to be only the oddity of our current mores that could prevent there being stronger reason for killing gravely defective children immediately after birth (because this was not the life they were promised) than for killing both the damaged and the undamaged *in utero.*

Green could perhaps support his conclusion when medical science is able to tell with certainty early in pregnancy the births which will result in seriously defective lives, for example, mongolism; but then his argument holds only in these cases. Since obviously there would be every reason for committing "fetal euthanasia" as early as possible, the simultaneous justification of infanticide would be avoided. Assuming that we need a moral argument for abortion that would not by its logic also warrant infanticide, the foregoing analysis does not pass this test (except

---

Times, editorial page, Feb. 18, 1967). There is secretly a reversed male-ism at work in the protest that the state has no business "dictating to a woman what she is to do with her own body and that which is a part of her own being" (*ibid.*). Even religious teachings that regard both sterilization and abortion as a means of birth control as *inherently* immoral also hold attacks upon fetal life to be the far more serious offense. One can only say that the present penchant for abortion (upon the woman) as solution to family and other social problems reflects a more patriarchal and male-centered attitude in our present culture than ever influenced the moral doctrines of our religious communities.

perhaps in the case noted). Indeed, it is doubtful whether any argument *can* do so if it simply bypasses "fruitless controversy" concerning whether and when a fetus is human and proposes no particular answer to that question.

Another extraordinary attempt to construct a morality of abortion is contained in an unofficial study pamphlet issued by the Church Assembly Board of Social Responsibility of the Church of England in 1965. In cases where there is possibility of grave deformity or where pregnancy has resulted from rape or incest, this pamphlet does not allow abortion on these grounds *alone*. Instead it concludes that these factors rarely stand alone and so declares that abortion is morally to be permitted or even advised on the ground of a "prognosis concerning the mother as affected by the pregnancy in question; not the possibility of deformity itself, not simply the fact (if established) of the act of incest or rape." [28] In other words, this study adopted a premise that "because of its potential future, there is a *presumption* that we ought to do what we can to preserve the foetus." This premise, however, is put only as a presumption in favor of the fetus; there may be good reasons for setting it aside. Still this pamphlet asserts "as normative, the general inviolability of the foetus"; defends "as a first principle, its right to live and develop"; and then lays "the burden of proof to the contrary firmly on those who, in particular cases, would wish to extinguish that right on the ground that it was in conflict with another or others with a higher claim to recognition." [29]

This approach meant that the distinguished committee of British philosophers, theologians, and medical men who prepared this report had to reject any outright program of fetal euthanasia. They held that "the concept of a human being is to some extent indeterminate"; that, for example, from applying the standard of rationality one would get a different result than using as a test "the capacity to reciprocate love in a typically human way, which

28. *Abortion: An Ethical Discussion*, Church Information Office, Church House (Westminster, England) 1965, p. 62.

29. *Ibid.*, pp. 31–32. This presumption in favor of the fetus, which would seem to be more pliable than trying to base a moral argument on the concept of the fetus as a human being, is said actually to be "not so pliable" (p. 31) — because, beginning with that concept one can go in the direction of denying the fetus *any* due consideration as easily as one can go in the direction of attributing *equal* moral claims to the fetus.

might be possessed even by a mental defect." [30] Yet the committee concluded that. "to grant to the 'whole' the power to kill the deformed, unconsulted, or against the general wish of those capable of being consulted, on the ground that it was in their own interest for them to be killed, would be as unethical as it would be socially dangerous."

The committee did locate a possible justification of abortion in a conflict of presumptions to a right to live and develop. Its reason was that conflicting presumptions in favor of life could have unequal weights. Granting that "the fact that a child (following rape or incest) ought not, in law or in morals, to exist affords no justification *per se* for depriving it of its right to live," the committee refused to bring to bear upon the woman any merely "notional insistence that she be obliged to carry it to term." Instead the committe proposed a rebuttable presumption that she should bear the child; she might be able "to 'forgive' the child for being where and what it was, and accept it as her own." The institutions of society and the influences surrounding her might strengthen her and enable her to do this, if none of these institutions acquiesced in reducing the presumption in favor of nascent life or yielded to a reduced estimate of human nature and capacity. Still, a medical assessment could be made of the probable effects upon the mother if she had a "determined rejection and resentment of the child"; this might place her own life or health or development in such jeopardy as to be overriding, and she could be advised accordingly. Indeed — and this would seem a conclusion well warranted by this pamphlet's reasoning — where the patient was still a girl-child, a doctor would feel free to terminate the pregnancy as constituting an overriding threat. He "constructively" could determine that she had an irremoveable inability to acknowledge the child with which she was pregnant to be hers and that she would be overcome by the threat of it. However, "if the patient were not a child, and the fact of rape were similarly clearly established, the doctor could accept an invincible aversion to the pregnancy as good evidence of such a threat, and terminate." [31] Similarly, the risk of bearing a gravely defective child could constitute a direct and invincible threat to

30. *Abortion: An Ethical Discussion*, p. 30.
31. *Abortion: An Ethical Discussion*, p. 47.

the mother's health and to the development of her other children. These would be "accessible indications"; to abort in this case would not be the same as when, in fetal euthanasia, the warrant is "an *a priori* and non-medical assumption about the supposed interest of the unborn child" in not being born.[32]

What has been forgotten in this very sensitive analysis is the correctness of a statement made earlier in the report, namely, that "it is difficult to envisage a moral argument for or against killing the foetus immediately before birth which would not apply with equal or almost equal force to the child newly born." [33] If there is a strong presumption in favor of fetal life and development, this presumption would seem to give greater support to the practice of killing the gravely defective immediately after birth — not because these were *not* the lives promised them but because a general presumption in their favor is outweighed by an assessment of jeopardy to the mother's or family's health or well-being. If serious defects become certainly predictable by medical science, and only in such cases, would the structure of the argument of this report warrant abortion without entailing a possible justification of infanticide.

It is true the committee mentions "invincible aversion" and "determined rejection" only in its finding of possible warrant for abortion to terminate a pregnancy following incest or rape. The fact of a violation of the woman's "maternal capacity" in the

32. *Ibid.*, p. 49.
33. *Abortion: An Ethical Discussion*, p. 26. The corollary statement that "it is difficult to envisage a moral discourse appropriate to the cell immediately after conception which was inappropriate before it" is simply mistaken. An even more glaring error is on the next page. The committee here states its belief that "medical skill was now *able* to terminate pregnancy by direct action upon the foetus with a diminishing threat to the life of the mother." That is correct in fact. But from this was drawn the conclusion that the rapid progress of medical and surgical skill has "rendered obsolete earlier casuistry in so far as it had depended on a distinction between a 'direct' and an 'indirect' attack upon the foetus, and between the abortion of the foetus as a deliberate act and its happening as an unintended consequence of an act directed to another end" (p. 27, italics added). The latter is a *moral* distinction which medical skill only gives us the ability safely to *violate*. To say that what we are now *able* to do itself renders obsolete an earlier morality would be like saying that the fact that we are now *able* with nuclear weapons to annihilate a whole people, and perhaps to perform a direct abortion on the human race, renders obsolete all earlier conventions concerning *jus in bello* that are based on the distinction between discriminate and indiscriminate acts of war.

event of forced intercourse has an independent weight in the logic of this argument, as does the assessment to be made of the woman's capacity to "accept" the child as her own. The grounds of "invincible aversion" or "determined rejection" (actually or "constructively" assessed) would have always to be taken together with the fact of rape or incest. Both could be weighed, without waiting for the child to be brought to term. Therefore it cannot be said that the structure of the committee's argument in these cases has any further entailment.

Still it stands very close to the elbow to ask how many normal children would equal one seriously abnormal child in assessing real threat to the life and health of a mother and of her family. We have also come close to a border line on the other side of which is the weight to be given in law and morals to a man or a woman's invincible aversion to more children, and their determined rejection of them.

It looks as if we are not going to get very far in discussions of the morality of abortion by resolutely avoiding making some decision even a very rough, theoretically uncertain and practical one, concerning when the fetus is to be treated *as if* he is a human being. We are going to have to determine when, before birth or viability, the fetus already has a right of life and not only a presumptive right to be born, if our arguments justifying abortion are not to undercut the rational moral grounds mankind has for preserving the life of every viable product of human generation.

I therefore say that there is need for a rational moral argument for feticide that is not also an argument for infanticide. Many of the arguments in the current debate do not meet this test. The usual response to the proposal of this test is to cry silence in a loud voice. Where that is not the response, the answer is made that this proposal is only a "thin edge of the wedge" argument, and it is argued that men must trust themselves to be able to institute or acquiesce in the practice of one sort of thing without being driven inexorably to institute or acquiesce in the doing of another sort of thing. The "wedge" argument may often be a good argument. It says only that there may be good reasons adduced for doing or not doing something on account of what may predictably or possibly follow, that is, good reasons that need not be good inherent moral reasons. Anyone who dismisses altogether the pertinence of the "wedge" argument is dismissing a consideration on which human civilization very much depends.

But in the foregoing, the "wedge" argument has not been invoked. What is involved is a form of the "universalizability" argument; and that is a different matter. In the "wedge" argument we ask, What will likely be the case if I do X? or, What will come to be the case if our society does X? Will I actually influence others or many others to do other things? Will my action have consequences of a large order on the practices of others? Will this social practice have consequences on other practices? These are the questions the "wedge" argument raises.

The test of universalizability asks an entirely different question. It does not ask what will likely happen. It asks, rather, in regard to an individual act, What would be the case if everyone in a morally relevant, like situation did X as I am doing (whether there is any tendency for them to do so or not)? In regard to a social practice it asks, What would be the case if every possible X were done that fulfills the warrants now invoked to justify a present practice or reform, whether or not there is any causal connection between one practice and another. In the case of individual actions done in safe secrecy, having no influence upon others, the universalization-argument test still holds. In the case also of social practices, absent any causal influence upon the production of other practices, the universalization-test still holds. What is now being done or proposed to be done is tested by asking what would be the case if every case of this were established practice.

Until we are given a moral argument for abortion in certain sorts of cases that would not also be an argument for infanticide in the same sorts of cases, then the proposed abortion is now morally the same as that for infanticide, even granting there is no tendency toward the production of the latter institution. Abortion would be (unless and until we are clearly shown otherwise) morally the same sort of "slaughter of the innocent." Those who believe this is the case have every right to say so. No good reason can be advanced why the use of pungent language should be reserved for those who plead the cause of distressed, conscious lives needing the relief for which abortion is proposed.

VI. BIRTH, VIABILITY, AND THE PRACTICE OF FETAL MEDICINE

The rapid advancements in medical practice in caring for the unborn, and present and future possible ways to render him "born alive" long before the normal time of human birth, are depriving us of "birth" as a seemingly significant distinction in our moral reflection upon the care to be extended to new life. Everything has been accelerated, including the nine months that used to be required. Modern incubator methods have already pushed back the time of "viability." Future developments in this regard, and in the medical care that can be extended to the fetus *in utero*, are going to obliterate the distinction between the pre- and the post-natal period.

Cesareans plus earlier viability and other ingredients of medical progress have already taken away most if not all of those "indications" for abortion based on fatal birth-room conflicts between the lives of mother and child which some people still mistakenly think crucial. There are no theoretical limits upon man's scientific ability to push back the time of viability and to treat the patient *in utero* as a man alive. Not even an umbilical cord is required; a fetus can be profused through any vein. Science may soon simulate the environmental condition of living *in utero* to a degree that will make our present incubators antiquated. To speak of improved "incubators" may be too crude an image; it is better to say that science could create an artificial "placenta" with which to surround and nourish the nascent life. Such development will take place to some degree in the normal course of medical advancement.

That viability is a moveable line and medicine can be practiced upon the fetus *in utero* as an independent patient like any other human being have brought into actuality a form of the "reversibility"-argument test for resolving questions of right and wrong. The test of reversibility requires us, in claiming that certain actions are right, to reverse roles and put ourselves as agents in the place of another to whom the action should also apply if it is right, or to put another in our place. The reversibility "argument" is simply an imaginative way of making sure we have correctly applied the test of universability in reaching a moral conclusion. We today hardly need use our imaginations to put ourselves in the place of the unborn patient, or to place him in the land of the living like any other infant, and in this way to enable ourselves to reason correctly about what should or should not be done to him. Medical science has performed the experiment for us.

In face of the universalizability test and in face of the reversibility of unborn and born life which science daily makes manifest, anyone who wishes to make birth or viability the points at which a human life begins to have a right to life will find it necessary to provide himself with an arbitrary determination that such is the case, and he must then simply resolve to hold this decision firmly. This may be sufficient for law-making or for medical practice, but it can afford us neither a medical ethics nor a personal ethics.

Ancient Jewish thought found it necessary simply to set the time and lay down the law as to what "birth" meant. Anyone today must do the same, even if he simply pronounces that we must do everything we can to save every *viable* nascent life. He must legislate in face of the increasing interchangeability between born and unborn lives, between born and unborn patients of medical practice. He will still probably accuse theological moralists of being "legalists," obscurantist dealers in mysteries, subject to arbitrary and unscientific judgments. Yet if a medical practitioner simply holds firmly to the wavering and passable line of viability, he must do so despite the fact that he knows that it is not impossible for a doctor performing an abortion later than would generally be the practice to find himself face to face not with a dead, aborted fetus on the operating table but with a live fetus. Should he now in the light of consciousness attempt (even if vainly) to save a life which moments before in the darkness of the womb he meant to kill? Should he try to make it "viable" and therefore inviolate? Or shall he throw it out with the garbage as in principle dead already? Should mothers be induced instead to contribute these fetal lives to cancer research? Why not?

When we think about man's present capacity to place nascent life in the land of the living, there inevitably takes place a convergence of the moral issues arising from man's capacity to save nascent life "safely" and the moral issues arising from man's capacity to destroy nascent life "safely." The issue that must be urgently raised is whether we are going to continue relentlessly, and it may be indiscriminately, to save life in the beginning of it. There is no way to avoid bringing these two questions together; and when we do so we are compelled to seek for some grounds for what we are doing either in significant periodization within the time between conception and what used to be called "birth" or in the lineaments of a proper medical ethics governing the care of nascent and of dying lives.

The elements of an older medical ethics which today have again become meaningful and necessary are: the distinction between killing and allowing to die, the distinction between prolonging life and prolonging dying, and the distinction between using ordinary means to save life (which are affirmatively obliging) and extraordinary means to save life (which are binding neither upon the physician nor upon the patient, actually or "constructively"). Today men of medicine and moralists working together need to inquire what would be the meaning of these categories for modern medical practice. It may be that a scientific age is lacking in the apprehension of some categories necessary for the proper care of life both in the last of life and in the first of it.

In an article "Whatever the Consequences" Jonathan Bennett takes up a case presenting a straight choice between the woman's life and the child's life where the woman's life can be saved only by craniotomy.[34] A woman in labor will certainly die unless an operation is performed in which the head of the child is crushed and dissected; while if the operation is not performed, the child, he says, can be saved only by postmortem Cesarean section. The author is concerned to refute what he takes to be the Roman Catholic verdict in this sort of case. In this instance he denies that there is any moral distinction to be drawn between directly killing the child and allowing the woman to die. His is a modest if still significant thesis: he wants to refute the proposition that "it would always be wrong to kill an innocent human life, whatever the consequences of not doing so." I would judge that Bennett succeeds in demonstrating what he set out to demonstrate. Readers of his article, however, need to note that the consequences he has in mind are limited by the terms of this case, and that the

34. In *Analysis*, January 1966, pp. 83-102.

effect of removing the word "always" from this proposition leaves standing very much if not all of the moral force of saying that it is wrong to kill an innocent human life when *other* consequences are in view or believed about to supervene. Bennett calls himself a consequentialist; but from this article one can say that he is a remarkable consequentialist, and that the consequences in other sorts of cases may not have at all the decisiveness in moral judgment that is allowed in this case.

Not all "upshots" belong to the description of "what he did"; and in a proper description of "what he did" there is correct distinction to be made between "killing" and "allowing to die." The latter is an important element in the descriptions of acts from either of which death results. Moreover, Bennett seems not to deny that there may be moral significance in drawing the distinction in "what we do" between "action" and "refraining." He is only concerned to establish the fact that the action-refraining distinction does not have the moral impact it has been believed to have in the particular sort of case to which his article is devoted. These consequences (where *both* will die) nullify any alleged moral difference between killing the one and allowing the other to die, although the latter is still an apt and proper part of the description of what was done.[35] It is, therefore, possible for the action-refraining distinction to have moral import in other sorts of cases or situations. In fact, the author says at one point that "the reproach" suggested by the words "he lets her die" used to obliterate this distinction is "just an unavoidable nuisance, and I shall not

35. While granting Bennett's conclusion in the case before us, in the course of his argument he is mistaken, I believe, in saying that what is "aimed at" is the same in each of the alternative actions. This reveals an inadequate analysis of "intention" or an insufficient comprehension of the traditional analysis. Bennett's conclusion should nevertheless be endorsed. In an article entitled "The Sanctity of Life — In the First of It" (*The Dublin Review*, Spring 1967, esp. pp. 13–17), I reached the same conclusion from theological ethical premises. This was to justify *direct* therapeutic abortion to save the mother's life (even if today this would be rarely or never needed medically), in contrast to the justification in traditional Roman Catholic moral theology of only *indirect* therapeutic abortion to save the one life that can be saved under the assumed circumstances. Logically prior to what the present essay undertakes to set forth, that article also analyzed the Biblical and common Christian (Protestant and Roman Catholic) grounds for respect for the sanctity of nascent life. It has now been reprinted as a chapter entitled "The Morality of Abortion" in *Life or Death: Ethics and Options*, ed. Daniel H. Labby (Seattle, Wash.: University of Washington Press, 1968), a volume of addresses originally delivered by a number of scholars at a Reed College symposium on The Sanctity of Life.

argue from it." The author proceeds himself to propose more limited moral "rules of practice" in the area of medical ethics than the sweeping "It is *always* wrong" proposition which he refutes;[36] and in each case these are universal sorts of "killing the innocent" which, the author seems to say, should never be done.

In his discussion of the possibility of justifiable abortion, Karl Barth limits such abortion to cases of mortal or near mortal conflict of nascent life with the mother's life — or her health, he sometimes adds.[37] He does not take up the suggestion that abortion is justified if the child is likely to be born with grave mental or physical defects. We can only make suppositions about what Barth would say on this issue. Yet there cannot be much doubt that the substance of his entire special ethics under the heading of the protection of life would require him to agree with Father Gerald Kelly that the action proposed in such cases can be more accurately described as "fetal euthanasia" than as abortion.[38] Therefore, in order to tell what Barth might say on the subject of abortion for the sake of the child, we can refer to his treatment of euthanasia in general.[39] This will also give us the opportunity to examine a highly problematic moral situation in which, there being no other life in competition, Barth can find absolutely no justification for an "exception" from the duty to respect and care for life by preserving it — not, at least, until he is forced to distinguish between direct killing and allowing to die, and for him this distinction is no exception, but a merciful rule regulating behavior.

The incurably infirm, those suffering terminal illnesses or serious mental or physical deformity "cannot in any case be regarded as providing an exception," Barth writes. The question whether anyone ever has the right to declare another life useless "is to be answered by an unequivocal No." This would be "a type of killing which can be regarded only as murder." "The value of this kind of life is God's secret." ". . . The whole idea of unfit-

36. Bennett, "Whatever the Consequences," pp. 22, 100.
37. *Church Dogmatics* (Edinburgh: T. & T. Clark, 1961), III/4, § 55, 2: "The Protection of Life," pp. 415–423.
38. Gerald Kelly, S.J., *Medico-Moral Problems* (St. Louis, Mo.: Catholic Hospital Association, 1954), V, 16.
39. Barth, *Church Dogmatics*, III/4, § 55, 2: "The Protection of Life," pp. 423–427.

ness to live, is already transgression," even though "the sonorous Greek term 'euthanasia' " be used for the way it is proposed that we should deal with persons in whom we can find no worth to themselves or to others.[40]

It is at this point that, out of his unremitting effort to probe the ways in which human life may be sanctified and served, Barth's analysis brings him to a breaking point. First, he rules out any pettifogging distinction between directly killing and allowing to die. Then, he turns around and himself draws this distinction — both, it would seem, for sufficient reason.

In rejecting the distinction, Barth in part misunderstands the meaning of the indirect, unintended effects of an action. The suggestion that in the treatment of a patient (fetus or terminal case) anyone could "help him to die," not directly but "only in the form of mercifully not applying means for the artificial prolongation of his life," with or without the agreement of the patient, strikes Barth as raising "tempting questions" which "for all their impressiveness . . . contain too much sophistry for those who are directed by the command of God." Then it is that he misunderstands the essential meaning of the rule and the distinction which he seemingly rejects and ridicules. "All honor to the well-meaning humanitarianism of underlying motive! . . . The derivation is obviously from another book than that which we thus far have consulted [the Bible!]. Nor do subjectively well-meaning motives change wrong into right." [41]

Still, the motif that is powerfully at work in Barth's analysis and which accounts for the horrible impressiveness of his conclusions is not to be set aside as only a mistake in the intellectual order. The motif is rather that of a man who in his thought is seeking to conform in every way to the degree to which God has from all eternity surrounded with sanctity all these nascent and dying lives of ours. According to this measure of cleaving to the life of a fellowman, it would seem that one can "give up" the life of a sick or useless or horribly deformed person *no less* by "letting

40. *Church Dogmatics*, III/4, pp. 423–424.
41. *Church Dogmatics*, III/4, p. 425. This is the same mistake Jonathan Bennett makes in saying that the distinction between directly killing and allowing to die entails no difference in what is "aimed at." Both men confuse motive with intention and seem to be insufficiently informed concerning the analysis of intention in traditional moral theology.

his life ebb away" than by "encompassing his death." [42] Upon this basis, the attempted distinction between directly intending the death and allowing to die completely collapses in Barth's view into "deliberate killing" (just as was the case in the matter of "deliberate abortion"). "It can hardly be said," Barth concludes, that "this form of deliberate killing ['letting . . . life ebb away'] . . . can ever seem to be really commanded in any emergency, and therefore to be anything but murder." [43]

Then, finally, Barth sets down a fine-print paragraph in which he reverses himself on this crucial point. The first two sentences (one-third of the short paragraph) restate "strongly" and without qualification the conclusion to which Barth had arrived, to the effect that "the same truth" applies to "passive failure to apply the stimulants" (in heart cases) as to cases of "active killing." Then comes the reversal, and the consideration Barth suddenly introduces at this point deserves to be investigated by moralists and by medical doctors alike, and ought to be put to far greater use in moral theology; it cuts across the present-day medical ethics of always saving life, even as it cuts across Barth's own position. "The question also arises," Barth writes, "whether this kind of artificial prolongation of life does not amount to human arrogance in the opposite direction, whether the fulfillment of medical duty does not threaten to become fanaticism, reason folly, and the required assisting of human life a forbidden torturing of it. A case is at least conceivable in which a doctor might have to recoil from this prolongation of life no less than from its arbitrary shortening. We must await further developments in this sphere to get a clear general picture. But it may well be that in this special sphere we do have a kind of exceptional case. For it is not now a question of arbitrary euthanasia; it is a question of the respect which may be claimed by even the dying life as such." [44] If there is indeed

42. *Ibid.*, pp. 426–427. "It must be remembered that not only the patient but his relatives and the doctor are all dying men, i.e., those who after the expiry of an unknown period are doomed to die, and that they, too, will have to bear sufferings which might make the shortening of this period seem desirable to them" (p. 427). Then perhaps it is the case that in order for there to be a prudent application of this distinction between direct killing and allowing to die in analyzing moral action, one would have to find an important discrimination to be made in the patient and his illness between prolonging life and prolonging dying.
43. *Church Dogmatics*, III/4, p. 427.
44. *Ibid.*, p. 427.

Paul Ramsey

"a kind of exceptional case" in this matter it is not likely that Barth would allow, in the light of his whole discussion, the possible justifiability of a directly death-dealing action. The exception makes use of the distinction Barth has rejected up to this point, between "active killing" and "passive failure" to keep a dying patient forcibly alive. It becomes a case of love's casuistry spelling out and applying with practical wisdom the distinction between allowing to die and arrogantly using all the resources of medical science artificially to prolong dying. Out of respect for the dying life as such, there would arise a fresh understanding of the forbidden torturing of it. Then, within these limits and in the course of positing the courageous deed that respects life enough to stand aside from a man's dying and let him die, we might gather enough data to draw a relativistic line between what are "ordinary" means and what are "extraordinary" and therefore dispensable means of saving life in a particular situation, taking all factors, both as to the life and as to the state of the science of medicine, into account.

The moral tradition of Christendom was wonderfully wise in making this distinction between ordinary and extraordinary means of preserving life. According to it there was an affirmative obligation to use ordinary means only, and no obligation upon a patient to use extraordinary means (though he may choose to do so), or for a doctor to use them in saving life, unless, upon a clear presentation of the options, he were requested to do so. Perhaps beneath this distinction there was a recognition of the fact that we should try to distinguish between prolonging life and prolonging dying (which would be a forbidden torture).

Now, it may be that only in an age of faith when men know that the dying cannot pass beyond God's love and care will men have the courage to apply these limits to medical practice. It may be that only upon the basis of faith in God can there be a conscionable category of "letting die." It may be that in an atheistic and secular age the best morality men can think of is to make an absolute of saving life for yet a bit more spatio-temporal existence, as if death were only and always an unmitigated evil. If this has to be the conclusion of a secular age, then it is the root of many problems, since this would mean, as Barth suggested, that medical duty has become fanaticism. Together, medical men

94

and moralists need most urgently to renew the search for a way
to express both moral recoil from any arbitrary shortening of life
and moral recoil from arbitrarily prolonging dying. Since Christians believe that death and dying are a part of life and no less
than birth a gift of God, they have not to wrestle with the Al-
mighty with no holds barred for the dying man.

The meaning of the mandatory "ordinary means" for saving life
is of course a relative and a changing one, so also the meaning of
the permitted but dispensable "extraordinary means." For one
thing, an *artificial* means of prolonging life is not the same as
extraordinary means. Thus, J. V. Sullivan writes: "A natural
means of prolonging life is, per se, an ordinary means of prolonging life, yet per accidens it may be extraordinary . . . An artificial
means of prolonging life may be an ordinary means or an extraordinary means relative to the physical condition of the patient." [45]
Presumably this passage implies, among other things, that up to a
point the worse off a patient becomes, the more do extraordinary
and artificial means become "ordinary" and therefore morally mandatory. It is certainly required even in grievous illness that every
effort be made to save life. Since treatment is a necessary part of
good diagnosis, every effort should be made to save a patient, no
matter how difficult it may be to draw this line and to say when
this particular patient's dying has taken irreversible control, as
distinct from the general sense in which we are all dying men.
Medical conscience must learn to be willing to begin treatments
and then to stop them — a more difficult thing to do, or to justify,
than not to start a given treatment of an apparently hopeless case.
Medicine should instead accompany a man's dying with due respect for *that* as well, and seek only to benefit dying men as before
it sought to save the lives of men not yet seized by their death.

Does there not come a point past which the same means become, still relative to the patient's condition, "extraordinary," and
thus become means which no man has any obligation to employ
for prolonging his own life or the life of another? "There is an
absolute norm beyond which means are *per se* extraordinary,"
Sullivan writes; and "an aged woman sick unto death with cancer
would not have to use the same means toward prolonging life as

45. J. V. Sullivan, *Catholic Teaching on the Morality of Euthanasia* (Washington, D. C.: Catholic University of America, 1949), p. 65.

a young girl ill for the first time in her life with a hopeful future ahead. For this aged woman an operation which might prolong her life a few months or a year would be an extraordinary means."[46] Note that this last statement refers not simply to degree of illness in trying to determine whether a grievously assaulted life or its dying is predominant. It refers to the mere age of the patient as one of the factors dispensing from an affirmative obligation to use every means to save life — so far is a proper religious ethics from teaching that saving life is an absolute, or from saying that God may be merciful in allowing men to die but men cannot be.

Another of Sullivan's illustrations justifies a physician in cutting off intravenous feeding because it is an extraordinary means and therefore need not be used on a terminal patient in great pain.[47] Respect for life requires in this case that men accompany the patient's dying by affording relief from pain; it does not at all require the prolongation of his dying.

Finally, this distinction is relative not only to the condition of the patient but also to progress in medical science. "As science advances, the extraordinary means of a decade ago become the ordinary means of today. It would seem today that even the amputation of an arm or leg would be an ordinary means of prolonging life. In times past, such an operation was considered by theologians as an extraordinary means."[48] It is notable how tentative this religious ethicist is in reaching the conclusion about amputation that the present age would regard as obvious and a certain moral mandate! Sullivan is under no great compulsion to reach the conclusion that a man is obliged to choose life without his limb, though he does arrive at this verdict.

In the light of this, the following questions need urgently to be raised: Have we not gone too far in thoughtlessly supposing that any means for prolonging life, once it is made available, becomes ordinary and morally mandatory upon both patient and doctor? Is intravenous feeding extraordinary only for an incurable patient in great pain, or also for a patient in peaceful terminal coma? Is a quadruple amputee obliged to choose existence on such terms by submitting to the use of any means to save his life? If not, what

46. *Catholic Teaching*, pp. 64–65.
47. *Catholic Teaching*, p. 72, case (R).
48. *Catholic Teaching*, pp. 64–65.

right has a doctor (apart from the general benefit of pushing back the frontiers of medical science) to save his life forcibly? In the case of an ordinary man threatening to commit suicide, we restrain him on the assumption that his real will is different from his actual will, often well expressed, to die. But what is the correct assumption to make in cases of men who are sick unto death? May not the real will of a terminal patient be likewise known by his personal physician or rightly supposable even if never verbally expressed — his real will not to be forcibly maintained in existence as a cadaver? Whatever protections may be needed in the criminal law regulating medical practice, can it be denied that as a moral matter a physician may know enough and be morally sensitive enough to do in relation to the dying as he would be done by? Is there not an obligation to allow to die, limiting the exercise of a doctor's general responsibility to save life? Moralists and men of medicine must work together to enlarge again the category of extraordinary means which are morally dispensable, and to explore the difference between saving life and prolonging dying. Otherwise, what ought to be done for the patient and what doctors are morally required to do will continue to be a tight and impenetrable and ever-enlarging category of practices imposed without limit upon dying men. What ought to be done will continue to be a function simply of what can be done to prolong life; and the propriety of an action, the inexorable consequence of the physical power to do it. In this there is little ultimate respect for human life, and no sense that dying men have dignity too. Reason becomes folly, the assistance of life verges on forbidden torture, and the medical impulse to save life becomes an arrogant use and misuse of it. Unless, in short, doctors do more than hold death at bay, unless there is a morally justifiable category of actions that "allow to die," there is in the last of life no respect for human life or acknowledgment of the sanctity and the limitations God places on every human being.

These considerations need now to be applied to nascent life. Is there ever warrant for recoiling from the preservation of germinating life as well as from any arbitrary killing of it? Before we rush to the justification of direct "fetal euthanasia" if the child is likely to suffer from grave physical or mental defect, surely the first question is the morality of a relentless and unqualified effort to save fetal life. The first question to be asked is whether the respect which can be claimed for nascent life may include also the claim to be allowed to die, and not be kept alive by the application of all the extraordinary means by which medical science can now do this. With regard to nascent life as with all life, not everything that can be done ought therefore to be done. There is not always an affirmative moral obligation, whatever the law may say, to use extraordinary means to save the child.

In late July, 1965, a severely malformed infant girl was born to Mr. and Mrs. William McCauley. She needed surgery to increase her slender chances of survival. The doctors testified that even with surgery her chances of survival were exceedingly slim. The operation they wanted to perform would not significantly relieve the exceedingly grave deformity of the child's body; it only might enable it to survive. On petition of the Riverview Hospital of Red Bank, New Jersey, Judge Gene R. Mariano in Freehold, New Jersey, ordered the operation over McCauley's objections.

Some of us may not entirely agree with these parents. "I don't know that I could cope with it," said Mrs. McCauley. "I don't know what it will do to the four boys to bring her home, and after a while to put her away." Said Mr. McCauley: "I feel my wife is not emotionally geared to raise an impaired child." Said the Judge, "Life is a precious gift of God and only He shall be permitted to take it away. I cannot permit parents to determine if a child shall die or live. The infant is entitled to the protection of the law, even when its chances of survival are only 20 to 30 percent." But God in his mercy was beyond the jurisdiction of this human court. The child died before the operation could be performed.[49]

The question raised by this case is whether there is a moral distinction to be made between letting life ebb away and encompassing a child's death, between a passive failure to apply surgery and taking her life away. These questions are all ways of asking whether respect for the sanctity of life and therefore for nascent and for new-born life does not include sometimes keeping one's distance from its dying, protecting its dying no less than its life from arbitrary intrusion.

49. The *New York Times*, Aug. 6, 1965.

It is well known that spontaneous abortion, prenatal death, and infant mortality in some of their incidence include children who began their particular "dying" with the first of their lives. During the early stages of human life a number of seriously defective individuals normally die of these deformities as such, and not from extrinsic causes. A recent book gives a startling account of the power of modern medicine to save prenatal life. The author describes a new breed of medical men, the "fetologist." [50] The fetus is treated by the fetologist as fully human. He is in fact an "encapsulated spaceman." He perceives sensations, opens his eyes, dodges the painful prick of a needle (now that the blessings of a blood transfusion, always only inches away, have been visited upon him). He hears sounds, including his mother's lower tones of voice, and reacts with quickened heartbeat. He even begins to suck his thumb if he feels a bit insecure about all that's going on in and around his life.

Despite all that is indubitably to be praised in its accomplishments, fetology is apt to raise here at the first of life serious questions about the right of the fetus to be allowed to die, of the same order as those the practice of medicine has already raised concerning the last of life.

Some percentage of genetic defectiveness would, in the ordinary course of "nature's deliberations concerning the man," be eliminated by miscarriages. If more and more of these lives are brought to birth, and then to child-bearing age, and then to ability to engender or bear children of their own by the steady advance of the practice of scientific medicine, the result will be a steadily increasing number of seriously defective individuals among the population in all future generations. Fetology seems apt to accelerate this tendency. These considerations open serious medical and moral questions. The principal question is whether it is not morally responsible, or at least morally tolerable, to negate some of the negative consequences of the practice of saving life. Should not this practice be limited by the sort of respect that esteems life enough to allow it to die on occasion even if it technically could be saved?

In the future we are going to have to face the fact that the

50. Beth Day and H. M. I. Liley, *Modern Motherhood: Pregnancy, Childbirth, and the Newborn Baby* (New York: Random House, 1967 ed.), pp. 23–24.

fetus can be made a man among men by much earlier incubator methods, and can in any case be treated as a patient while *in utero* like any other person. We are morally ill-prepared for this situation. It is possible for the practice of medicine governed only by an undifferentiated resolve to save life to create as many problems by its interventions upon life in the first of it as have been created by the undifferentiated resolve to save life in the last of it. These interventions take the form of an otherwise unlimited impulse to save life and at the same time self-elected decisions to destroy life. Between these two, the middle ground of the justifiability of allowing to die and the unjustifiability of taking human life needs to be restored.

In terminal medicine the time is somewhat past in which very many people proposed that we should relentlessly prolong life, not allowing man to die humanly, and at the same time mounted schemes of euthanasia, or direct killing. Something like this is now the case with regard to the practice of fetal medicine and public policy in regard to the first of life. On the one hand, there are moral impulses behind an unremitting endeavor to save every new life that medically can be saved and, at the same time, it is alledged that men have moral warrant for planning the destruction of nascent life. Again, the middle ground justifying allowing unborn child-life to die and keeping our distance also from the destruction of child-life (born or unborn as they now indistinguishably are) needs to be recovered. This will not come to pass if we have only caring hearts, some abstract concept of the person, and technical competence. To limit an omnicompetent saving or destruction of life requires a sense of the significance of the bodily life to the person, a knowledge that a person is the body and the bodily process of his soul no less than he is the soul of his body. It requires a sense that to die is one way of being a human creature and to be allowed to die a precious human right.

JAMES M. GUSTAFSON

A Protestant Ethical Approach

In the ethics of abortion, the differences of opinion surface not only on the substantial moral question of whether it is permissible but also on the question of what is the proper method of moral reflection. The two questions are not entirely independent of each other, as this essay demonstrates. Catholics and Protestants have been divided on the question of method, as well as on the substantial moral judgment.

I. SALIENT ASPECTS OF TRADITIONAL CATHOLIC ARGUMENTS

Any Protestant moralist writing about abortion is necessarily indebted to the work of his Roman Catholic colleagues. Their work on this subject shows historical learning that is often absent among Protestants; it shows philosophical acumen exercised with great finesse once their starting principles are accepted; it shows command of the medical aspects of abortion beyond what one finds in cursory Protestant discussions; and it shows extraordinary seriousness about particular moral actions. Debt must also be acknowledged to the contemporary Protestant moralist who has learned most profoundly from the Catholics, namely Paul Ramsey, for his voluminous writing about problems of war and of medical ethics have introduced a note of intellectual rigor into Protestant ethics that was too often absent.[1]

Every moral argument, no matter who makes it and what is the issue at hand, must limit the factors that are brought into consideration. No one can handle all possible relevant bits of data, ranges of value, sources of insight, and pertinent principles in a manageable bit of discourse. What one admits to the statement of

1. See, for example, his essay, *supra*.

the moral issue in turn is crucial to the solutions given to it. The determination of which factors or principles are primary, or at least of greater importance than others, in the way one argues is also fairly decisive for the outcome of the argument. The traditional Catholic arguments about abortion can be characterized in part by the following delineations of the perspective from which they are made.[2]

First, the arguments are made by an *external judge*. They are written from the perspective of persons who claim the right to judge the past actions of others as morally right or wrong, or to tell others what future actions are morally right or wrong. To make the point differently, moral responsibility is ascribed to others for their actions, or it is prescribed or proscribed.

The perspective of the external judge can be distinguished from those of the persons who are more immediately involved in an abortion situation. It is clear, of course, that those involved, for example, physicians or mothers, might interpret their situations in terms that they have been taught by the external judges. Even if they do, however, the *position of personal responsibility* that physicians, mothers, and others have is different from that of the writer of a manual of moral theology, or of the priest who judges the moral rectitude of others and determines the penance that is to be required. To assume responsibility for an action is quite a different order of experience from ascribing responsibility to others for an action.[3] Physicians, mothers, and others are initiators of action, they are agents in the process of life who determine to a great extent what actually occurs. Their relationship to a situation involves their senses of accountability for consequences, their

2. The generalizations do not do injustice to the treatment of abortion in at least the following books: Thomas J. O'Donnell, S.J., *Morals in Medicine*, 2nd ed. (Westminster, Md.: Newman Press, 1960); Charles J. McFadden, O.S.A., *Medical Ethics*, 5th ed. (Philadelphia: F. A. Davis Co., 1961); John P. Kenny, O.P., *Principles of Medical Ethics*, 2nd ed. (Westminster, Md.: Newman Press, 1962); Gerald Kelly, S.J., *Medico-Moral Problems* (St. Louis: The Catholic Hospital Association, 1958); Allan Keenan, O.F.M. and John Ryan, F.R.C.S.E., *Marriage: A Medical and Sacramental Study* (New York: Sheed and Ward, 1955). They apply also to manuals of moral theology that are more comprehensive than these which focus on medical care.

3. Albert Jonsen, S.J., in *Responsibility in Modern Religious Ethics* (Washington, D.C.: Corpus Books, 1968), demonstrates the importance of the distinction made here. See pp. 36ff.

awareness of particular antecedents (for example, the conditions under which a pregnancy occurred), their sensibilities and emotions, their private past experiences and their private aspirations for the future, their personal commitments and loyalties.

Second, the arguments are made on a basically *juridical model.* The action is right or wrong depending on whether it conforms to or is contrary to a rule, a law, and the outcome of a moral argument. The rules or laws, of course, are defended on theological and philosophical grounds; they are not arbitrary fiats imposed by an authoritarian institution. Traditional authorities are cited; theological and philosophical principles are given to support the rules; the consequences of different possible courses of action are considered. The argument's principal terms and its logic, however, are directed toward the possibility of defining a morally right act and a morally wrong act. As with the civil law, there is a low tolerance for moral ambiguity. The advantages of this for the person whose behavior conforms to the outcome of the authoritative argument is that he probably can act with a "clear conscience," and he can justify his actions on the basis of authorities other than himself. His own responsibility for his actions, including its consequences, is decisively limited, for with reference to the juridical model of morality he has done what is determined by those whose authority he accepts to be correct. If the primary agents of action, mothers and physicians, for example, do not judge themselves only in the light of the rules, if they exercise the virtue of prudence, and the virtue of *epikeia*, or equity in interpreting the law in a particular case, they are in a slightly different situation. Their own degree of responsibility is increased, and yet they have the advantage of the clarity of reflection that is given in the moral prescription.

The juridical model can be distinguished from others that view the justification for the moral rectitude of actions in different ways or that have different views of how moral judgments are to be made. Some persons have sought virtually to quantify the good and ill effects of courses of action, and as a result of this have suggested that action which assures the greatest good for the greatest number is right. Others have relied heavily on "moral sentiment" to be sensitive to the moral issues in a situation, and relied upon compassion, the sense of altruism, or the sense of moral indignation to determine the act. Some have relied upon insight and rational intuition to size up what is going on in a time and place and to discern what the proper human response ought to be. Or "love" has been asserted to have sufficient perspicacity and motivating power to enable one to perceive what is right in a situation. It has been cogently argued that morality develops out of experience, and that when laws become abstracted from experience, their informing and persuasive powers begin to evaporate.

Third, the traditional Catholic arguments largely confine the relevant data to *the physical*. The concern is with physical life, its sanctity and its preservation. Obviously, other aspects of human life depend upon the biological basis of the human body, and thus the primacy of this concern is valid. But on the whole, the arguments have not been extended to include concern for the emotional and spiritual well-being of the mother or the infant. The concern has been largely for the physical consequences of abortion.

Fourth, the arguments are limited by concerning themselves almost *exclusively with the physician and the patient* at the time of a particular pregnancy, isolating these two from the multiple relationships and responsibilities each has to and for others over long periods of time. The obvious basis for this is that the physician has to decide about abortions with individual patients as these patients come to him. But he also has responsibilities for the well-being of the whole of his society, and for the spiritual and moral well-being of the patient's family. It could be argued that there is no dissonance between what would be decided in a particular relationship between two people and what is good for society, but that is not self-evident. The focus on the mother's physical condition, and on her as a statistical instance of a general and uniform category of mothers, makes it difficult to consider this particular mother, her particular relationships, and her past spiritual as well as physical history. For example, arguments pertaining to "saving the life of the mother" do not admit as important evidence such factors as whether she is the mother of six other children dependent upon her, or no other children. In some other ways of discussing abortion such information might make a difference in the argument. I am suggesting that the time and space limits one uses to isolate what is "the case" have a considerable effect on the way one argues.

Fifth, the traditional Catholic arguments are *rationalistic*. Obviously to make an argument one has to be rational, and to counter an argument one deems to be rationalistic he has to show what would be better reasons for arguing differently. What I refer to as rationalistic can be seen in the structure of many of the sections of the manuals of moral theology that deal with questions such as abortion, or the structure of manuals of medical ethics. One often finds brief assertions of "fundamental truths" which include definitions of terms used in these truths or in subsequent arguments. This might be followed by "basic principles" which will include distinctions between the kinds of law, principles pertaining to conscience, principles of action, a definition of the principle of double effect, and others. The principle of the sanctity of inviolability of human life is discussed at great length since its application is primary to particular cases.

One must recognize that any argument about abortion will use principles. But the rationalistic character of the arguments seems to reduce spiritual and personal individuality to abstract cases. The learning from historical experiences with their personal nuances seems to be squeezed out of the timeless abstractions. The sense of human compassion for suffering and the profound tragedy which is built into any situation in which the taking of life is morally plausible are gone. Individual instances must be typified in order to find what rubric they come under in the manual. While it is eminently clear that any discussion must abstract facts and principles from the vitality and complexity of lived-experience, the degree of abstraction and the deductive reasoning of the traditional Catholic arguments remove the issues far from life. The alternative is not to wallow in feeling and visceral responses, nor is it to assume that one's deep involvement with the persons in a situation and one's awareness of the inexorable concreteness of their lives are sufficient to resolve the issues. But an approach which is more personal and experientially oriented is another possibility.

James M. Gustafson

Sixth, the traditional perspective seeks to develop arguments that are based on *natural law*, and thus ought to be persuasive and binding on all men. Intentionally the particular historical standpoint and substance of the Christian message is subordinated to the natural law in the arguments. To be sure, arguments can be given for the consistency between the natural law and particular Christian affirmation; also any one who would begin with particular Christian affirmations would have to show their viability on moral questions to those who did not share his religious outlook and convictions. To indicate that arguments from natural law can be distinguished from arguments that place particular historical aspects of Christian thought at a different point in the discussion is not to assert that the answer to questions about abortion can be found in "revelation," or that the use of human reason is less necessary. It is to suggest, however, that one's basic perspective toward life might be altered, and one's ordering of values might be different if the first-order affirmations dealt with God's will not only to preserve his creation, but to redeem it. One's attitude toward the persons involved might well be more tolerant, patient, loving, and forgiving, rather than judgmental. One might look for consistency between one's principles and the great themes of the Christian faith at a more central place in the discussion than the traditional Catholic arguments do. To predict that the outcome of the argument would be greatly different in every case would be folly, though it might very well be in some cases. Since theologically based moral arguments, like all others, are arguments made by human beings, many other factors than commonly held convictions enter into them.

These six points are meant to provide a descriptive delineation of salient aspects of traditional Catholic arguments. I have sought to indicate that alternative ways of working are possible with regard to each of them. To claim them to be insufficient or invalid without providing an alternative would be presumptuous. As a way of suggesting and exploring an alternative, I shall describe a situation, and indicate how I would go about making and justifying my moral judgment pertaining to it. In its basic structure it is in accord with the situations of persons who have sought me out for counsel, although for various reasons I have made a composite description.

106

II. A DISCUSSION OF A HUMAN CHOICE

The pregnant woman is in her early twenties. She is a lapsed Catholic, with no significant religious affiliation at the present time, although she expresses some need for a "church." Her marriage was terminated by divorce; her husband was given custody of three children by that marriage. She had an affair with a man who "befriended" her, but there were no serious prospects for a marriage with him, and the affair has ended. Her family life was as disrupted and as tragic as that which is dramatically presented in Eugene O'Neill's *Long Day's Journey into Night*. Her alcoholic mother mistreated her children, coerced them into deceptive activity for her ends, and was given to periods of violence. Her father has been addicted to drugs, but has managed to continue in business, avoid incarceration, and provide a decent income for his family. The pregnant woman fled from home after high school to reside in a distant state, and has no significant contact with her parents or siblings. She has two or three friends.

Her pregnancy occurred when she was raped by her former husband and three other men after she had agreed to meet him to talk about their children. The rapes can only be described as acts of sadistic vengeance. She is unwilling to prefer charges against the men, since she believes it would be a further detriment to her children. She has no steady job, partially because of periodic gastro-intestinal illnesses, and has no other income. There are no known physiological difficulties which would jeopardize her life or that of the child. She is unusually intelligent and very articulate, and is not hysterical about her situation. Termination of the pregnancy is a live option for her as a way to cope with one of the many difficulties she faces.

The Christian Moralist's Responsible Relationship

In indicating that the position of writers of moral argument about abortion in traditional Catholicism is that of an external judge, I did not wish to suggest that priests are not compassionate, understanding, and loving in their relationships to physicians and to mothers, nor did I intend to suggest that they overrule the liberty of conscience of others through authoritarian ecclesiastical sanctions. No doubt some have acted more like rigorous judges than loving pastors, but many have been patient, tolerant, loving, and aware of the limitations of any human authority. (This is not the place to raise the difficult problem of the magisterial authority of the Church, which logically could be raised here, an authority still used to threaten, coerce, and suspend dissident voices.) I do wish to suggest, however, that I believe the responsible relation of a Christian moralist to other persons precludes the primacy of the judgmental posture, either in the way we write or in the way we converse with others.

The moralist responding to this woman can establish one of a number of ways of relating to her in his conversations. The two extremes are obvious. On the one hand, he could determine that no physiological difficulties seem to be present in the pregnancy, and thus seek to enforce her compliance with the standard rule against abortions. The manuals would decide what right conduct is; her predicament would be defined so that factors that are important for others who respond to her are not pertinent to the decision about abortion. Both the moralist and the woman could defer further moral responsibility to the textbooks. On the other hand, he could take a highly permissive approach to the conversation. In reliance on a theory of morality that would minimize the objective moral considerations, and affirm that what a person feels is best is morally right, he could affirm consistently what her own dominant disposition seemed to be, and let that determine the decision.

Somewhere between these is what I would delineate as a more responsible relationship than either of the two extremes. It would recognize that the moralist and the woman are in an interpersonal relationship; this is to say that as human beings they need to be open to each other, to have a high measure of confidence in each other, to have empathy for each other. Obviously the moralist, like any other counsellor, is in a position to have more disclosed to him than he discloses of himself to the other, and he has professional competence that enables him to be relatively objective within the intersubjectivity of the relationship. But as a Christian moralist his obligation is first to be open and to understand the other, not to judge and to prescribe. He will recognize that his judgement, and that of others who have informed him, while learned, mature, and hopefully sound, remains the judgment of a finite being with all the limitations of his perspective. He will, in a situation like this, acknowledge the liberty of her conscience, and will not immediately offer an authoritative answer to her question; indeed, the context of her question, and its nuances might make it a subtly different question than the one the textbooks answer. All this is not to say that he has nothing to contribute to the conversation. As a moralist he is to help her to objectify her situation, to see it from other perspectives than the one she comes with. He is to call to her attention not only alternative courses of action with some of the potential consequences of each (including the violation of civil law), but also the value of life and those values which would have to be higher in order to warrant the taking of life. He is to help her to understand her past, not as a way of excusing anything in the present, but as a way of gaining some objectivity toward the present. He is to find what constitutes her moral integrity and convictions, her desires and ends. He may find himself bringing these into the light of other ends which he deems to be important, or he may find himself inquiring whether potential courses of action are more or less in accord with the values and convictions she has. It is his obligation as a Christian moralist to bring the predicament into the light of as many subjective and objective considerations as his competence permits, including concerns for the wider moral order of the human community of which she is a part as this is sustained in civil laws.

Salient Facts in One Christian Moralist's Interpretation

The relationship of a moralist to a person who seeks conversation with him is by no means simple. Thus it is not easy to isolate what the salient facts of the predicament are, and to give a ready valence to each of them. Efforts at this analytical task are incumbent upon him, but he also *perceives* the person and the situation in some patterns or in a single whole pattern which already establish in his perception some of the relationships between the factors. He never confronts the salient facts as isolates, or as discrete entities that can be added arithmetically into a sum. The person confronts him not as isolable elements, and her experiences are not detached moments only chronologically related to each other. He does not respond to her any more than he responds to a portrait first of all as a series of colors, or a series of lines. He can in reflection discriminate between the colors and talk about the lines, but even then these are in particular relationships to each other in the portrait, and in his perception of it. He does not perceive the woman in pure objectivity, nor as she perceives her own predicament, though obviously he seeks to have his own perception informed by the actual predicament insofar as possible. Even in this, however, his perspective conditions how he "sees" and "feels" the relationships between factors that can be abstracted and isolated. This preface to a statement of salient facts is important, for it precludes both oversimplification and dogmatic analytical authority. He can never say to another person, "In comparable situations find out the answers to the following factual questions, and you will have an accurate picture of the predicament."

In the personal situation under discussion, it is clear that if medical factors alone were to be considered grounds for an abortion, none would be morally permissible. The woman had three pregnancies that came to full term, and the children were healthy. To the best of her knowledge there are no medical problems at the present time. Periodic gastro-intestinal illnesses, which might be relieved with better medical care, would not be sufficient medical grounds. Although the present pregnancy is disturbing for many reasons, including both the occasion on which the pregnancy occurred and the future social prospects for the woman and the child, in the judgment of the moralist the woman is able to cope with her situation without serious threat to her mental health. The medical factors insofar as the moralist can grasp them, would not warrant a therapeutic abortion.

Legal factors potentially involved in this situation are serious. First, and most obvious, the woman resides in a state where abortion of pregnancies due to sexual crimes is not at present legally permissible. Since there are not sufficient grounds for a therapeutic abortion, a request to a physician would put him in legal jeopardy. Even if abortion was permissible because of the rapes, this woman was unwilling to report the rapes to the police since it involved her former husband and had potential implications for the care of her children. To report the rapes would involve the woman in court procedures which seem also to require time and energy that she needs to support herself financially. To seek an abortion on conscientious moral grounds would be to violate the law, and to implicate others in the violation. Not to press charges against the rapists is to protect them from prosecution. Disclosure of the rapes would make the abortion morally justifiable in the eyes of many, but it might lead to implications for her children. The legal factors are snarled and are complicated by social factors.

The moralist has to reckon with the financial plight of the woman. She is self-supporting, but her income is irregular. There are no savings. Application for welfare support might lead to the disclosure of matters she wishes to keep in confidence. If a legal abortion was possible, the physician would receive little or no remuneration from the patient. There are no funds in sight to finance an illegal abortion, and the medical risks involved in securing a quack rule that out as a viable prospect. The child, if not aborted, could be let out for adoption, and means might be found to give minimum support for the mother during pregnancy. If she should choose to keep the child, which is her moral right to do, there are no prospects for sufficient financial support, although with the recovery of her health the woman could join the work force and probably with her intelligence earn a modest income.

The spiritual and emotional factors involved are more difficult to assess. While the moralist is impressed with the relative calm with which the woman converses about her predicament, he is aware that this ability is probably the result of learning to cope with previous inhumane treatment and with events that led to no happy ending. Socially, she is sustained only by two or three friends, and these friendships could readily be disrupted by geographical mobility. She has no significant, explicit religious faith, and as a lapsed Catholic who views the Church and its priests as harsh taskmasters, she is unwilling to turn to it for spiritual and moral sustenance. She has a profound desire not merely to achieve a situation of equanimity, of absence of suffering and conflict, but also to achieve positive goals. Her mind is active, and she has read fairly widely; she expresses the aspiration to go to college, to become a teacher, or to engage in some other professional work, both for the sake of her self-fulfillment and for the contribution she can make to others. She has not been defeated by her past. She can articulate the possibility of keeping the child, and see the child as part of the world in which there would be some realization of goals, especially since she has been deprived of her other children.

She has confidence, she has hope, and she seems to be able to love, though she wonders what else could happen to make her life any more difficult than it is. She carries something of a guilt load; the courts gave custody of her three children to the husband because of adultery charges against her. Yet, her interpretation of that marriage in her youth was that it freed her from her parental home, but that the marriage itself was a "prison." She responds to the rapes more in horror than in hatred, but is too close to that experience to know its long-range impact on her.

The more readily identifiable moral factors are three, though in the ethical perspective of this paper, this constitutes an oversimple limitation of the "moral" and of the nature of moral responsibility. One is the inviolability of life, the sanctity of life. My opinion is that since the genotype is formed at conception, all the genetic potentialities of personal existence are there. Thus it is to be preserved unless reasons can be given that make an exception morally justifiable. A second is rape — not only a crime, but a morally evil deed. The sexual relations from which the pregnancy came were not only engaged in against the woman's will, but were in her judgment acts of retaliation and vengeance. The third is the relation of morality to the civil law. If abortion were considered to be morally justifiable, to have it done would be to break the civil law. It would be an act of conscientious objection to existing laws, and is susceptible to scrutiny by the moral arguments that pertain to that subject in itself.

All of these factors in isolated listing, and others that could be enumerated, do not add up to a moral decision. They are related to each other in particular ways, and the woman is related to her own ends, values, and to other beings. And the moralist's relationship is not that of a systems analyst sorting out and computing. His relationship is one of respect and concern for the person; it is colored by his perspective. It is necessary, then, to state what seem to be the factors that are present in the perspective of the moralist that influence his interpretation and judgment.

Salient Aspects of the Moralist's Perspective

The perception and the interpretation of the moralist are not a simple matter to discuss. It would be simpler if the author could reduce his perspective to: (a) theological and philosophical principles; (b) moral inferences drawn from these; and (c) rational application of these principles to a narrowly defined case. But more than belief, principles, and logic are involved in the moral decision. A basic perspective toward life accents certain values and shadows others. Attitudes, affections, and feelings of indignation against evil, compassion for suffering, and desire for restoration of wholeness color one's interpretation and judgment. Imagination, sensitivity, and empathy are all involved. For Christians, and many others presumably, love is at work, not merely as a word to be defined, and as a subject of propositions so that inferences can be drawn from it, but love as a human relationship, which can both move and inform the other virtues, including prudence and equity (to make a reference to St. Thomas). All of this does not mean that a moral judgment is a total mystery, it does not mean that it is without objectivity.

The perspective of the Christian moralist is informed and directed by his fundamental trust that the forces of life seek the human good, that God is good, is love. This is a matter of trust and confidence, and not merely a matter of believing certain propositions to be true. (I believe certain statements about my wife to be true, including the statement that she wills and seeks my good, but the reasons for my trust in her cannot be described simply by such a statement.) Yet the way in which I state my convictions about this trust defines in part my moral perspective and my fundamental intentionality. (What I know *about* my wife sustains my trust in her, and in part sets the direction of our marriage.) Life, and particularly human life, is given to men by God's love: physical being dependent upon genetic continuity; the capacity of the human spirit for self-awareness, responsiveness, knowledge, and creativity; life together in human communities, in which we live and care for others and others live and care for us.

God wills the creation, preservation, reconciliation, and redemption of human life. Thus, one can infer, it is better to give and preserve life than to take it away; it is better to prevent its coming into being than to destroy it when it has come into being. But the purposes of God for life pertain to more than physical existence: there are conditions for human life that need delineation: physical health, possibilities for future good and meaning that engender and sustain hope, relationships of trust and love, freedom to respond and initiate and achieve, and many others. The love of God, and in response to it, the loves of men, are particularly sensitive to "the widow, the orphan, and the stranger in your midst," to the oppressed and the weak.

These brief and cryptic statements are the grounds for moral biases: life is to be preserved, the weak and the helpless are to be cared for especially, the moral requisite of trust, hope, love, freedom, justice, and others are to be met so that human life can be meaningful. The bias gives a direction, a fundamental intention that does not in itself resolve the darknesses beyond the reach of its light, the ambiguities of particular cases. It begins to order what preferences one would have under ideal conditions and under real conditions. One would prefer not to induce an abortion in this instance. There is consistency between this preference and the Christian moralist's faith and convictions. But one would prefer for conception to arise within love rather than hate, and one would prefer that there would be indications that the unknowable future were more favorably disposed to the human well-being of the mother and the child.

The perspective of the Christian moralist is informed and directed by his understanding of the nature of human life, as well as his convictions about God. Abbreviated statements of some convictions are sufficient here. These would be first, that moral life is a life of action, in which intentions, judgments, the exercise of bodily power and other forms of power and influence give direction to our responses to past events, and direction to future events themselves. Persons are active, responsive, creative, reflective, self-aware, initiating. The second would be that we can discern something of the order of relationships and activity that sustains, preserves, and develops our humanity. The child conceived in love, within a marriage (an order of love), within an order of society that maintains justice, is more likely to have a higher quality of life than one who is conceived in other conditions. The decision to seek an abortion is human, the act of abortion would be human, the relationships before, during, and after the abortion are human. The consequences are not fully predictable beyond the physical, and yet the human is more than perpetuation of the body. A moral order was violated in rape; are the human conditions present that would sustain and heal the humanity of the child and the mother in the future? The answer to that question is a finite, human answer, and how it will be answered by the mother and others deeply affects a most decisive act.

A third pertinent affirmation about human life is important: to be a creature is to be limited, and the good and the right are found within the conditions of limitation. Present acts respond to the conditions of past actions, conditions which are usually irrevocable, unalterable. Their consequences will be projected into the future and quickly become part of other actions and responses so that the actors in the present cannot fully know or determine the future. The limitations of knowledge, both of potentially verifiable facts and of good and evil, while no excuse for not knowing what can be known, nonetheless are present. Thus not only physical risk, but moral risk is fundamental to human action, and this risk in the life of this woman involves potential tragedy, suffering, and anguish. But her condition itself is the fruit both of events beyond her control (for example, the rapes) and events that have occurred because of choices (for example, earlier adultery). What many men find out about the dark side of existence through novels and dramas, she has experienced. Action is required within the limits; the good or the evil that is involved will be concrete, actual. Thus there is no abstract standard of conduct that can predetermine without moral ambiguity what the right action is in this predicament. Since predicaments like this have emerged before, however, one's conscientious moral interpretation can use those generalizations that have emerged out of the past for illumination, and for direction. They may present values or principles so universally valid that the present decision, if contrary to them, must be justified as a clear exception. Since action is specific, either the following of established rules, or the finding exceptions to them refer to specifics. Specificity of good and evil is the human condition (I never know either in the abstract); choices are agonizingly specific. The moralist has the obligation conscientiously to assess the specific in the light of principles and arguments that pertain to it; the woman is entitled to see her predicament and potential courses of action in the light of as much distilled wisdom and experience as she can handle. Indeed, the principle of double effect (preferably multiple effects none of which are totally evil, and none of which are totally good) might assist in the reflection. But the choice remains in the realm of the finite, the limited, and the potentially wrong as well as right.

Pertinent Principles That Can Be Stipulated for Reflection

Neither the moralist nor the woman comes to a situation without some convictions and beliefs that begin to dissolve some of the complexity of the particularities into manageable terms. Perhaps the traditional Catholic arguments simply assume that one can begin with these convictions and principles, and need not immerse one's self in the tragic concreteness. The pertinent ones in this case have already been alluded to, but here they can be reduced to a simpler scheme.

1. Life is to be preserved rather than destroyed.
2. Those who cannot assert their own rights to life are especially to be protected.
3. There are exceptions to these rules.

Possible exceptions are:

a. "medical indications" that make therapeutic abortion morally viable. Condition not present here.
b. the pregnancy has occurred as a result of sexual crime. (I would grant this as a viable possible exception in every instance for reasons imbedded in the above discussion, if the woman herself were convinced that it was right. In other than detached academic discussions I would never dispatch an inquiry with a ready granting of the exception. If the woman sees the exception as valid, she has a right to more than a potentially legal justification for her decision; as a person she has the right to understand why it is an exception in her dreadful plight.)
c. the social and emotional conditions do not appear to be beneficial for the well-being of the mother and the child. (In particular circumstances, this may appear to be a justification, but I would not resort to it until possibilities for financial, social, and spiritual help have been explored.)

In the short-hand of principles this can be reduced to an inconsistency between on the one hand the first and second, and on the other hand 3.b. and perhaps 3.c. While I am called upon to give as many reasons for a decision between these two as I can, the choice can never be fully rationalized.

The Decision of the Moralist

My own decision is: (a) if I were in the woman's human predicament I believe I could morally justify an abortion, and thus: (b) I would affirm its moral propriety in this instance. Clearly, logic alone is not the process by which a defense of this particular judgment can be given; clearly, the facts of the matter do not add up to a justification of abortion so that one can say "the situation determines everything." Nor is it a matter of some inspiration of the Spirit. It is a human decision, made in freedom, informed and governed by beliefs and values, as well as by attitudes and a fundamental perspective. It is a discernment of compassion for the woman, as well as of objective moral reflection. It may not be morally "right" in the eyes of others, and although we could indicate where the matters of dispute between us are in discourse, and perhaps even close the gap between opinions to some extent, argument about it would probably not be persuasive. The judgment is made with a sense of its limitations, which include the limitations of the one who decides (which might well result from his lack of courage, his pride, his slothfulness in thinking, and other perversities). [4]

Continuing Responsibilities of the Moralist

The responsibilities of the moralist, like the consequences for the woman, do not end at the moment a decision might be made in favor of an abortion. Some of them can be briefly indicated, since they have already been alluded to in the discussion. Since the moralist concurs in the decision, and since the decision was made in a relationship in which he accepts limited but real responsibility for the woman, he is obligated to continue his responsible relationship to her in ways consistent with the decision, and with her well-being. He cannot dismiss her to engage in subsequent implications of the decision on her own and to accept the consequences of such implications on her own. First, he is obligated to

4. This procedure can be applied to cases other than pregnancy due to rape, obviously, and *might* lead to similar conclusions in instances of unwed girls, or older married women with large families, etc.

assist, if necessary, in finding competent medical care. In such a situation as the one described, with abortion laws as they now stand in most states, this is not necessarily an easy matter and not a trivial one. Second, financial resources are needed. To put her on her own in this regard would be to resign responsibility prematurely for a course of action in which the moralist concurred, and might jeopardize the woman's health and welfare. Third, the woman needs continuing social and moral support in her efforts to achieve her aspirations for relief from anguish and for a better human future. To deny continued support in this case is comparable to denying continued care and concern for the well-being of those who have large families as a result of a moral doctrine prohibiting contraception, or for children born out of wedlock, both reprehensible limitations of responsibility in my judgment. Fourth, the moralist is under obligation, if he is convinced of the propriety in this human situation of an abortion, to seek reform of abortion legislation which would remove the unjust legal barrier to what he believes to be morally appropriate. Other considerations must be brought to bear on the discussion of legal reform, such as the crucial matter of the legal and moral rights of the defenseless unborn persons, but it is consistent with the moral judgment in this case that the laws permit an action which is deemed to be morally approvable. To judge an action to be morally appropriate, and not to seek the alteration of legislation which would make such an action possible without penalties would be a serious inconsistency in the moralist's thinking and action. It would be comparable to approving conscientious objection to specific wars on moral grounds and not seeking to make such objection a legal possibility.

These points are made to indicate that the time and space limits of a moral issue extend beyond the focal point of a particular act. Indeed, the focal point has not been the abortion, but the well-being of the woman over a long range of time. If such a delineation of the situation is made, the responsibility of the moralist must be consonant in its dimensions with that. These points are made to reiterate an earlier one, then, namely that the delimitation which a moral issue receives from its discussants is a crucial factor in determining what data are significant and what the extent of responsibilities is.

III. THE LOCATION OF THIS DISCUSSION ON THE CURRENT MAP
OF MORAL THEOLOGY

This essay began with a description of salient aspects of the traditional Catholic arguments. With reference to each of these, I have emphasized a different way of working. The discussion of this paper does not provide a totally different way of thinking about the matter; indeed, the concerns of traditional moral theology are brought into it.

In place of the external judge, the position of the persons who must assume responsibility for the decision has been stressed. This requires empathy with the woman and the physician who might become involved. But the moralist himself is responsible for · his decision: if he offers recommendations he is responsible to all who accept and act upon them. If an abortion is induced, he shares moral responsibility for it. Moral decisions, however, are not made wallowing in sympathy and empathy. The element of disinterested objectivity is a necessity, something of the stance of the external judge or observer is involved. In a process of conversation with one who has the serious moral choice, however, the interpersonal relationship not only establishes the possibilities of open communication, but provides insight and understanding, and sensitizes the affections.

In place of the determination of an action as right or wrong by its conformity to a rule and its application, I have stressed the primacy of the person and human relationships and the concreteness of the choice within limited possibilities. There can be no guarantee of an objectively right action in the situation I have discussed, since there are several values which are objectively important, but which do not resolve themselves into a harmonious relation to each other. Since there is not a single overriding determination of what constitutes a right action, there can be no unambiguously right act.

Whereas the moral theology manuals generally limit discussion to the physical aspects of the human situation, I have set those in a wider context of human values, responsibilities, and aspirations. While this does not make the physical less serious, it sets it in relation to other matters of a morally serious nature, and thus qualifies the way one decides by complicating the values and factors to be taken into account.

I find it difficult in discussing possible abortions to limit the personal relationships as exclusively to the physician and the patient as do the manual discussions, and to limit the time span of experience to the fact of pregnancy and action pertaining to it alone. Most significantly in the instance discussed, the conditions under which the pregnancy occurred modify the discussion of the abortion.

The role of compassion and indignation, of attitudes and affections in the process of making a decision is affirmed in my discussion to a degree not admitted in traditional moral theology. Indeed, I indicated the importance of one's basic perspective, and the way in which one's perception of a situation is conditioned by this perspective. Situations cannot be reduced to discrete facts; one's response to them is determined in part by one's faith, basic intentions, and dispositions, as well as by analysis and the rational application of principles.

Although I have only sketched most briefly the theological convictions that inform the perspective, they perhaps have a more central place in the ways in which I proceed than is the case in traditional moral theology. I wish not to suggest that there is a deposit of revelation, supernaturally given, which I accept on authority as a basis of moral perspective; such a position is not the alternative to natural law. Ampler elaboration of this, however, is beyond the bounds of this paper.

Although the structure I have used as a model differs from that model used by the Roman Catholic manuals of moral theology, in a specific instance a Catholic moralist might reach a conclusion not strikingly dissimilar from my own in counselling the woman. He could do so by means of the classic Catholic doctrine of "good faith." As expounded by Alphonsus Liguori, a confessor is not to disturb the good faith of the penitent if he believes that telling the penitent he is committing a sin will not deter him from his course of action, but will merely put him in "bad faith," that is, in a state of mind where he is aware that what he is doing is opposed to the will of God. There are exceptions to this doctrine where the penitent must be informed of what is necessary to salvation, or where the common good is endangered by the proposed actions. These exceptions, however, do not seem applicable to the special kind of case I have outlined. Consequently, a Catholic moralist faced with a woman who believes she is doing what is right in seeking an abortion, and who in all probability would not be deterred by advice to the contrary, might well conclude that his responsibility was not to put the woman in bad faith.[5]

This Catholic approach to a particular case accords with mine in recognizing a principle of personal responsibility which the moralist must honor. He cannot coerce the person; in some sense each person must decide for himself. This approach differs from mine, however, in the analysis of the act of abortion, which is treated in a special sense as a sin. Elucidation of this difference would require extensive discussion of the relation of religion and morality in the two approaches, in the uses of the concept of sin, and other matters too large to be developed here. This Catholic approach also differs from mine in the limits it would impose on cooperation with the act by the counsellor.

A Catholic moral theologian, if he approved of the outcome of the discussion presented here, might compliment it by indicating that it is an example of prudence informed by charity at work, or that it is an exercise in the virtue of *epikeia*, applying principles to particular cases. If such generosity were shown, I would not be adverse to being pleased, for it would indicate that some of the polarizations of contemporary moral theology between ethics of law and situational ethics are excessively drawn. I would also suggest, however, that there is a different valence given to prudence and equity, indeed, to the moral virtues, in the order of ethical analysis here than is the case in the treatises on medical ethics. There is a sense in which the present discussion subordinates law to virtue as points of reliance in making moral decisions.

Since there is no fixed position called "situation ethics," it would be futile to distinguish the approach taken here from what cannot be readily defined. I would say in general that in comparison with Paul Lehmann's ethics of the theonomous conscience,[6] with its confidence in a renewed sensitivity and imagination to perceive what God is doing in the world to make and keep human life

5. See Bernard Häring, *infra.*
6. Paul Lehmann, *Ethics in a Christian Context* (New York: Harper & Row, 1964).

human, the approach of this paper is more complex, and ultimately less certain about its answer. Further, the weight of responsibility for reflection and for action rests heavily upon the actor, since no perceptive powers I have enable me to overcome the distance between God and the action that I respond to. I cannot claim to perceive what *God* is doing. The polemical force with which Lehmann attacks "absolutist ethics" is foreign to this approach; [7] while I clearly believe that abstract principles and logic alone do not contain the dynamics of suffering and evil, or of love and good, their utility in bringing clarity to discussion is much treasured.

As the morally conscientious soldier fighting in a particular war is convinced that life can and ought to be taken, "justly" but also "mournfully," [8] so the moralist can be convinced that the life of the defenseless fetus can be taken, less justly, but more mournfully.

7. *Ibid.*, pp. 124–132.
8. See Roland H. Bainton's discussions of the mournful mood of the just war theorists, in *Christian Attitudes toward War and Peace* (New York: Abingdon Press, 1960), pp. 98, 112, 139, 145, and 221–222.

BERNARD HÄRING

A Theological Evaluation

This paper does not claim to propose *the* Catholic position on the problem of abortion. However, the author believes that the arguments and distinctions presented here are possible within the frame of Catholic doctrine and thought.

My intention is to be thoroughly "a professional thinker about morals" [1] but in full awareness of the specific Catholic tradition as well as of cultural traditions. A "professional thinker," deliberately confronting all the realities of the situation, does not forget the impact of environment, of sociological group, and of the Church to which he belongs in loyalty. But aside from a sense of gratitude for the traditions that give him a starting place and ground for his personal efforts, there must also be a critical attitude toward all those elements of tradition and group solidarity that might make him deviate from sincere and courageous thinking.

As a Catholic of the post-Vatican II era, one cannot easily avoid the sharp distinction that must be made between doctrines which are considered to be irreformable dogmas, and teachings which, at least to some degree, are open to questioning and to more or less substantial changes. The discussions now going on within the Church about birth regulation are indicative of the wide range of development, shift of emphasis, and sharp distinctions which were not always seen in times past.

The characteristic note in Catholic theology today is one of critical searching. But while themes as diverse as church structures and divorce are subject to intense studies which to some extent challenge traditional teaching, I see no indications of this

1. *The Terrible Choice* (Washington, D.C.: Joseph P. Kennedy, Jr., Foundation, 1968), p. 82.

123

kind regarding the problem of abortion, at least insofar as its morality is concerned.

The severe judgment of the Church about abortion, repeated through Vatican II,[2] is commonly accepted. There is, however, a certain difference between a vast number of writers who simply repeat the teaching of the Popes and the common formulations of the manuals[3] and those who think that the teaching of the Catholic Church might be "susceptible to gradual development through a process of refinement"; yet even these latter also insist that "one ought not to suggest that the Catholic Church's teaching is about to change in a substantive way."[4] Since this is also my own conviction, I shall try to point out cautiously what type of refinement of the Catholic theology might realistically be expected.

Sharper distinctions may depend on increasing knowledge of such physical details as development of the ovum from fertilization to implantation in the uterus, and so on, a growing understanding of what is human life, what is personal life and a person, and on a more precise focus on the moral malice of abortion, its definition, and reasons for the asserted malice. If we have determined the nonvalue of malice that leads us to condemn abortion so severely, we ask whether this malice can be shown in all cases which we commonly call "abortion." For this we must either distinguish the medical, legal, and the moral concept or definition of abortion or else show that there is no substantial difference between the different concepts.

2. *Constitutionis Pastoralis de Ecclesia in mundo huius temporis* (*The Constitution on the Church in the Modern World*), art. 51: "Therefore from the moment of its conception life must be guarded with the greatest care, while abortion and infanticide are unspeakable crimes." (Unless otherwise noted, all translations are the author's.)

3. We may compare the article by J. Piltz, "Abtreibung," in *Lexikon für Theologie und Kirche*, 1 (1957), cols. 97–100, and T. J. O'Donnell's article on abortion in *The New Catholic Encyclopedia*, vol. 1, pp. 27–29. Both articles very similarly take the position that discussion among orthodox Catholics may be only about the argumentation in order to strengthen the doctrine and about the distinction between direct and indirect abortion: whether some cases fall under one or the other category. O'Donnell explicitly brings into the condemned category the termination of an ectopic pregnancy, being even more severe than Pilz, but he does not state, as Pilz does, that we are faced with a truth of faith taught at least by the ordinary Magisterium, applying this to all kinds of directly intended and induced abortions. In the same line of thought, among many other recent Catholic publications, is, e.g., Peter Flood O.S.B., "The Abortion Act 1967: Some Moral Implications," 53 *Clergy Review* (January 1968), 42–48. Flood is quite firm about the validity of this natural law teaching for all men.

4. *The Terrible Choice*, p. 88.

After the discussion of the malice of abortion I shall try to trace the direction in which further thought and refinement of the doctrine might be possible or even needed. A quite different question is the value we attribute to the legal regulation and what we think about the "art of the possible."

I. THE NONVALUE OF THE MALICE OF ABORTION

About abortion, many if not most Catholic theologians would say that since theology is confronted by a clear and unchangeable doctrine of at least the ordinary Magisterium, there remains only the necessity of explaining clearly the reasons behind the doctrine and discussing whether some complicated cases might be considered as "indirect abortion." This, according to the principle of the "double effect," can be justified when the directly intended action is not abortion but a licit medical intervention that has the character of a remedy for the mother. The first necessity is indeed a clear expression and discussion of the reasons why abortion is considered as intrinsically evil. From such discussion may arise some clearer distinctions whereby we may then see whether the reasons for asserting malice do apply to all possible cases.

As to the reasoning about the malice of abortion, my own way of arguing is almost identical with the one expressed by Protestant thinkers such as Paul Ramsey. Although our language distinguishes between abortion and infanticide,[5] it seems arbitrary to draw the line of moral judgment between a born and an unborn child. The child in the mother's womb is alive and has almost the same qualities before being born as it has after birth.

There seems to be almost the same common agreement that the line cannot be drawn between the time before and the time after viability. Not only can medical skills constantly progress and possibly affect the viability at an earlier stage, but the real difference is then only whether the fetus can or cannot live outside the womb of the mother. The mere fact that it cannot live outside its natural environment cannot justify the action of depriving it of this life-preserving environment. However, there remains a certain doubt about the moment of conception or animation. Is it

5. *The Constitution on the Church in the Modern World*, art. 51, makes this distinction but expresses the same condemnation of both.

the moment of the fertilization of the egg (ovum) or is it during or after implantation? We shall return to this question later.

The following fundamental values are at stake here: (1) the recognition of the right of each human being to the most basic conditions of life and finally to life itself; (2) the protection of this right to live, especially by those who have cooperated with the creative love of God; (3) the preservation of a right understanding of motherhood; (4) the ethical standard of the physician as one who protects and cares for human life and never becomes a destroyer of human life. The whole argumentation derives its vigor from our belief in the *dignity of each human being*, created to the image and likeness of God, and in man's calling to universal brotherhood in mutual love, respect, and justice.

All these values come to a focal point and special urgency in the family, in the relationship between mother and child and between father and child. The intimacy of human solidarity and dependence on the other person's love and protection is never more strongly disclosed than during the nine months the embryo or fetus lives in one bloodstream with the mother. The psychological and moral maturity of the mother, as mother, affects greatly her attitude toward the child she is bearing. Whether she considers the fetus as only a tissue, or entertains motherly feelings toward this living being, makes a tremendous difference. The humanization of all mankind, the totality of relationships among all human beings, cannot be dissociated from this most fundamental and life-giving relationship between mother and unborn child. All forms of arbitrary rationalization that might make acceptable what in the strict sense is abortion must lead to other forms of rationalization about the relationships among men.

The power of all these arguments stems from belief in God as Creator and Redeemer of man, the only Lord over life and death: God Who is love and Who calls man to mutual love, respect, and care.

II. HOW CERTAIN ARE THE PRESUPPOSITIONS OF THE CATHOLIC DOCTRINE?

Holy Scripture does not provide us with clear-cut teaching about all the questions and solutions regarding abortion. It does teach the basic values on which we ground our arguments: the dignity of man, protection of innocent life, the concept of motherhood and fatherhood, and the commandment to love, which becomes an urgent imperative of love whereby the life of the neighbor can and must be protected. There is at least a probability that the word *pharmakeia*, which Paul includes in his catalogue of the fruits of self-indulgence (Gal. 5:20), condemns abortion along with any other use of drugs with magical or inimical intentions. (See also Rev. 9:21; 18:23; 21:8; 22:15.)

But whatever may be the evidence of the biblical texts, it is sure that ever since the times of the apostles Christianity has taken a very severe stand against abortions, equating abortion and homicide.[6] Abortion, like infanticide, is considered as direct transgression of the commandment "You shall not kill" (Exod. 20:12). It is in plain opposition to the commandment to love one's neighbor. In speaking on abortion, the Church Fathers often called it homicide or parricide,[7] thus showing that in their view abortion added to the sin against life another sin against the fundamental relationship between parents and offspring.

The presupposition for condemning abortion as homicide and parricide is, of course, that the life which is attacked is believed to be a human life. Does this hold true only under the condition that the embryo or fetus can be considered a human person, a human being with an immortal soul? There was no doctrine about the moment when the fetus is "ensouled" or "formed." Christians have shared the common opinions or common doubts about the moment when the embryo is animated. But in any event it is life-to-be, a man, under the protection of the Giver of life.

Evidently it should make a great difference in the moral judgment whether one considers the embryo or fetus as already endowed with a human soul — thus possessing fully the status of a person — or only a tissue or living entity on the way to becoming a human being. Jerome and Augustine were already acutely aware of this difference in qualifications.[8] However, they remained

6. See John T. Noonan, Jr., "An Almost Absolute Value in History," *supra;* J. Palazzini, *Jus fetus ad vitam eiusque tutela in fontibus ac doctrina canonica usque ad saeculum XVI* (Urbaniana, 1943).

7. Noonan, *supra.*

8. Jerome, *Epistles,* 121, 4 *Corpus Scriptorum Ecclesiasticorum Latinorum* 56, 16; Augustine, *De origine animae,* IV, 4 *Patrologiae Cursus Completus, Series Latina,* 44, 527.

very firm in the disapprobation of abortion, whether before or after the period in which it was thought ensoulment took place.

As long as the common convictions within the culture strongly favored the opinion that ensoulment takes place in a later stage of the development of the fetus, the theologians, while still firmly condemning abortion in general, could think there might be grave reasons in extraordinary cases that could justify the abortion of an unsouled fetus. Many theologians did indeed express such opinions without being condemned by the Church. Thomas Sanchez,[9] who developed a detailed casuistry, could follow many previous famous theologians.[10]

Since the first centuries, the Church issued grave sanctions against those Christians who would dare to commit the crime of abortion. When the moralists treated those cases which, in their view, did not involve the malice or evil which makes abortion such a grave sin, they drew the conclusions that these extreme cases did not fall under the sanctions of the Church.

It is interesting to consider an effort of the highest authority of the Catholic Church to legislate about sanctions while ignoring this sharp dispute among the leading theologians. In the bull *Effraenatam*, Sixtus V (Oct. 29, 1588) decreed that all penalties of canon law and secular law should be applied to all those committing abortion, whatever the age of the fetus. Absolution from excommunication was reserved to the Holy See. Even a therapeutic abortus seemed to be included, although the chief purpose of the bull was to fight against prostitution in Rome. But since the

---

9. Thomas Sanchez declared the abortion of an unsouled fetus lawful for several grave reasons, e.g., after a conception through adultery, if this would expose the woman to great risk not only of her honor but also of her life (*Disputationum de matrimonii sacramento*, bk. IX, Disp. XX, 8 (Brescia, 1624), vol. III, p. 229). Very interesting also is his argumentation in the matter of saving the life of the mother in extreme danger: "In this case the moral lawfulness of abortion seems to be the more probable opinion, since it is not truly a homicide while the fetus belongs to the intestines as a part of it, being not yet informed by a rational soul; therefore there is no reason why it should be preserved with such great and imminent risk of death for the mother, especially in view of the circumstance that the fetus will anyway not be ensouled if the mother dies" (*ibid.*, Disp. XX, 9, p. 230). We find similar opinions among several other renowned Catholic moralists of that and the later epoch, e.g., Laymann, *Theologia moralis*, bk. III, treatise III, chap. IV, 4 (Bamberg, 1969), p. 293.

10. A considerable list of them is quoted by Sanchez, *Disp. de matrimonii sacramento*, and Laymann, *Theologia moralis*. See also the masterly summary history of Noonan, *supra*.

bull met strong opposition among moralists and canonists and did not have the hoped-for success, Gregory XIV decided that the earlier legal situation should be restored.[11]

I come now to the question: How sure are we today about one of the main presuppositions for the severe moral judgment against abortion: a judgment that does not easily allow exceptions if we are faced with a human person, a human being with the full dignity and status of personhood?

Many circumstances have favored a rather strong conviction among Catholics about the ensoulment of the embryo from the very first instant after fertilization. Conception as a privileged moment was celebrated regarding the humanity of the Lord Jesus Christ and in the case of His mother. But the moment of ensoulment, or the moment of "conception" in the fullest sense as the beginning of a human person, does not belong to the data of the revelation. A certain awareness of this fact comes through in the *Constitution on the Church in the Modern World* of Vatican II. The Commission responds to the amendment or modi that the expression "from the moment of its conception life must be guarded" is not meant to determine the time of animation.[12] The Commission felt also that it could not easily fulfill the petition of those who desired an accurate definition of abortion.[13]

In the end it must be said that the question about the precise moment after which we are faced with a human being in the full sense is not yet settled and will probably not easily be determined. For this the Magisterium relies on the data of science and on philosophical thought. The theory of a successive ensoulment of the embryo, which was the more common opinion before St. Albert the Great is gaining ground once more.[14] We shall not

11. The cases under dispute, and generally the abortion of the fetus which was considered as not yet ensouled, were not any longer to fall under the sanctions. The expression with which the bull of Sixtus V was invalidated is interesting: the respective part should be considered as if it had never issued (ac si eadem constitutio in hiusmodi parte numquam emanasset) *Sedes apostolica, Magnum bullarium romanum* (Luxemburg, 1742), vol. II, p. 766.

12. Second Vatican Council, *Schema constitutionis pastoralis, De ecclesia in mundo huius temporis: Expensio modorum* pt. II, notes 101a and b; Response to a, p. 36.

13. *Ibid.*, Response to n. 101c, p. 36.

14. See W. Ruff, S.J., "Das embryonale Werden des Individuums," in *Stimmen der Zeit*, vol. 181 (1968), pp. 107–119; "Das embryonale Werden des Menschen," *ibid.*, 327–337. R. J. Gerber, "When is the Human Soul Infused?" in *Laval théologique et philosophique*, 22 (1966), 234–247.

again reach a naïve certainty that would permit us to determine the precise moment of the event such as the fortieth day or the eightieth day, as many did in earlier time, following Aristotle and other thinkers.

Science provides us some bases of thought regarding animation: (1) The fertilized egg is still open to a development toward duplication in twins; this may induce us to doubt whether there is already a determined human individuality when further development can produce two human beings; (2) Experiments with animals have shown that the prenatal loss from the time of fertilization averages about 40 percent to 50 percent. In view of the higher organization of man the losses may be even greater. At least one-fifth or even one-fourth of the fertilized eggs may perish before implantation in the uterus or during this process;[15] (3) Thought can be entertained that a certain analogy occurs between the development of the embryo and the long process of hominization in evolution.

The material substrate for any spiritual activity or the appearance of human nature seems to be the central nervous system. Before a certain specifically human cerebral development, does the embryo show sufficient specification in the direction of a human being with the potentialities of spiritual activity? The first differentiation in this direction begins probably between the twentieth and fortieth day. This is a decisive time as to the normality of the future development or deviations. But until the fifth month, the surface of the brains of the fetus is not yet fully distinct from the structure of the brains of lower mammals.[16]

From all this we do not derive a knowledge that before a certain day or moment the embryo is not yet a human being. In my view, however, it does follow that we must confess that we are not so sure about the time of animation or endowment of the embryo with a human soul. Though we are not sure whether we are already faced with a fully-human being, the development of this individual toward an ever clearer appearance of all the characters of the human person may be compared with the marvelous

15. See, e.g., H. D. Pache, "Pränatale Gefährdung," in *Handbuch der Kinderheilkunde* (Berlin, 1966), pp. 1094–1103; G. Martius, "Die pränatalen Schadigungen des Kindes," *Klinik der Frauenheilkunde*, vol. 3 (Munich, 1965), pp. 69–164.
16. W. Ruff, "Das embryonale Werden des Menschen," p. 332.

"miracle" of evolution up to the first break toward hominization.

However, there is an aspect which cannot be compared simply with that long evolution. At least after the twentieth day there is an *individuum;* and there is an inborn dynamism, a principle of life in this *individuum* developing toward the full organization of a human person. This individual being deserves our complete respect and loving care, as an expression of adoration before God the Creator of human life. The uncertainty about the status of person does not at all justify an arbitrary destruction of such a living being on the way to ever greater development of humanness. To interrupt such a process of growing life is not only to destroy a hope for human life but also to risk destruction of what is already created as a person made to the image and likeness of God.

III. CAN OTHERS BE CONVINCED ABOUT THE CATHOLIC POSITION REGARDING ABORTION?

In 1961 John J. Lynch, S.J., deplored the "professed inability" of our separated brethren to understand our cogent argumentation about the intrinsic immorality of contraception.[17] He thought that ecumenical dialog demands only a great effort to explain to our separated brethren the meaning of "our immutable position" [18] as an exigency of our faith, though he was quite pessimistic about the possibility of convincing even the most open-minded Protestants. Meantime theological discussion has helped greatly to distinguish what is immutable in our position and what can and must be further developed and better grounded.

I do not think that we can compare the discussion about abortion with that on contraception. There is a wide area of common ground among Catholics and Protestants about abortion in general, even though there are different positions in view of difficult situations. I think that the position of Paul Ramsey, which is very close to my own, is shared by many Protestants in all countries. And perhaps we can say that the position of James M. Gustafson[19]

17. "Notes on Moral Theology," *Theological Studies,* 22 (1961), 255.
18. *Ibid.,* p. 256.
19. "A Protestant Ethical Approach," *supra,* where Gustafson, in his comparison of soldiers taking life in a war of whose justice they are convinced and of taking the life of the innocent fetus "less justly but more mournfully," comes close to thoughts of earlier Catholic moralists.

Bernard Häring

is at least not very far from the position of Catholic thinkers of the past which we have reviewed.

My feeling is that there could develop a large area of agreement if we, on our part, were able to distinguish very carefully and thoroughly the essence of our doctrine from some less sure conclusions and arguments. The official position of the Catholic Church, which in most respects is well grounded, will be weakened in the eyes of Protestants and of many critical Catholics unless we give a clear account of the different degrees of certainty of our general presuppositions, and acknowledge the intellectual difficulties regarding some hard cases which are now falling under the official condemnation of the Church, although they were freely discussed in earlier centuries.

To my knowledge, Protestant writers affirm unambiguously the same basic moral values as those on which we ground our own argumentation; there is therefore a broad agreement about the immorality of abortion in general. Disagreement arises chiefly about hard cases where Protestants hold that, because of special circumstances, other moral values dominate in such a way that what is still called abortion does not show the specific malice of abortion.[20]

It is true that since the end of the last century the Holy See has more and more eliminated milder opinions which were proposed by renowned Catholic moralists.[21] The Catholic theologian will manifest loyal adherence to these decisions. However, scientific attitude and concern for credibility and for earnest ecumenical dialog force him to discuss important distinctions: What is the

20. St. Alphonsus Liguori asserts that *epikeia* (which frees from the particular law if there is a certain or truly probable opinion that the legislator, acting wisely, could not have intended to include such an extraordinary case in his law) can be used even in matters of *natural law* (*ubi actio possit ex circumstantiis a malitia denudari*), where owing to the situation, the action would not be characterized by that malice which is the reason for the immorality asserted in the principle (*Theologia moralis*, bk. I, treatise II, n. 201, ed. Gaudé, 1905, vol. I, p. 182). Following this view, Alphonsus did at least consider the probability of the opinion that the need to save the life of the mother in imminent danger of death might free the therapeutic abortion from the typical malice of abortion, though on the practical level he favored the safer opinion of those who were teaching that a direct intention of abortion should be excluded. But his final argument is puzzling, since he repeats twice in the context, "why expel it [the fetus] directly since it is lawful and sufficient to do it indirectly" *ibid.*, pp. 644, 646).
21. Noonan, *supra*.

essential and abiding part of the official teaching and what is a special pastoral aspect or a less convincing application? To what extent is a part of a doctrine, presented in the name of "natural law," binding for all times if the arguments given by the Magisterium are not fully convincing and if theology is not able to supply more convincing reasons? Finally, how can the Magisterium maintain a part of its official teaching if the arguments are not fully cogent or convincing? If it is really a matter of natural law, then it is chiefly a matter of human experience, reflection, and insight.

However, I want here to explain my own approach clearly. If I try to argue about questions which seem to be decided by the Magisterium, though not in an irreformable way, I do not recommend my tentative opinion as one to be followed in practice. I insist that the presumption is in favor of the position of the teaching of the Magisterium; a doubt by some theologian does not invalidate the official position. Later discussions may even strengthen it and bring forth more convincing arguments. It is in this attitude that I propose some thoughts about possible directions for a refinement of the actual teaching of the Catholic Church about abortion.

IV. EXPLORATIVE POINTS OF REFINEMENT OF THE CATHOLIC TEACHING ON THE INTRINSIC MALICE OF ABORTION

The foregoing considerations about the degree of certainty of our presuppositions, along with the historical survey, may have already provided some indications for further searching thought. In the following section I shall give special attention to some characteristic questions, confronting myself loyally with the official teaching of the Catholic Church.

V. SHARPER DISTINCTION BETWEEN ABORTION AND CONTRACEPTION

In the past, contraception and abortion were somehow put on the same or equal level: as a crime against nature and against the procreative function of sexuality. Thus the specific malice, the reason for the immorality of abortion, did not appear clearly. This lack of a total distinction was understandable at a time when moralists were abiding by the opinion that the fetus of the male was ensouled on the fortieth day after fertilization and the female fetus on the eightieth day, and when they sharply distinguished the abortion of an ensouled and an unensouled fetus.

The encyclical *Casti connubii* is probably the most classical official text that condemns contraception and abortion with almost the same severe expressions. This was so because the encyclical was especially directed and worded in opposition to the permissive teaching of the Lambeth Conference about contraception, and was inspired by a widespread fear that a contraceptive attitude might not only cause serious problems of population (imbalance between old and young) but also destroy the very ideal of parenthood and conjugal chastity.[22] There was evidently a strong conviction that the tendency toward abortion could not be conquered without first fighting against the source of the evil, the contraceptive attitude.

Between the encyclical *Casti connubii* (1930) and the teaching of Vatican II (*Constitution on the Church in the Modern World*, article 51) lie thirty-five years of rich experience, of sociological and psychological studies, and reflection. It is no wonder, then, that the teaching of Vatican II shows an acute awareness of the total difference between birth regulation by contraception — especially if inspired by responsible parenthood — and abortion.

If rigoristic formulations of the teaching on contraception, and even more rigoristic pastoral application of that teaching, were among the causes of an increase in abortions among groups of the Catholic population (for example, in Latin America), then there arises an urgent need for more careful and sharper distinctions between actions as totally different as abortion and contraception. Although a contraceptive attitude, which manifests a depreciation of the parental vocation and of the child, is one of the chief causes of abortion, a conscientious use of the best possible ways of birth regulation, in the spirit of generous responsible parenthood, can remove many temptations of abortion.

22. Pius XI, encyclical *Casti connubii, Acta Apostolicae Sedis,* 22 (1930), 539–592. The encyclical calls contraception without any distinction: "fascinorosa licentia" (criminal license), "turpe quid et intrinsece inhonestum" (turpitude and infamy by its very meaning), p. 559; "turpis labes" (mark of infamy), "gravis noxae labes" (stain of grave guilt), p. 560. Then it introduces the argument on abortion with the words: "aliud quoque gravissimum facinus" (another extremely grave misdeed), p. 562.

The Church's condemnation of abortion is only fully credible if at the same time all possible effort is made to eliminate the chief causes of abortion. These efforts should include truly pastoral wording of the doctrine as well as all kinds of social action in favor of those who are especially exposed to the danger of "resolving" their hard problems by abortion.

VI. CLEARER DEFINITION OF THE MALICE OF ABORTION

The traditional moral theology has sharply distinguished direct and indirect abortion, condemning the first and condoning the latter. However, indirect abortion can be lawful only under the condition that it is not an abortion in the moral sense: if it does not bear the moral malice or nonvalue of abortion.

Many moralists of past centuries spoke on indirect abortion in a very broad sense.[23] Their teaching was applied in one way or another to almost all cases where the chief and decisive intention was directed toward another good — the health and life of the mother. The taking away of the life of the fetus was then only the secondary effect of the intention and action: secondary insofar as it was not willed in itself. In accordance with the principle of the double effect, there had also to be a very evident proportion between the danger to the life of the fetus and the motives justifying the danger and the action.

It was chiefly out of pastoral concern that the Holy See — in several responses to bishops who had informed the Roman authorities that "a way had been found to abort the fetus by means which did not directly tend to its killing in the mother's womb but to its expulsion, so that it would die as soon as it came to the light" — took position against any therapeutic abortion.[24]

In their pastoral concern, and faced with a multitude of people either unable to distinguish or else inclined to all too subtle distinctions, Pius XI and Pius XII condemned, with the strongest expressions, any kind of direct abortion and declared the absolute invio-

23. See Noonan, *supra.* See also my note 20. Augustine Lehmkuhl was still asserting in 1888 that an abortion (an expulsion) of a nonviable fetus to save the mother's life would scarcely be "a direct abortion in a theological sense, any more than yielding a plank in a shipwreck to a friend is direct killing of one's self." *Theologia moralis* (Freiburg-i-Br., 5th ed., 1888), sec. 841.

24. Denzinger-Schönmetzer, *Enchiridion Seymbolorum,* 32nd ed. (Freiburg/Breisgau and New York, 1963), n. 3298, seen. 3258.

lability of life, allowing no exception.[25] One of the results of this was that Catholic gynecologists, because of the necessity for extraordinary effort, made special contributions to the saving of life of both the mother and the fetus.

But the question of what is direct and what is indirect abortion was even then not settled in Catholic moral theology. The standard case of the cancerous uterus found approval by the majority of Catholic moralists. The physician is surely allowed to perform all the medically accepted operations with the standard procedures, insofar as they appear necessary and urgent to remedy an acute, hazardous, morbid condition of the expectant mother, even if these medical procedures entail a probable or even certain danger to the life of the fetus as an undesired and indirect consequence. In all cases there is the condition that there is no real probability of saving both the mother and the unborn child.

The distinction between "direct" and "indirect" abortion has sometimes resulted in too literal or mechanical applications. A gynecologist tells of a typical case: "I was once called upon to perform an operation on a woman in the fourth month of pregnancy, to remove a malign uterine tumor. On the womb there were numerous very thin and fragile varicose veins which bled profusely, and attempts to suture them only aggravated the bleeding. Therefore, in order to save the woman from bleeding to death, I opened the womb and removed the fetus. Thereupon the uterus contracted, the bleeding ceased, and the woman's life was saved. I was proud of what I had achieved, since the uterus of this woman, who was still childless, was undamaged and she could bear other children. But I had to find out later from a noted moralist that although I had indeed acted in good faith, what I had done was, in his eyes, *objectively* wrong. I would have been allowed to remove the bleeding uterus with the fetus itself, he said, but was not permitted to interrupt the pregnancy while leaving the womb intact. This latter, he said, constituted an immoral termination of pregnancy, though done for the purpose of saving the mother, while the other way would have been a lawful direct intention and action to save life. For him

25. Pius XI, *Casti connubii, Acta Apostolicae Sedis*, 22 (1930), 262–265; Pius XII, Address to Catholic Society of Midwives, Oct. 29, 1951, *Acta Apostolicae Sedis*, 43 (1951) 838f.

preservation of the woman's fertility and thereby, under some circumstances, preservation of the marriage itself, played no decisive role." [26]

My solution in a similar case would follow a different line of reasoning. The malice of abortion is an attack on the right of the fetus to live; but since the doctor in this situation can determine (with great moral certainty) that there is no chance for both the mother and the fetus to survive if he does not intervene directly, he accepts the only chance to protect and serve life which Divine Providence has left to him. He saves the life of the mother while he does not truly deprive the fetus of its right to live, since it would not survive in any event if he failed to save the mother's life. Moreover, the preservation of the mother's fertility is an additional service to life.

As we already distinguish between abortion (or interruption of a pregnancy) in a *medical* and a *legal* sense, I propose the further distinction of abortion in a *moral* sense. Abortion in the moral sense would designate all cases which bear the characteristic malice or nonvalue which justifies our severe condemnation of abortion. Practically, this solution would not go much further than the casuistic solutions of those moralists who undertake the problem with only the principle of the double effect and indirect action, but my argumentation seems to me — at least in some cases — less artificial.

I do not, however, deny the value of those common distinctions. They allow, for example, a quite reasonable solution to the case of an ectopic pregnancy. The reason for terminating the pregnancy cannot be the fetus as such, but only a dangerous development of the organ such as a pathological pregnancy in the fallopian tube. But even in this case my own argumentation seems to me simpler and more convincing. The physician should do his best to preserve the fetus in the case of an ectopic pregnancy, but as soon as it becomes sure that intervention is necessary to save the mother, and there is no chance to save both by waiting, the intervention does not truly deprive the fetus of the right to live, since it has already no chance to survive. The fact that the biological death occurs

26. H. Kramann, "Umstrittene Heilmethoden in der Gynekologie," *Arzt und Christ*, 5 (1959), 202f. See my book *The Law of Christ*, 3 (Westminster, Md.: Newman Press, 1966) 212.

some days earlier than if the physician allowed both to die does no harm to the right of the fetus, since it is not deprived of any personal activity.

VII. THE DEFINITION OF A HUMAN BEING

Hitler destroyed hundreds of thousands of human persons because he considered them to be "unfitting life." His criterion was the utility of man for the type of economic and political society he wanted to produce. He did not believe that suffering, and the loving care of suffering persons, can enrich the whole of mankind. But the distinction cannot be between socially useful persons and socially "unfitting" persons. Whether useful for earthly purposes or not, the life of the human person is always sacred.

I cannot, therefore, see any truly moral justification for the interruption of pregnancy because of a probability that the child might be defective (as in the case of the thalidomide children), unless it could be proved sufficiently that the embryo is not at all human life. Neither can I see that such a proof would be possible at our present level of medical knowledge.

But another question cannot be avoided by the modern moralist. Is a totally deformed fetus that is even lacking the biological substrate for any expression of truly human life, still to be considered a person? Is it wholly clear that we must preserve, with tremendous effort and inconvenience, a biological life born of a human mother if there is not and never will be the slightest expression of humanity? Would it be an abortion in the full moral sense if the doctor, after a clear diagnosis of such a total deformation (no development of the central nervous system and human brain) would interrupt a pregnancy?

I am not sure whether this question can find a safe and certain response at the present stage of discussion;[27] but it is worth consider-

27. See W. Ruff, S.J., "Das embryonale Werden des Menschen," *Stimmen der Zeit*, 181 (1968), 331–335. The medical data for this question are new, but the question itself is not totally new. Alphonsus Liguori, following older moralists, responds to the question about the abortion of a totally deformed fetus that has no chances of survival: "As Sporer and Holzman rightly assert, there must be made an exception in the case of a corrupted fetus, because if it is deformed to an extent that it is no longer apt to be ensouled it is no more a fetus, but just a putrid substance" (*Theologia moralis*, bk. III, treatise III, Doubt IV, n. 394, in the critical edition of Gaudé, vol. I, p. 645). Of course the problem presented itself to

ation, since our concern is not just for biological life but for *human* life. Putting this question does not suggest at all any justification of euthanasia. Though a person may suffer deeply in the last days or month of his life, this can still be a blessed human life; there can be most important manifestations of the human person in faith, trust, patience, gratitude. On the other hand, I do not see any need for *artificially* keeping the biological life of an adult person or of a child for days and months if there is no hope whatever that this person would regain consciousness or be capable of any personal manifestation.[28] There is, however, an essential difference between killing and allowing a human being to die in dignity.

VIII. MORAL PRINCIPLES AND PASTORAL COUNSELLING

James M. Gustafson has made a major contribution to the discussions of situation ethics by distinguishing the different levels of discourse.[29] One should clearly realize on what level he wishes to conduct his discourse.

Most of the paper of Professor Gustafson is on what he calls the second level, the reflective question of a man asking, "What ought I to do in this situation?"[30] The woman who, after being raped, seeks advice and her counsellor are going to discuss the question in a discourse which remains essentially on the same level.

Up to this point my article has been on Gustafson's "third or ethical level" where questions are raised about the rules or considerations that justify a particular moral judgment.[31] In Catholic theology there is a long tradition for these clear distinctions of the levels on which one confronts a problem. We distinguish the level of moral theology and the level of pastoral counselling. This distinction is somewhat different from that of Gustafson, but it can be compared.

---

these moralists in a somehow different perspective, because their casuistic solutions were based on the theory of a successive animation. The articles quoted in *supra* n. 14 (W. Ruff) are giving a modern evaluation to these theories.

28. See Cardinal Michele Pellegrino, "Questioni deotnologiche nella practica cardiologica," *Minerva Medica*, vol. 59, no. 28 (1968), pp. 1591–1599 (esp. pp. 1594–1596 on reanimation).

29. In "Context Versus Principles. A Displaced Debate in Christian Ethics," 58 *The Harvard Theological Review* (1965), 171–202.

30. *Ibid.*

31. *Ibid.*, p. 174.

Bernard Häring

On the level of pastoral counselling a Catholic moralist might come to almost the same conclusion and even to almost the same way of friendly discourse as Gustafson. Pastoral prudence looks not only to the general principles but also to the art of the possible. By looking for the real step that can be taken by the person in the concrete context, the pastoral effort of the moral theologian does not betray his own "objective" principles, since the whole of moral life is characterized by the "law of growth," by the need of a constant conversion, step by step. The milder tradition of moral and pastoral theology expresses an important aspect of this dynamic approach by its discourse on "invincible ignorance."

Invincible ignorance should not be interpreted in the sense of mere intellectualism but rather in the light of a theory on conscience, which emphasizes the existential totality of man. Invincible ignorance is a matter of inability of a person to "realize" a moral obligation. Because of the person's total experience, the psychological impasses, and the whole context of his life, he is unable to cope with a certain moral imperative. The intellectual difficulties of grasping the values which are behind a certain imperative are often deeply rooted in existential difficulties. The human person is ever in the condition of the disciples to whom the Lord says, "There is still much that I could say to you but the burden would be too great for you now" (John 16:12). According to the very different stature and situation of people, this can be the case not only as to highest ideals and goal-commandments of the Gospel but also as to the concrete and existential understanding of a prohibitive moral norm.

Alphonsus Liguori expresses the basic principle of moral counselling in such cases in the following way: "The more common and true opinion teaches that the confessor can and must refrain from admonition and leave the penitent in good faith whenever he is confronted with an invincible error, whether in matter of human law or of divine law, if prudence tells him that an admonition would not do any good but rather harm the penitent." [32] The concern of pastoral counselling must always be the conscience of the person and not abstract rules. Alphonsus explains that "the reason is that there must be more care for avoiding the danger of a formal sin

32. *Theologia moralis*, bk. VI, treatise IV, n. 610, ed. Gaudé (1905) vol. III, p. 634.

140

than of a material sin. God punishes only the formal sin, since He takes only this as an offence." [33]

Since Gustafson has used in his moral discourse the example of a woman who seeks counsel after a heinous rape committed against her by her ex-husband and a group of scoundrels, I may be allowed to note my own way of approaching a similar case before I had knowledge of Gustafson's approach.

On the "third level," as moralist expressing opinion about the objective norms, I wrote: "In cases of rape, it is morally allowable to cleanse away the sperm, which is considered to be an extension of the initial act of aggression. Abortion, however, is not allowed if conception has already taken place. It has not been adjudged that the fetus, which would not have been formed except for the presence of the "aggressive" sperm, is itself an "aggressor." [34]

Then, turning to the level of pastoral counselling I continued: "Nevertheless, we must recognize that although the fetus is innocent, the girl is likewise innocent. We can therefore understand her revulsive feeling that this is not 'her' child, not a child that she is in justice required to bear. We must, however, *try to motivate her* to consider the child with love because of its subjective innocence, and to bear it in suffering through to birth, whereupon she may consider her enforced maternal obligation fulfilled and may give over the child to a religious or governmental agency, after which she would try to resume her life with the sanctity that she will undoubtedly have achieved through the great sacrifice and suffering. If, owing to the psychological effects of her traumatic experience, she is utterly unable to accept this counsel, it is possible that we may have to leave her in 'invincible ignorance.' Her own salvation may depend on it because of her near despair. If she has already yielded to the violent temptation to rid herself as completely as possible of the effects of her experience, we can leave the judgment of the degree of her sin to a merciful God and try to build

33. *Praxis confessarii*, chap. I, n. 8. However, Alphonsus states some important exceptions to this principle: If there should arise danger to the public good, princes, judges, and prelates who gravely neglect the duties of their office, even if they would be stubborn, must be warned. If the penitent asks explicitly about the objective rule and solution, the priest should tell the truth; the very fact of such an insistent and explicit question may indicate that the ignorance is not thoroughly invincible (*ibid.*, n. 9).
34. B. Häring, *Shalom: Peace. The Sacrament of Reconciliation* (New York: Farrar, Strauss, and Giroux, 1968), p. 181.

up her willingness to integrate both her suffering and her fault with the sufferings and sins of the world that Christ took upon Himself on the cross." [35]

It is true that the mode of expression differs from the style and approach of Gustafson, since my references are within the frame of the specific Catholic tradition of pastoral theology. But I do not see that the two positions are irreconcilable as to their essence. I did not write that the confessor or counsellor must tell her first the objective principles. My expression, "we must *try to motivate* her" excludes a pastoral approach that starts out immediately with the abstract principles and an imperative according to them. It is above all a matter of motivation. Then it will become clearer how far the person can bear a word of concrete appeal to accept the heroic solution.

However, in my pastoral approach I would never go so far as to advise the person to abort the fetus. Neither would I say to the person involved that this is the right decision if she has made up her mind. Gustafson puts his accent on the "more mournfully." I would even more emphasize the "less justly." [36] But during the pastoral counselling I would refrain from all rigid judgment once I could see that the person cannot bear the burden of a clear appeal not to abort.

IX. THE MORALITY OF LEGISLATION

Legislation and approved customs have played a large part in the formation of consciences in homogeneous and closed societies, and especially in the less developed parts of the societies. The admonition of the state by Pius XI can be understood in view of such a historical situation. He charged the state "in legislating to take into account what is determined by the divine law and by Church legislation, and to proceed with penal sanction against those who have sinned. For there are people who think that whatever is allowed by civil legislation or not subject to penal sanctions may also be allowed according to the moral law; or they may put it into practice

35. *Ibid.*, p. 182.
36. Speaking on counselling in the most complicated situations, Gustafson says: ". . . the moralist can be convinced that the defenseless fetus can be taken, less justly, but more mournfully" in "A Protestant Ethical Approach," *supra*, that is, less justly than the taking of innocent life in a way which is considered to be just.

even against their conscience, since they do not fear God and would not have to fear anything from human legislation." [37]

In a pluralistic society one of the most urgent duties of the churches and of humanist ethicists is to contribute to the formation of a mature conscience. Every mature person must be clearly aware that true morality and penal sanctions — or the absence of penal sanctions — lie on two quite different levels. Legislation or custom must not be allowed to determine our moral judgment; this must be formed by the Gospel and by insight into moral values. It is true that the combination of law with custom provides one of the easier sources of accessibility to moral insight, but in a pluralistic society the role of this source has greatly diminished. As a result, a shift toward more direct insight into the levels and urgencies of moral values is most necessary for all. We should consider this shift as offering a greater impetus toward maturity and depth, although it may also entail dangers for the weak ones.

Many factors contribute to the event that the modern pluralistic state, especially in the United States, will be less and less able to enforce the penalties against abortion, especially in the numerous cases where the citizens, and Christian ethicists also, no longer are in agreement about the hierarchy of values and its principal applications. Under such circumstances the Church's undue emphasis on a battle for penal legislation could sacrifice an opportunity to work for a deeper formation of the consciences of the faithful. The present discussions should lead to an awakening of the conscience of many about their responsibilities in the whole issue.

Formation of conscience demands good and absolutely honest argumentation and a fairly clear distinction between the existence of an official teaching and intrinsic reasoning about values, urgency of values, and so on. Only within the Church itself is the existence of a teaching a strong argument; in the dialog with others it has little bearing. However, since legislation in a modern democratic state depends greatly on public opinion, all who are convinced about the need for certain legislation to protect the innocent life of the fetus should give due attention to the art of influencing public opinion by appropriate methods and arguments.

37. Pius XI, *Casti connubii, Acta Apostolicae Sedis*, 20 (1930), 589. The context of this text is the Lateran Concordat with the Italian state in 1929, to which the encyclical refers explicitly as a hopeful event.

Bernard Häring

A battle for better public opinion and for laws protecting the life of the unborn children is only credible, honest, and effective to the extent that all other genuine opportunities for social help in difficult situations are used to the utmost. Since the protection by penal legislation may be more and more weakened, in spite of all our efforts, there should be more intelligent efforts to remove the chief causes of abortion and to enlighten public opinion about the whole problem. The combining of teaching with action would at the same time work out as part of an effective motivation.

As far as legislation itself is concerned, it should be discussed chiefly in terms of the common good, justice toward the weak ones, and protection of those basic values without which society would be exposed to great risks of self-destruction. It cannot be the task of a pluralistic state to protect the religious teaching of a church where this does not coincide with the common good of the respective society. If we argue on the basis of natural law, this can be effective only to the extent that we give, besides the official teaching of the Church authority, reasons and motives that could be convincing to sincere and intelligent people who are not under Church authority.

I am not at all enthusiastic about the Abortion Act of Great Britain of October 27, 1967. While there is a conscience clause — as there should be — so that no one can be forced to participate in any abortion if he has conscientious objection to it, I disagree with the restriction in this clause which deprives of its benefits anyone who "has a duty to participate in treatment which is necessary to save the life or to prevent grave permanent injury to the physical or mental health of a pregnant woman." This is most deplorable if it may be interpreted as obliging a Catholic doctor, under penal sanctions, to terminate pregnancies by procedures which can be judged as directly abortifacient.

On the other hand, if it is a matter of discussing the qualities of the legislation *as* legislation, I do not find the following type of discussion very helpful: "Mother and child have an equal right to life and no action is moral that favors the life of one against that of another. No Catholic, or indeed anyone — for the law of God governs all men — may take part in this type of abortion . . . Direct abortion is always against the positive and natural law of God. Indirect abortion may sometimes be permitted for a sufficiently grave reason." [38] I do not deny the value which, at least for Catholic theologians, is behind this argument, but it does not reach the partners of the dialog and does not seem to be to the point of legislation as such.

I, too, would argue strongly against the restriction, but rather in this line of thought: One of the great values and fundaments of a religiously pluralistic state is the respect for the moral and religious convictions of loyal and most serious citizens. There is no good reason, in view of the common good and the fundamental right of all citizens, to disregard the upright moral conviction of many Catholics who on this point abide by the official teaching of their Church. This disregard for the conscience of many Catholics, and others who share their convictions, is the more deplorable as the restriction of the conscience clause is worded in a way that might open the way to pressure against doctors for not having prevented "grave permanent injury to the physical or mental health of a pregnant woman." This law seems also to be in contradiction to common practice of modern states not to encourage people to invoke legal processes against conscientious physicians.

The state preparing new legislation on abortion should study with great care the foreseeable impact on the common good, on respect for another person's life, and on all other values that could be affected by changes being considered; but this is not the duty of the legislators alone. It is likewise the responsibility of members of the Church, of Church authorities, and of ethicists who wish to make concrete suggestions about the content of a law, to study on all levels the matter of probable consequences. Besides this, there remains always the "art of the possible" in the best possible direction.

38. Peter Flood, "The Abortion Act 1967," p. 46.

GEORGE HUNTSTON WILLIAMS

The Sacred Condominium

ETHICAL ACCOMMODATION OF INDIVIDUAL AND SOCIAL
PREROGATIVES IN A PLURALISTIC DEMOCRATIC SOCIETY

Developing religious attitudes as to the components of personhood
with special reference to abortion help to explain both the active
principles and especially the moral residues that condition many
Americans as they approach the current abortion debate. The
author has traced the historical background from patristic times
to the present under the title "Religious Residues and Presuppositions in the American Debate on Abortion." [1] The task here is to
reflect upon this not entirely homogeneous heritage and to recast
it with reference to modern categories and some quite new social
concerns in an updated Christian fetology in Protestant perspective.

We shall then set forth a basis for a politics of abortion that
emerges from this updated fetology and that will heed the rights
of minorities and the consensus of the majority, endeavoring out
of a Protestant's experience with his collective past to supply or
identify a model for the execution of responsible decisions amid
a complex of factors and values. The proposed model for a politics
of abortion is a sacred condominium[2] in which parents and the

1. In *Theological Studies*, 31 (Woodstock, Md., March 1970). The present essay
constitutes in effect Part II of the larger essay published there.
2. The author has previously expressed himself in print on abortion only in
"The No. 2 Moral Issue of Today," *America* (25 March 1967), pp. 452f. This
two-page piece was actually an enlarged letter in commendation of an earlier
article in *America* by Dean Robert F. Drinan of the Law School of Boston College. Since then Dean Drinan, confident that faithful Catholics will in any case
follow the lead of the Church and concerned with the pedagogical role of the
law and worried that the state might become involved in setting up therapeutic
and even eugenic standards, at the International Conference on Abortion, sponsored by the Harvard Divinity School in cooperation with the Joseph P. Kennedy, Jr., Foundation, held in September 1967 and subsequently, has expressed

body politic are understood to share sovereignty in varying degrees and in varying circumstances. The model will be set forth as something distinctively American, though exportable, and as an elaboration and conceptualization of what in fact already subsists latently in our pluralistic, constitutional commonwealth.

Next, the roles in the sacred condominium of the various functionaries like physicians, lawyers, social workers, and clergymen will be specified and clarified.

Finally, various types of abortion cases will be dealt with in what is envisaged as the common court of the cosovereigns, presumably best located in a hospital. It should be remarked in advance that the concept of the sacred condominium and its application is conservative in intent, although it affords a theoretical and procedural rationale for a somewhat larger number of abortions than is now legally permissible in most states.

I. AN UPDATED CHRISTIAN FETOLOGY: THE GENETIC AND SOCIAL COMPONENTS OF PERSONALITY

On the biological level, Patristic, classical Protestant, and especially Papal asseverations as to the fully human character of the fetus from the moment of conception have been more than vindicated. For, once the haploid generation of sperm and ovum have joined in the diploid generation of the zygote, the biological essentials of the inchoate person are in order fixed, the definitive genetic code has been arranged and set. Whereas in traditional Jewish thought even the well-formed fetus still required for completion the essential *neshamah* and hence *nephesh* at birth, and whereas in the traditional Aristotelian-Thomist thought (before post-Tridentine adaptation) the fetus required the rudiments of a body in order to be rationally informed or animated, in the under-

---

preference for no law either way on abortion of the fetus before quickening. The slight accommodations in the present paper which go beyond what I endorsed in my earlier letter are prompted by the same fear as that of Father Drinan about state control. But over against his call for less legal specifications with respect to abortion prior to quickening, I am proposing a somewhat new legal principle, or application thereof, the condominium, in which the expectant mother is recognized as having a unique status with respect to the state. This proposal of a condominium was made by me in the legal section of the Conference partly out of recognition of the social dimensions that before the Conference I had not understood so well.

standing of modern biology the fetus only needs time! In third-century Carthage Tertullian was really quite close to our present genetic understanding: "He is a human being [in essence] who will be one." [3] Viability, the term used for the susceptibility of the fetus to being brought to babyhood outside the womb, is being pushed ever backwards by the refinement of the incubator and the auxiliary skills of fetology.

At the same time, modern embryology since Karl von Baer and Edouard van Beneden, over against the sire-centered theory of both Thomas Aquinas and Martin Luther, have demonstrated the precise equality of the two progenitors in shaping the genetic character of the fetus. But despite this genetic equality, still other factors highly valued in modern society have tended to make the mother, whether a wife or unwed, the determining voice as to the fate of the fetus.

An updated sacred embryology must take cognizance of these several shifts along with new sociopsychological definitions of personality which would supplement or even, in extreme formulations, replace the purely genetic definition of the life in the womb. Partly because modern physiology and medicine are unable to distinguish any validly distinctive nodal point in the continuum from the implantation of the blastocyst in the lining of the uterus to birth, much of the modern argument for the legitimacy of abortion, as distinguished from infanticide, is beginning to revolve around the rather new category provided by social science: the conception of person and personality as a consequence of socialization.

For example, an important factor in the shaping of a personality is firstness among the siblings, or the middle position, and so on. On this view, the abortion of a possibly defective fetus in a young mother afflicted with rubella would still allow for that uniquely social element of firstness (or secondness) to perdure in the succeeding fetal personality. That incommensurable factor of being the first or second or third offspring to be received by expectant parents (and any other members of the family) is, according to the situationalists, a societary component of personality. Some-

3. See Williams, *ibid.*, n. 36, in a section where traducianist Tertullian is enlarged upon among the Fathers because of his later influence on Luther and "Protestant embryology and sexual ethics."

what like the "rational soul" emergent in or infused from without into the "formed fetus" of Aristotelian-Thomist embryology, the "social" soul, that is, the family pattern or imprint, would remain intact, despite a therapeutic abortion, to shape instead the mother's next embryo brought to term. Obviously, this modern view of the completed person as partly a socialized being (an idea which has Jewish antecedents and Protestant social gospel support) goes far beyond such an incommensurable as firstness and secondness to embrace the whole range of psychosocial considerations, from the health of the mother during the pregnancy to the character and mood of the mother and of all the others who would constitute the early environment of the wanted or unwanted, the cared for or neglected, or, even, battered child.

There now tends to be a rapid polarization of thinking between those who (in the Catholic and classical Protestant line) hold that the fetus is genetically a complete human being and potential personality from conception (or at least implantation of the blastocyst) and those who (in the traditional Jewish line) hold that it becomes such primarily when the infant draws its first breath among the living.[4] Further, in so-called liberal Protestant and secular espousal of this second position, an accepting attitude on the part of the mother or the family and in the social context is being allowed to play an increasingly important role in the politics of abortion. It is possible that conserving Christians, alike Catholic and Protestant, and indeed theistic ethicists in general, could, updating their theories, make use of both these stages of "personification," genetic and social, as they present to the religiously neutral lawmakers their reconsidered rationale for their own nuanced religious code of behavior in this difficult area and their preferred terms for a politics of abortion in the public domain.

Surely the fact that the laws and canons in various lands, times, and traditions have always distinguished between the crime of abortion and the crime of infanticide indicates that there has been felt to be some moral difference in the status of the fetus and that of the newborn infant. This is evident not only in rabbinical Judaism

---

4. I have traced the interrelationship of the genetic-embryological development and the three Christian theories of ensoulment (the preexistence of souls, creationism, and traducianism) with the evolution of Western sensibilities about abortion in my essay, "Religious Presuppositions," pt. I, cited in n. 1 above.

but also even in the Catholic tradition, especially from Augustine through Aquinas to Alfonso Liguori, that is, before modern papal pronouncements.

It could be argued that the moral and legal difference between the fetus and the newborn child and hence between feticide and infanticide is ultimately based upon the fact that up to the decisive moment of birth (the severing of the umbilical cord), the life of the fetus is biologically the creation of its progenitors and that society instinctively senses a difference of some degree between the murder of a full member of society and the termination of the life of a presocialized fetus not yet subject in all respects to the laws governing society at large. Anciently, in the Roman tradition, for example, the paterfamilias had plenary power over the unborn and the young, the right to extinguish or sell unto slavery his offspring, not to say merely the right of life or death over the fetus in the womb of his spouse. In the Old Testament are preserved clear traces of the parental sacrifice of the first fruit of the womb not only to Baal but also to Yehweh. Then, after centuries of moral tutelage we came to understand the parents in wedlock (and otherwise residually the mother alone) as sharing with the state — in varying degrees in different societies — the mutual responsibility for the *protection* of an unborn life. On this view, the fetus is not merely a part of the mother like a limb or not merely an extension of the domain of the paterfamilias (to summarize a venerable rabbinic and an ancient Roman theory) but is, as it were, both a subject and ward of two coordinate sovereignties: the progenitor(s) and the body politic. Authority over the unborn life today can be best understood as a primordial condominium with preponderance shifting now to the state, now to the progenitor, depending upon the circumstances.

Unless we insist on this sacred condominium we can foresee such extremes in some future society, in effect statist or feminist, as that the state would demand eugenic or even demographic abortion[5] or that the mother could acquire by legal concession that complete control over her progeny which was once exercised in patriarchal society (pagan Roman and pre-Abrahamic) alone by

5. Cf. Ralph B. Potter, Jr., "The Abortion Debate," *The Religious Situation:* 1968, ed. Donald R. Cutler (1968), pp. 112–161.

the sire. She would, moreover, be facilitated in the assimilation or arrogation of virtually sole control of intrauterine life by the increased availability of chemical abortifacients which would enable her, if she so willed, to act without the approbation of her doctor or even her mate.

Both of these extremes, statist and feminist, are abhorrent for most Christians to contemplate. But a completed Christian theory of the politics of abortion should recognize the rights alike of the mother, the fetus, and society. We must affirm and elaborate the principle that safeguarding the life of the unborn does, in fact, in the evolution of society, represent a unique condominium in which the state and the married couple or the single mother can in various circumstances work out literally the modus vivendi.

The writer's own Christian fetology is here presented in the larger quasi-political construct of the sacred condominium of the progenitors and the state over the fetus.

II. THEORETICAL CONSTRUCT: THE SACRED CONDOMINIUM OF PROGENITOR AND STATE

The politics of abortion implies a social institution or set of conventions by which society can reach the best possible resolution of a moral dilemma that is difficult because unborn lives are at stake. Since politics is the "art of the possible," we must strive in the special sector of it relating to abortion to find the most humane solution among the demands of the common good, the autonomy of the individual conscience, and the various voluntary collectivities like the Church which especially nurtures that conscience. It is as a foundation to such a politics of abortion that we identify and develop the concept of the sacred condominium, already implicit in society's conventions.

The present American legal use of the term and concept of condominium is largely limited to housing, that is, to joint ownership of apartment houses and the like. The term has, however, a richer historical meaning. In the Middle Ages a condominium referred to the corule of two princes over a territory — a rule that could alternate yearly, one prince governing and collecting revenues from the land one year, and the other the next. This kind of condominium could be inherited from generation to generation. It is this venerable usage of corule or cosovereignty that we revive as a theoretical basis for a politics of abortion.

Condominium in this august sense is the cosovereignty of the progenitor and the state over the life of the fetal person. Both progenitor and state have their proper responsibility for the nurture and tutelage of the child and consequently their own proper authority in the preservation of its life.

This is a primordial cosovereignty which we are identifying, and it is especially appropriate that it be recognized in a pluralistic society and in a republic shaped by a covenantal constitution that understands the state to have but limited powers. For our federal government and society have from the beginning respected primordial social entities, like the Church and the University that antedated the American nation, entities whose charters — literal (the Dartmouth College Decision, 1819) or metaphorical (the First Amendment) — have been constitutionally acknowledged and confirmed. Furthermore, our federal and state constitutions recognize that there are inalienable rights reserved to private citizens; and numerous personal predilections are respected as zones and sectors of our being and action on which our governments, whether local, state, or federal, may not trespass, whether in the realms of conscience and the pursuit of life,[6] liberty, and happiness, or in the more public realm of voluntary association.

In our society the family also partakes constitutionally (the Oregon or *Pierce* decision, 1925) of this same primordial character, which is acknowledged in the Church and the University. But to a greater degree than they, the family is a mixed realm. For, although to some it is a diminutive or molecular commonwealth; for others, an *ecclesiola;* for others still, a cultural entity with its own customs and usages — the same family nevertheless participates also in the public domain and is both protected and remotely supervised by the state. Into the sphere of the nurture and education of the family's children — prospectively participant citizens — the state can extend its sovereignty in the case, for

6. On the constitutional right to life see J. T. S., "In Defense of the Right to Live: The Constitutionality of Therapeutic Abortion," 1 *Georgia Law Review* (Summer 1967), 693.

example, of a battered child who may be removed from an irresponsible parent.

Thus the social constitution of our nation can be said already to recognize a condominium of progenitor and state over the lives of children, including the unborn. And we can add that it is a sacred condominium, quite apart from theistic presuppositions, on the ground that all who are seriously concerned with social and personal responsibility consider human life sacred. Looking, then, to the sacredness of human life, which is at stake in the abortion controversy, our appeal is that this sacred condominium, as a principle already legally and socially recognized except for the term, may be further articulated into a legal doctrine and system which will serve as a foundation for a humane and democratic handling of the abortion problem.

The corule being discussed here is not that limited sovereignty over self which a freeman as distinguished from a serf or slave has over his own body and over what he does, constrained by the state only where that "sovereign" person (1) may be required to offer his life in the defense of the state, (2) trespasses upon another person or society at large, or (3) attempts to take his own life. In the last case the state and other persons are indeed commonly held to have the preemptory right to intervene by force or guile to protect any "sovereign" person from an attempt at suicide. Different from this limited sovereignty over self and of a different order is that cosovereignty or condominium in the unique realm of the procreation of new life. Here the corule of the mother or of the two progenitors rests upon the fact that they have voluntarily or involuntarily brought a protoperson into being. In a sense the progenitor is the last sovereign in a democratic society, for the fetus, as creature of the progenitor biologically, is organically, physically also a *subject*. Of the democratic state the fetus really is but a *ward* in the same condominium. Although the quasi-political theory of the condominium presupposes that the fetus is at least an inchoate person in consonance with the patristic-papal line of development, the theory of corule also reinstates something of the scriptural-rabbinical view that the mother is sovereign over the fruit of her womb, even if she can no longer maintain anatomically and hence morally that the fetus is merely a limb or growth. Our updated theistic fetology thus combines the patristic-papal and the scriptural-rabbinical lines of development in a Protestant quasi-political construct. Herein is stressed individual accountability. The mother or the two covenantly joined progenitors presume preeminence over the fruit of their intercourse no longer on the embryologically untenable ground that the fetus is but a growth until it has received "breath among the living" but on the ground that the mother or the two progenitors at once incur new responsibility and acquire a certain primordial cosovereignty with society the moment their intercourse results in a new life.

It would be a mistake to consider the condominium in the sphere of fetal life as completely analogous to the venerable Christian conception of the Two Powers (*Duo quippe sunt*), going back to Pope Gelasius (d. 496) and beyond to the beginnings of the Church as an *imperium in imperio*, because it and the related Two Kingdoms theory rest on a distinction between the eternal and the temporal, the spiritual and the mundane, the inner and the external, the church and the state; in the sacred condominium the state and that other limited sovereign, the progenitor(s), are alike concerned with the ultimate and the immediate welfare of another person, namely, whether that fetal person is to be or not to be.

The legal and institutional development of the progenitorial–political condominium over the unborn could have for the modern family and for the mother as cosovereign person what the evolution of sacred embryology achieved for the full humanity of the fetus as homo in *Casti connubii* (as late as 1930). The recognition of such a condominium as exercised by the progenitor(s) and society in mutual concern for the right of all persons involved (the incipient person, the progenitors, and the community at large) could be a distinctly American contribution to establishing a balance between individual and professional autonomy and general social control. In the ideal situation the authority of the progenitor(s) and of society would be balanced in the normal presumption of mutual concern (personal and abstract) for the prospective child as heir and citizen. But in certain instances, as we have already intimated and will detail below, the state could find occasion to withdraw from the condominium to allow the mother or the parents together to make a self-sacrificial decision in accordance with their ideals (religious or other). In other instances, the state could feel obliged to maximize its role or prevail in the condominium to protect, sometimes the fetus from the parents, sometimes the mother from the imperilling fetus (if she calls for help).

A German jurist in 1889 suggested one dimension of the condominium in his juridical theory for legitimating perforation of a fetus to save a mother's life, arguing in terms of Prussian citizenship. The state, he said, had an interest in protecting the fetus from hostile assaults, but the fetus, not being a "belonger of the state" (*Angehöriger*) could not demand protection from the state over against the mother, who as "member of the state" (*Mitglied*) had the right at least of self-defense when threatened from within. Therefore "in a collision between the two the state should *withdraw* its protection from the fetus."[7] The doctrine of the sacred condominium now being more carefully articulated recognizes with the German jurist the right of the state to protect the mother as citizen. Going beyond that right, neutralizing its inherent statism, and indeed insisting upon a quite different political metaphor for the politics of abortion, the doctrine demands the acknowledgment of two sovereignties, both ideally concerned with fetal life, but in case of conflict, the orderly adjudication of the right of the mother and that of the fetal person in a medical court.

An acceptable medical and legal code, implementing the balanced forces of the condominium over unborn life, presupposes accountability and knowing consent on the part of the progenitors, *at least the consent of passion.* The condominium would be considered abnormal or unbalanced if the procreative partners, especially the female, were unaware that their sexual act could lead to the formation of another human being. Awareness could be wanting either because of the minority of the progenitors or because of the rapaciousness or the imbecility or the insanity of one or both of the progenitors. Not only is witting consent absent in some sexual acts leading to conception, but also even passion. (An adultress and an adulterer, in contrast, would know the possible consequences of their act even when carried into it by passion, however irrational.) The same concern of Catholic moral theologians with the fetus as person with rights before the law must now

7. Joseph Heimberger, *Über die Straflosigkeit der Perforation,* Inaugural dissertation at Munich (Berlin, 1889), 33 pp.

be extended to the innocent victim of intercourse who has not willingly or knowingly participated in the biological act that leads to the creation of another human being. But the fact that the progenitor is not necessarily responsible for what has taken place within her does not dismantle the condominium but requires only that it be more fully articulated. Full recognition of the legal-political principle of the condominium in the cosovereignty of progenitors and the body politic involves some further revision of our conceptualization and terminology.

Thus the sacred condominium is not to be thought of as collapsing in the case of the progenitor's immaturity or defectiveness any more than in the paradigm of the royal sovereign and his prerogatives during minority or incapacitation. A woman whose sovereignty over her body has been violated, perhaps by rape, or a child whose body has been imposed upon by reason of her immaturity or defectiveness of mind stands in need of a kind of *regency*. A regency in the context of our political metaphor would be the collective term for those specialists and others — doctors, asylum or orphanage directors, parents, social workers — who ad hoc or over a period of time would be acknowledged by the state and in many cases designated and salaried by the state as speaking on behalf of the girl or incapacitated woman whose sovereignty had been in any way encroached upon.

Ordinarily, however, the two sovereignties would each be represented in a medical court by medical magistrates engaged by each, physicians (and other specialists) each in the service, respectively, of the mother and the body politic: the one, advocate and defender of the rights of the mother as limited sovereign and the other the advocate and defender of the fetus[8] on behalf of the state.

The use of the term "medical magistrate" or advocate is drawn, of course, from the analogy of law. Before a court the criminal has not only the right to be represented by a lawyer to defend

8. I find an analogous proposal by J. T. S., "In Defense of the Right to Live," p. 706: "Theoretically even a complete stranger should be able to act for the child [fetus], with the court's permission. A petition to the court for appointment as guardian ad litem should be a feasible procedure." For a discussion of the somewhat analogous Georgia statute see David W. Louisell and John T. Noonan, Jr., "Constitutional Balance," sec. III *infra*.

himself against the state prosecutor but also the right, if he be indigent, to choose from a panel of advocates maintained by the state.

Another analogy suggests itself from the sphere of marriage, an institution of concern to civil society as well as to religious communities. In other lands where state and church are separated the civil and religious ceremonies are distinct. The king of the Belgians, for example, must submit to civil services in his two official languages as well as to being joined with his queen in the nuptial mass. In the United States, in contrast, where church and state are constitutionally separated, it has been possible nevertheless for civil society to regard the celebrant of the nuptial mass, the minister, or the rabbi as a magistrate ad hoc, whose religious act can be taken as a binding legal action so long as, in whatever the religious context, he complies with what civil society deems sufficient for the solemnization of marriage as also a civil contract. By the same token civil society can regard the physicians deliberating as medical magistrates, by standards deemed sufficient by both the medical profession and the state.

In the sacred condominium the advocate for the mother or the advocate for the fetus should be acknowledged as such, first by his peers and then respectively by the patient (the pregnant mother) and by the state (for the fetus). Let us now look more closely at these "medical magistrates" and others who might appropriately discharge roles in the sacred condominium.

III. THE ROLES OF PROFESSIONALS IN THE SERVICE OF THE TWO SOVEREIGNTIES IN THE SACRED CONDOMINIUM

A hospital room could be thought of as the medical court where the sacred condominium of the pregnant mother and society become, as it were, jurisdictionally visible. It is now our task to see how the medical, the legal, the sociopsychiatric, and the clerical professions and callings function in the deliberations of this *condominial court*. These persons, professional and otherwise, are not to be thought of collectively either as a *panel* of specialists seeking some consensus or as a *court proper* with judge, jury, and advocate seeking a verdict, but rather as a confrontation of two sovereigns, clarifying and assessing their respective rights and duties with professional help from various quarters.

The Medical Profession in the Sacred Condominium: Physicians as Magistrates

The hospital has been envisaged as the place for an abortion case to be resolved because it is a public institution architecturally and emotionally associated with the mission of mercy and the preservation of human dignity in life and death. Here physicians are in their own setting, gynecologically and fetologically competent. Here they sustain their professional relationships to their patients and their peers. Here, too, they may be said to be ethically competent against the background of the long tradition of ethical awareness that has imbued the profession since Hippocrates. However, this is not their chief competence, which is medical; and it would be unfair to place the entire burden of ethical decision upon them.

It is being belatedly perceived in today's discussion of abortion that physicians are being called upon to bear too many moral and legal burdens that become inextricably involved in their medical expertness. Doctors must as of now consider at one and the same time, often in trying circumstances, the viability and the condition of the fetus, the circumstances of the conception, the condition of the mother, and the strictures of the law. A decision must often be made up of many components ranging from prudence to compassion. Although it has often been agreed that a panel of two or three physicians should be involved in any decision to abort, a clear differentiation of the roles of these physicians has not hitherto been insisted upon. With the legal recognition of the sacred condominium doctors could divide their roles, just as do lawyers, the one becoming in a given case an attorney for the defense, another the attorney for the prosecution, each within the confines of legal procedure. By analogy there should be a doctor–advocate for the fetus or the unborn life,[9] as well as, in difficult cases, an advocate for the mother or the parents together, seeing things from the

9. In her spirited summons of Americans to turn aside from our slippage into the "Hard Society," Eunice Kennedy Shriver makes a similar request. "When Pregnancy Means Heartbreak: Is Abortion the Answer?" *McCall's Magazine*, April 1968.

maternal side. Moreover, as physicians and surgeons are inured by their profession to doing difficult things to restore health that an ill person could never bring himself to do, so in hard cases of fetal or maternal priority a physician for the mother or parents together could do something for them in their name and interest that could not be easily articulated by them. But doctors should have their individual roles clarified so that they would understand their specific professional relationship in the condominium, lest they be confused as to whether they are deciding and acting according to their personal medical code, the Hippocratic oath, their patient's intimated intention, the statutes of the state, or the accepted usage of the hospital. Thus the compassionate involvement of physicians and their professional autonomy would be explicit, safeguarded, and enhanced, if in a given difficult case two doctors faced each other as spokesmen in the condominium respectively of the progenitor and of the fetus and society's concern for it.

These medical magistrates would have the official responsibility of voicing a medical judgment as to whether an abortion in the case before them would be licit, or if not as to what provision should be made for the mother and the fetus. But the burden of the moral decision whether to proceed to abortion would not be theirs alone, for others specialists should participate in the deliberations in varying strengths, broadening the context in which the decision is to be made and assisting from their various professional perspectives.

The Legal Profession: Moderation and Arbitration

The first function of the legal profession would be to establish the sacred condominium as a legal doctrine in the constitutional theory of the land, to define the jurisdiction of the condominial court in the hospital, and to help construct specific state abortion laws appropriately in these terms. If these efforts should succeed, one can envisage lawyers also specialized in medical law being named by the medical magistrate to serve as career moderators and arbiters in hospital courts and as additional counselors for the two concerned parties. In many circumstances it would be incumbent upon these legal moderators (or arbiters but never judges) to establish contact between the hospital court and other independent legal jurisdictions: juvenile, criminal, and probate courts. Without infringing on the magisterial functions of the two physician-magistrates representing respectively the mother and the state on behalf of the fetus, the legal moderator could expedite what could often prove to be an emotionally taxing process. The legal moderator, as one familiar with the evaluation of evidence and the procedures of regular courts, would preserve the records of each case and thus build up a body of medical-moral clarifications of issues and precedents to be duly edited, bound, and shelved in the hospital chamber established for these deliberations. It is possible that the hospital court and its legal moderator could serve also for the many other hard moral cases that with increasing frequency will be coming before men of medicine in the years ahead.

The Sociopsychiatric Professions

Psychiatry has been increasingly involved in abortion proceedings when endangerment of the life and health of the mother includes psychological indications. Social work has more recently emerged to join psychiatry as a profession with its own distinctive character and mission. These two professions, the one a little more conspicuous in abortion cases involving the affluent, the other in those involving the poor or the marginal, are alike relevant to the proceedings of the condominial court because in present-day discussion emphasis has for good or ill shifted from preoccupation with the soul of the fetus to the psyche of the unwed or overproductive mother, from ensoulment of the fetus and sire-centered embryology to social conditioning of the mother and to a concern with the irresponsibility of the father. Thus in many abortion cases in the hospital court the insight and testimony of the psychiatrist and the social worker would constitute useful background for sound and informed moral judgment.

The "social history," as a distinct genre of assessment developed by the social worker, should be part of the proceedings when indicated, reflecting as it often would the effect of social stratification upon life style, of economic pressures, of social mobility, of anonymity upon interpersonal relations, and of the moral accountability of individuals and society itself ever being molded by these and other forces even more difficult to sort out and estimate.

The Clarification of the Clergy in the Sacred Condominium and the Condominial Court

The balancing and adjustment of the respective authorities of the progenitors and the state in the condominium over the unborn, must be worked out on the basis of the common humanistic and democratic concern for the rights of the mother as individual and the otherwise unprotected person of the fetus and not on the basis of generally theistic convictions or specifically Christian or Jewish views as to the nature and destiny of man. But in recognizing the cosovereignty of the progenitor in the condominium, the state recognizes also the right of the mother or the parents to call upon the counsel of their rabbi, priest, or minister prior to and during the hospital court session. Indeed the clergy as religio-ethical professionals could function as advisors in the sacred condominium not only on the side of the indisposed or overwhelmed or conscientious mother but also on the side of the state in behalf of the fetus. It is important to reserve a place for the professional ethicist as counselor for the medical magistrates. The presence of a clerical figure in the hospital court would tend to conserve in the deliberations that dimension of concern and sanction to which more than two millennia in the development of "sacred embryology" [10] testify. Increasingly, religious communities might place at the disposal of the state and religiously uncommitted but conscientious persons involved in the dilemma of an abortion such specialized ethicists as might give additional counsel within the contingencies of our pluralistic society.

The religious community, acknowledged by our constitutional society as having certain prior claims on those citizens who freely avow loyalty to it, will never become irrelevant to the discussion of the issue of abortion merely by being once removed from the basic parental–political condominium. The religious community can be energized as it works freely and indirectly through the clergy by suasion within a society where the state has already acknowledged that the parents have rights prior to the state with respect to their child and its nurture. Moreover, the whole doc-

10. The phrase echoes the highly influential *Sacra Embryologia* (Palermo, 1745) of Archbishop Francesco Cangiamila, dealt with by me in the already cited "Presuppositions" at n. 85.

trine of the sacred condominium and the condominial court would represent mutatis mutandis a repristination in modern institutions and social conventions of some of the perennial concerns of the religious community in dealing with the nature and destiny of personhood.

IV. THE OPERATION OF THE CONDOMINIUM IN SELECTED CASES

On the basis (1) of recognizing that there is properly a condominium of a responsible society and consenting progenitors in the procreation of a new human being, (2) of recognizing as valid both the genetic and the social component in the human soul or personality, and (3) of recognizing that in the complicated issue of abortion the rights of persons in different degrees of accountability and sensibility and articulateness have to be adjudicated — in other words with the express purpose of allowing more than one moral principle to operate — we may turn to several specific cases where abortion could be variously legitimated or restrained. It is understood at the outset that the operation of the three foregoing principles in concert, although it might allow for a few exceptions to the traditional moral and legal formulations against abortion, would not affect a majority. The theory of the sacred condominium would primarily clarify the politics and procedures of limited abortion. The author has hoped to supply the outline of an ethical and social theory for only those few cases where many conscientious people feel the legitimation is most clearly indicated without violence to the main body of "sacred embryology." Intensified sex education on all social levels, the extension of the knowledge and use of birth control, and imaginative and concerted public and private support for supernumerary or unwanted children are the only proper ways in his view to solve the bulk of the problem before us in America if Christians and others are earnest about preventing abortion from establishing itself as an acceptable "second line of defense" for birth control.

Abortion to Save the Mother's Life

Abortion to save the life of the mother is apparently scarcely more than a theoretical question in the present stage of gynecology. It is in any event not a legal issue in the United States and has largely ceased to be a moral issue for theologians. In traditional Jewish and Catholic thought, the mother-threatening fetus was called an "innocent pursuer" or "innocent aggressor." Traditionally the force of the adjective in the Jewish *responsa* was to describe the kind of "assailant" from which the mother had a right to have her life defended. In contrast, in Catholic casuistry the same adjective had the force of protecting the fetus, since in law an innocent or irresponsible person, like a madman, might not be punished for what would otherwise be a crime. Modern Catholic moral casuistry, however, by virtue of the doctrine of the indirect effect, confirmed by a widespread instinctive sympathy of Catholic theorists and practitioners with the endangered mother and her family, has been able to justify the removal of cancerous wombs and ectopic pregnancies on the ground that the intention of the operation is to save the mother, not directly to destroy the fetus. In any event, in many another situation the saver of life is often confronted with the necessity of a swift choice for life between persons whether assailed by flames or water, in emergency wards, among the wounded on the battlefield, or during disaster at sea when traditionally women and children are saved first. The decision for abortion in case of absolute necessity for the life of the mother is now swift and humane. The suggested implementation and apparatus of the sacred condominium is here nonfunctional except to recognize that in an emergency the life of one of the principals in the condominium takes precedence over the fetus (subject of the joint protectorate).

But there is always the theoretical possibility that the imperilled mother would herself wish, under the influence especially of Catholic tutelage, to lay down her life for the life within her. As an ordinary sovereign individual she could be prevented by the state from making a decision that would lead to her own death. But as a cosovereign with the state she should, without obstruction, be able to make that self-sacrificial decision, sustained by the religious sanction for freely laying down one's life for another. Although an anguished husband as coprogenitor and the attendants from several professions might intercede with her not to give up her life for the child, in this most poignant of moments, the mother would be sovereign in her final decision and without peer. The state may not interfere with the exercise of a religious conviction in conscience, and even the husband, "one flesh" with her in the bonds of marriage, would not have that final power to restrain her decision as to her own soul.

Conception from Felonious Intercourse

It is in the area of felonious intercourse that the condominium begins to function substantially in helping us to draw distinctions in terms of the genetic-social definition of person and the minimal requirement of the consent of passion on the part of the progenitor and thus to allow for abortions in certain limited cases.

In the case of rape the victim has not consented even by passion. One person has been misused by another. Without at least the consent of passion the insemination that has resulted from the violation of one person by another is as misplaced as a begonia planted in someone's ear. In such a case an immediate curettage has been allowed also by Catholics. Society's role in this phase of the condominium would be limited to ascertaining the validity of the charge of rape. Here the principals in the condominium could be at odds in assessing the case and require specialized arbitration. If this were the case, the medical and the legal professions could be called upon together with that of social work. But even if rape is demonstrable, the mother may surely assent to the continuance of the misplaced life within her; and society represented in the condominium by the medical magistrate should make her affirmative decision as easy as possible by being prepared to help socially and economically. Although the intercourse is felonious, the state has no reason to resist the innocent fetus so long as the violated mother herself chooses to give it birth.

In contrast, in the case of incestuous pregnancy, the role of society through the agencies of the state should probably take precedence in the condominium because here one or both partners in the felonious intercourse have violated the code of society and engaged in a genetic felony which, once committed, the state has no reason further to condone by perpetuating the consequence of that relationship. The conceptive act of both progenitors being felonious, the illicitly formed fetus should probably be removed. Although genetic defects from incestuous pregnancies are not so common as often supposed, society has a tremendous stake in the maintenance and the protection of the family as a basic institution and may plausibly refuse as a cosovereign to extend to incestuous progenitors recognition as cosovereigns in a *sacred* condominium.

The Mentally or Physically Defective Fetus

Indication of a serious physical or mental deformation of the fetus creates a far more difficult situation to assess than does the question of abortion by reason of rape or incest. Fetology will irresistibly advance its skills in prognosis, prophylaxis, and therapy. A viable theory as to the limits of licit abortion must take it into consideration that increasingly fetology will be able to ascertain well in advance of birth and with ever decreasing incidents of error the presence of a defective fetus. To the demographic will be added with ever greater urgency the eugenic demand for the abortion of the demonstrably defective fetus for the sake alike of the mother (and her family) and society at large, and to an extent out of compassionate consideration of the gravely defective embryo itself. It will be at this point that humanistic and theistic groups will most quickly divide. But the legal principle of the sacred condominium is especially useful here.

Christians, presupposing the soul or/and working with the idea of the worth of each person regardless of his potential or achievement, may enter the public domain with their *theistic* (and humane) convictions only by recasting their argument in terms of the right of all persons before the law. They must, too, alert society to the imminent hazard to all human life whenever or wherever any society (as with the Nazis) presumes to make a life-and-death value-judgment about any classes of human beings before birth and hence, by implication, about any classes in asylums and hospitals for both the young and the aged (euthanasia). For many Christians, the most serious objections to a eugenic (though often called a "therapeutic") abortion are the direct involvement of the state in setting standards for human life and the frequent willingness of the proponents of "eugenic" abortion to run the risk of sacrificing, for example, in the case of rubella statistically as many as three normal fetuses when it is recognized that there is only one chance in four that a fetus will be defective.

In the difficult case of gravely defective embryos the concept of the sacred condominium over unborn life is especially helpful with the provision of medical and other specialists standing by in compassionate support of the two principals. Where, for example, the medical magistrate representing society's interest in the condominium has proven a given fetus to be seriously defective physically or mentally beyond any doubt, the state, it could be argued, might well withdraw from the condominium on the ground that it may legitimately act to check a gross intrusion upon itself. Thereupon the state would release full authority to the mother or the two parents together within the condominium, leaving it to them with their medical and clerical counsel to make the momentous decision. At the same time, in order to attenuate the eugenic implication of this relinquishment of its own protective role (having assured itself through its own medical counsel that the case be indeed *with utter certainty* that of a gravely defective fetus), the state should be sufficiently concerned with sustaining the right of the mother or the parents (and their supportive community of faith) to proceed with the pregnancy to term if her or their consciences so dictate to offer adequate care in state institutions for defective offspring.

Statutory Rape

There may be two more cases where the operation of the condominium might legitimate an abortion. What is called statutory rape, consenting intercourse of a minor female, could be carefully redefined and restricted so that it would fully cover, but in a more limited way than customary, those pregnancies of girls who by reason of age (say twelve and thirteen) or of mental retardation *demonstrably* (by psychological tests and social data) could not possibly have known or foreseen how their (immature) bodies could produce another human being. Under the provisions for general protection of minors and the mentally undeveloped or erratic, the pregnancies of mentally disordered or dependent adults could be terminated where intercourse could not be said to have been based upon knowing consent or passion. In the condominial court the professional regency for a minor or a mentally retarded adult could argue that her limited sovereignty over her own body had been violated or misused.

What might be called a Protestant disposition in this paper is perhaps most apparent in the foregoing paragraph of the exposition. Protestantism with its classical emphasis upon the priesthood of all believers, and subsequently upon the accountability of morally sovereign individuals, is not so willing as Catholicism with its special understanding of nature and the natural to accord to an unwitting and even unimpassioned mingling of two mentally irresponsible human beings the same legal, moral, and biological status as that of responsible persons. It would, however, in most cases have the same aversion as Catholicism to the direct tampering with nature, for example by compulsory sterilization. Protestantism would prefer to work with persons rather than nature and its processes and, where persons were either by age or mental underdevelopment completely irresponsible, spare both them and society from the consequences of their imbecility.

Adulterous Pregnancies

There is one final case which seems appropriate to be introduced into any redrawing of the licit bounds of abortion. It is the case of an adulterous pregnancy. A large percentage of actual abortions in the United States are carried out for married women. The recently proposed or enacted relaxation of certain state codes on abortion do not affect this large group as a class, nor does the author of this paper so intend. Within this class there is, however, the morally distinguishable category of adulterous pregnancies. In terms of both moral offence and psychological distress an adulterous pregnancy is for the husband the nearest equivalent of rape for the woman. As in the case of adultery, it could be argued that the state should withdraw from the condominium, after being satisfied by blood tests in order to rule out a deceptive charge or claim, and leave the sole authority with the two legal partners, in this case with the offended husband-nonfather in the prevailing role. As the husband and wife are of one flesh by law and religious covenant or sacrament, it could be argued that, as in the case of rape, so here in the case of another kind of violation, the husband would ultimately have the right either to call for abortion of the misconceived fetus (or to demand a divorce) or to assent to the completion of the pregnancy to term and of then either accepting the child as his own or of placing it for adoption. Again, one would hope that the violated husband's conscience informed by his religious community would persuade him to affirm intrauterine life and that both church and society would assist institutionally and psychologically to help the estranged couple to be reconciled to each other and to the misconception. But one could argue that in the case of an adulterous breach of the family, an ever imperilled institution to be protected by law, society could formally withdraw from the condominium and leave the final decision to the compassion of the usurped progenitor.

V. CONCLUSION

We may conclude that, as medicine recognizes physiologically ectopic pregnancies which must be terminated for the sake of the life of the mother, perhaps ethics, with a combined genetic-social definition of the human person, and the state, with its recognition of the shifting roles of state and progenitors in a unique condominium, could argue with restraint that there are also some instances of socially or psychologically ectopic pregnancies, namely, those issuing from felonious, unwitting, or adulterous intercourse, or those issuing in demonstrably and gravely defective embryos, warranting the removal of the unformed or unviable fetus either out of concern for the progenitors or society at large and in a few cases of extreme deformation out of a humane concern for the still unsocialized or perhaps unsocializable fetus itself. But the composite of three principles: (1) the genetic-social definition of the person, (2) the ranking of innocent or unwitting or unconsenting women and girls along with the fetus as alike entitled to protection by society, and (3) the primordial condominium of authority in the realm of procreation and early nurture has in it both that restraint and flexibility which could open up a few new ways of getting at difficult problems in this area without repudiating the venerable Judeo-Christian and humanistic tradition in law, medicine, and religion concerning the right to protection of the unborn fetus, now understood as never so clearly before as a complete human being from the moment of the setting of the genetic code in the first fusion of the successful sperm and the waiting ovum.

The sacred condominium, as here described, is not so much an arrangement, like a panel of doctors and others for deciding on a given case, as it is a concept or model by which all persons concerned may clarify their proper roles in a primordial covenant. Fundamental in the condominium is the recognition that the mother or the two progenitors are corulers constituting with the state a joint protectorate over the new life. Thus the condominium is undoubtedly a unique social concept in acknowledging a kind of partial sovereignty of the mother over her own body and the new creation therein. In according this recognition of a joint sovereignty to the mother, the condominium would represent a notable achievement in the long evolution of the rights and dignity of woman. But the condominium presupposes the woman's as well as society's concern to safeguard the life within her. If, therefore, the mother is an extreme minor or an imbecile and therefore incapable of sustaining the normal role in the condominium, her parents, her lawful or institutional guardians, or the equivalent among social workers, could discharge that role in her stead. In any case, society, as the other member of the condominium, has a responsibility not only for the innocent fetus but also for the innocent mother, immature or permanently non compos mentis et corporis.

Over the recent Christian centuries the mother as a person and especially as an innocent person has suffered relative to the fetus from moral preoccupation at her expense with the soul, the salvation, and latterly the temporal life of the fetus within her. Yet the theory of sacred condominium presupposes the hard-won completed Catholic view of the fetus as on principle a human being from conception, leaving it to fetological experts, of course, to draw or redraw at the very lowest reaches the precise line beyond which an act would no longer come within the scope of licit birth control (that is, more accurately, conception control). In its modification of creationism from Aquinas to Pius XII Catholic moral theology has indeed kept pretty close to the genetic and embryological facts. Protestantism, without knowing exactly when, long since abandoned the traducianism of Luther and Calvin's clearly articulated abhorrence of abortion; and it must now rally in general to the Catholic position concerning the fetus (not, however, to the Pian-Pauline position on contraception!) in its latest, its Pian form, remotely influenced as that may have been by classical Protestantism and in any case substantiated by modern genetics.[11]

Quite Protestant and Jewish, however, in the delineated sacred condominium is the recognition of the mother as an accountable and, with limits, sovereign person above nature, rather than wholly ruled by nature, state, or church.

Alike neo-Protestant or sectarian Protestant and Catholic in the concept of the sacred condominium is the recognition that the state is not omnicompetent in the temporal realm and that the progenitors, bearing the awesome responsibility for each new creation, have within circumscribed limits a voice over against the state where their conscience (in solidarity perhaps with their church) dictates the bringing into the world life considered by society's standards as inferior. In implementing the parents' rights to bring such life into the world, a humane in contrast to a hard society as the other partner in the condominium would in case of need provide the means for upholding the conscientious parental decision. In the condominium any eugenic (as distinguished from therapeutic) decision would rest with the progenitor alone. The state through its fetological experts would be limited to establishing the *certainty* of a major defect in the fetus before withdrawing in favor of the sovereign parental decision. The parents would be helped by the mother's doctor, religious counselor, and other professionals.

Thus in every sector in every new situation the concept and procedures of the sacred condominium would help clarify the sometimes quite disparate roles of parents, religious advisors, doctors, social workers, and jurists in considering and carrying out a substantial but still limited number of cases of justifiable abortion. At the same time the vaster number yearly reported or surmised of cases of abortion or attempts at abortion for any less compelling reasons would not fall outside the concept of the con-

11. Elsewhere I have pointed to the possible Protestant impact upon latter-day papal teaching on abortion, which goes beyond medieval Aristotelian-Thomist view in adapting creationism so as to construe human ensoulment as coincident with conception. Not only did the emergent Catholic dogma of the Immaculate Conception of Mary have implications for all intrauterine life but also Lutheran traducianism, refurbished from Tertullian, in insisting on the integrity of body, mind, and soul from the moment of conception, gave the Lutheran medical faculties a new theological basis for opposing abortion before quickening. "Religious Presuppositions," pt. I, §§ 3 and 4.

dominium. They would instead be constrained by it. Society, becoming automatically a partner in every new condominium as soon as life is conceived, should be ever more vigilant in its duty through its representatives (jurists, doctors, social workers, and clergymen) to safeguard the life of the fetus lest the perceptible moral evolution toward increased concern for unborn life over more than two millennia of our civilization be suddenly reversed all in the name of human dignity and freedom(!) by a technologically potent, and affluent, and strangely harsh generation.

Over the millennia mankind has tried to explore the ethical problem of abortion, ever held back from clarity of view by the obscurity of the biological process, until in fairly recent times biologists have made clear the distinction between the haploid generation of life represented by the sperm and the ovum and the diploid generation represented by the zygote with the plenary set of chromosomes, complete with genetic code. All the zygote/ fetus needs to be one of us is time.

It is an anomaly of the development of the moral conscience of society at the very moment when we know the most about fetal life and when we are, in our reverence for life, reviewing such formerly major instruments of society as capital punishment and war, that many in the name of humaneness and humanity would be disposed to let go centuries of ethical concern about prenatal life and the accumulated legal and medical safeguards thereof. The reason for this slippage or insensitivity precisely in those circles and professions traditionally associated with moral definitions is surely in part the fact that in the atmosphere of the current sexual revolution many are mistakenly subsuming abortion under the general heading of contraception and sexual freedom.

Tragically, an overriding issue of life and death concerning the zygote-become-fetus has been either trivialized or confused because the "right" to or the opposition to abortion has come to be almost inextricably linked either with sexual freedom and "women's rights" or, on the papal side, with birth control.

Yet the acknowledgment at law of the emergent principle of the sacred condominium over prenatal life could constitute an integrated movement forward in the evolution of both fetal rights and the rights of women and parents.

JOHN M. FINNIS

Three Schemes of Regulation

My theme is the legitimacy of various legal schemes for dealing
with abortion. Legitimacy in one sense is secured simply by com-
plying with the formal criteria for valid law-making: enactment
within power and in due form. But jurists have learned (or re-
learned) that more can be said about legitimacy, without betray-
ing the purity of their discipline by moralizing and advocacy.
From this development in jurisprudential thought emerges the
range of questions and criteria deployed in the present study.

Max Weber discerned three types of legal legitimacy: that
deriving from the sacredness of tradition; that deriving from
the charisma of saviours, prophets, or heroes; and that deriving
from the rationality of general rules.[1] In the last-mentioned case,
there stands behind every official and legal act "a system of
rationally discussable 'grounds,' i.e.. either subsumption under
norms or calculation of means and ends."[2] Formal rationality is
content to subsume particular cases under general norms; but
unrestricted rationality demands that the general norms themselves
should have more than merely traditional or charismatic authority, and so subjects all legal material to the substantively
rational coordination of means with ends.[3] Now jurisprudence is
committed, at the very least, to unrestrictedly rational discussion
of legal materials and legal experience. So a society in which jurisprudence is a socially recognized discipline is likely to be or
become one in which the principle of legal legitimacy is substan-

1. Max Rheinstein (ed.), *Max Weber on Law in Economy and Society* 336;
also xxxix–xlii (Harvard University Press, 1954).
2. *Id.* at 355.
3. On the distinction between substantive and merely formal rationality, see
Weber on Law supra n. 1 at 63–64, 351–356; also Rheinstein's intro., *ibid.* xlvii–
lx. "Unrestricted rationality" is not a Weberian category

tive rationality in Weber's sense. The raising of theoretical questions about law and legitimacy breaks the spell of pure tradition or mere charisma.[4]

In modern Western societies, jurisprudence is a recognized discipline, and legal legitimacy is sought to be measured by rationality. Official acts of administration or legislation are questioned, and in response are legitimated by appeal to more general norms and higher ends. These societies exist in a real tension toward the ideal of substantive rationality in law. Jurisprudence, in the pursuit of its own rational questioning, and without imperilling its purity, can examine actual legal material and proposed legal projects in the light of this working ideal. To say this is not to say that the most general norms and ultimate directive ideals of Western society are derived from, or justifiable by, jurisprudence. It is simply to say that even a jurisprudence which prides itself on rigorously restricted analysis of mature Western legal systems will have absorbed into its account many of the techniques, conceptual structures, distinctions, and procedures by which those systems strive to secure a working rationality in the coordination of ends and means and in the concretization of general principles and values.[5] Such a jurisprudence can examine actual and proposed schemes for regulating abortion and assess them in the terms of that working rationality, if nothing more.

That is my present purpose, and in carrying it out I shall discuss in turn three model schemes of legal regulation of abortion. At this point I shall characterize the three only roughly and, as we shall see, insufficiently: (1) the prohibition of all abortions, except where the life of the mother is threatened; (2) the permission of abortion when previously authorized, by independent officials, under defined but ampler categories of medical, psycho-medical, or quasi-medical conditions; (3) the permission of all

4. See Eric Voegelin, *The New Science of Politics* 59–60 (University of Chicago Press, 1952). On the inadequacy of Weber's analysis of the relation between rationality and charisma, see Talcott Parsons, *The Structure of Social Action* 658–672 (McGraw-Hill, 1937).

5. An obscure sense of this seems implicit in John Austin's doctrine that analytical jurisprudence should concern itself with "the ampler and maturer legal systems." Austin, *The Province of Jurisprudence Determined* 367, H. L. A. Hart, ed. (Weidenfeld and Nicolson, 1954). If law were to be regarded simply and solely as sovereign command, it would be difficult to see how it could be more (or less) mature at one time or place than at another.

John M. Finnis

abortions save those performed by persons unqualified to carry out the medical procedures involved.

I. THE "RIGHTS OF THE CHILD": STRICT CRITERIA AND EX POST CONTROL BY CRIMINAL LAW

The first scheme of regulation is that which until recently prevailed throughout the English-speaking world and much of the continent of Europe.[6] In this scheme, the inducing of abortion is prohibited, under penal sanction, except where the life of the mother is in danger or, at most, her health threatened with imminent, grave, and lasting impairment.[7] In various jurisdictions the width of these exceptions is uncertain; to interpret them it is necessary to know the accepted objectives of the scheme. These objectives and values do not appear unambiguously from a mere statement of the formal criteria for lawful abortions. That is why my rough classification of the three model schemes, by reference mainly to the breadth of those formal criteria, needs modification and amplification. Again, in a number of European jurisdictions there exist exceptions in favor, not only of the life and health of the mother, but also of eugenic (that is, in respect of presumed

6. The law in most English-speaking countries is similar to that in most of the United States, on which see the appendix to Eugene Quay, "Justifiable Abortion — Medical and Legal Foundations," 49 *Georgetown Law Journal* 395 (1960). The law under the Abortion Act 1967 (U.K.) seems to us to approximate to the third model scheme, for reasons discussed in the text *infra* at nn. 56–60, in nn. 56 and 73, and in Appendix A. For the law in most European states, see Marguerite Rateau, "Etude de Droit Comparé sur l'Avortement dans Quelques Pays Européens," [1959] *Revue Internationale de Droit Pénal* 265.

7. Where, as in England and California even before their recent legislative reforms, an exception to the general prohibition is admitted in favor of the *health* of the mother as well as of her life, the first scheme becomes more or less unstable, depending on the strength and content of medical ethics and the interpretation put on the law by the medical profession and the public. In England, a vaguely defined exception was admitted under *Rex v. Bourne* [1939] 1 K. B. 687, in favor of the mother's mental health, but the scheme was saved from collapsing into a permissive scheme of the third type by the cautious attitude of the medical profession: see Bernard M. Dickens, *Abortion and the Law* 98–100 (MacGibbon and Kee, 1966). In California, the exception in favor of mental health was not expressly admitted, but the scheme was made unstable by the creation of a presumption that any abortion performed by a licensed practitioner was necessary to preserve the life of the mother, which moreover need not be imminently threatened. *People v. Ballard,* 167 Cal.App. 2d 803, 335 P.2d 204 (Dist. Ct. App. 1959).

malformation of the child) and "ethical" (that is, in respect of pregnancies by rape or incest) indications. If not too many questions are raised about the principle on which these exceptions are based, their existence seems compatible with the first scheme (as well as with the second or third);[8] but the raising of these questions is liable to make the first scheme seem incoherent in its principles and objectives, and so gradually to topple it over into the third scheme. However, the defined grounds for lawful abortion within a scheme are less directly relevant to a jurisprudential discussion than are the general objectives of the scheme and the appointed techniques of deciding, policing, sanctioning, and adjudicating in the light of those objectives. So I shall not here spell out precisely the exceptional grounds for abortion that may or may not be compatible, in a more or less anomalous fashion, with the first of the three model schemes.

To understand any of the three model schemes, and their approximations in actually operative schemes, it is better to proceed straight to the root questions: What is the point of this scheme? Does it secure its objectives in a rational way?

The main objectives of the first scheme seem to be two: (1) the protection of children in the womb from destruction; (2) the protection of the mother from bungling operators. In short, the life of unborn children and the health of mothers are the main values that the scheme seeks to realize; the general principles or norms under which it can be subsumed are that the life of such persons should not be taken, and that people should not be permitted to risk their lives for inadequate cause.

The difficulty of formulating the last-mentioned principle without begging the question immediately reveals that in this scheme the first objective must be primary, and the second objective

---

8. Cf. *infra* n. 19. See Rateau, "Etude de Droit" *supra* n. 6 at 287–288. Cf. American Law Institute, *Model Penal Code* s.230.3 (*Proposed Official Draft*, 1962). Not least because of their comparative rarity in practice, the "ethical" and eugenic indications are compatible with the second scheme, but only if not too many questions are raised about their integration into medical ethics, which at present has not perhaps absorbed them: see *Report of the Committee of the British Medical Association* [1966], 2 *British Medical Journal* 40, 42. And in the third scheme they are virtually redundant; the Abortion Act 1967 (U.K.) omits the "ethical" indication because it is catered for by the "mental health" indication: see *Parliamentary Debates* (*House of Commons*) 13 July 1967, cc. 1174–1178.

secondary and in part subordinate and dependent.[9] For people
are generally permitted to risk their lives for adequate reasons;
so the postulated inadequacy of abortion as a reason for risking
one's life must be explained in terms of the undesirability (at
least relative) of killing the unborn child — and this is the undesirability with which the first objective or value or principle is
concerned.[10] (Notice that this argument in no way depends on
any assumption about the effectiveness or ineffectiveness of this
legislative scheme in achieving its second objective.)

The primary objective of this first scheme is to be interpreted
as a particular modality of a more general principle of mature
Western legal systems: that all human life is to be free from
deliberate or negligent attack. The assertion that the objective
of the scheme has generally been the maintenance of a sufficient

9. Courts and writers who maintain that the primary objective of the first
scheme is the protection of the mother misunderstand the scheme; the prevalence
in any society of such explanations forebodes the collapse of the first into the
third scheme. See the comments in Basil Mitchell, *Law, Morality and Religion
in a Secular Society* 81 (Oxford University Press, 1967), on the remarks of Lord
Chief Justice Goddard in *Rex v. Tate, Times* (London), 22 June 1949.

10. Zad Leavy and Jerome M. Kummer, "Criminal Abortion: Human Hard-
ship and Unyielding Laws," 35 *Southern California Law Review* 123, 134–135
(1962), seek to prove that the primary goal of American abortion law is protection of the mother. Their first proof is that the basic exception places the
life of the mother above the life of the child: but this is inconclusive, for most
of the abortions forbidden by the law remain cases where preserving the life of
the mother is not the reason for the abortion and where the law prefers the
life of the fetus to the mother's desires. The other three proofs concern rules
developed by the courts for the technical purpose of facilitating conviction of
abortionists: the woman's immunity from prosecution where her testimony is
needed for the prosecution; the irrelevance of the occurrence of actual miscarriage in a prosecution for abortion; and the classification of the woman as
victim rather than as accomplice for the purpose of circumventing State laws
requiring corroboration of the evidence of accomplices. Leavy and Kummer's
point is made only by suppressing the technical legal purpose of those three
rules: see the annotations in 139 *American Law Reports* 993, 997–1001. Notice
that in 1918–19 French law granted immunity to women who testified against
abortionists; yet the motive of French law of this period was protection of the
child for reasons of population policy: Pierre Bouzat, "La Politique Criminelle
Française en Matière d'Avortement et de Propagande Anticonceptionnelle," in
Institut de droit comparé, Université de Paris, *Les Principaux Aspects de la Politique Criminelle Moderne, Recueil d'études en hommage à la mémoire du Henri
Donnedieu de Vabres* 183, 187 (Editions Cujas, Paris, 1960). Still, Leavy and
Kummer grant that the "historical objective" of the law was to protect the unborn
child, and they have a point when they argue that if the objective has been
abandoned, the whole scheme stands in need of revision.

birthrate scarcely bears historical examination.[11] In any event, a scheme so motivated would be unstable and liable to abandonment in the event of overpopulation. So here I shall consider this scheme of regulation in its stable form, as motivated primarily by concern for human personality and hence for the person of the unborn.

Now the law can obtain its ends in a variety of ways, of which taxation, civil or tortious liability, and criminal or penal liability might conceivably be relevant. In fact, it is always the last-mentioned technique that has been employed in this scheme of abortion regulation.[12] Is it a reasonable technique?

That jurisprudence can differentiate concepts such as "tax," "tort," and "crime" is a mark of its partnership in Western rationality.[13] Indeed, a modern analytical jurist such as H. L. A. Hart has denounced as inadequate any jurisprudence, such as Hans Kelsen's, that in the name of scientific and value-free purity hesitates to differentiate such concepts because their differentiation

11. See Dickens, *Abortion and the Law supra* n. 7 at 11–15. Population policies influenced the growing severity of French law from 1914 to 1945, but abortion was a considerable crime long before the genesis of these policies: Bouzat, *Politique Criminelle supra* n. 10. See also *infra* n. 85.

12. The law can grant a civil action in tort to the husband whose marital interest in the life of his child has been invaded by the secret actions of his wife and her abortionist: cf. *Touriel v. Benveniste* 30 *United States Law Week* 2203 (Los Angeles Sup. Ct., 1961); "Comment," 110 *University of Pennsylvania Law Review* 908; 14 *Stanford Law Review* 901 (1962). But it is hard to see what other civil actions would usefully be available in respect of the abortion itself; the child is usually dead, the mother a consenting party. Cf. B. J. George, Jr., "Current Abortion Laws: Proposals and Movements for Reform," 17 *Western Reserve Law Review* 371, 388–390 (1965). Note that George also suggests treating abortion "within the framework of civil provisions affecting the medical profession rather than the penal concepts of the criminal code," *id.* at 397. But such a civil scheme would still have to approximate to one or other of our three model schemes, and would still require penal sanctions against abortions performed by persons outside the medical profession. And to try to hold the medical profession to the first scheme only by professional disciplinary proceedings would (a) weaken the symbolic force of the law, (b) place on the disciplinary procedures a role they are not structured to discharge either efficiently or with due process, (c) place on the profession an excessive burden in deciding a controverted social question. Note: all the articles on abortion in 17 *W. Res. L. Rev.* may now be found in David T. Smith, ed., *Abortion and the Law* (Case Western Reserve University Press, 1967).

13. "Western rationality" is not meant to deny rationality to other cultures, but simply to indicate conveniently a form of thought and culture familiar to us all. On the more general question see Eric Voegelin, *Order and History*, esp. vol. II, pp. 1–24 (Louisiana State University Press, 1957).

turns on value-laden differences of function.[14] For Hart, attention to such functional differences is the very mark of a fruitful jurisprudence. Yet such distinctions were not always drawn; they spring directly from the rational demand for justification in terms of norms and values.[15] Now the classical Western notions and justifications of penal action are today commonly declared to be obscure. So if our present question is to be answered jurisprudentially, a few clarificatory remarks and even definitions seem to be in order here.[16]

In the fully developed concept of "crime," an act or forbearance will be criminal in a strict sense only if it is taken to manifest an indifference to, and thus publicly to affront, all or some of a considerable set of values upheld by society. "Prosecution" and "punishment" are stages in society's attempt to vindicate those values. "Vindication" is the process by which "good" citizens are encouraged in their habitual readiness to prefer the socially approved values implicit in the law to any competing value. Vindication involves also the instructing of the teachable in the approved ramifications of those values, the deterring of the recalcitrant, and the reform of the amenable. Above all, vindication is the binding together of this complex of aims and processes into the distinct general form of punishment: a meeting of manifested waywardness of individual will by manifested subjection of that will to the will of those responsible for upholding the values which society prefers but to which that individual has failed to give due weight.

It is not too difficult to discern the range of values with which penal law is concerned. There is the value of the welfare of the

14. H. L. A. Hart, *The Concept of Law* 38–39 (Oxford U.P., 1961). For Kelsen's doubts about the jurisprudential ultimacy of the distinction between tort and crime, see Hans Kelsen, *General Theory of Law and State* 50–56, 207 (Harvard U.P., 1945). Holmes had doubts that were even less nuanced than Kelsen's: "The Path of the Law," 10 *Harvard Law Review* 457, 461 (1897).

15. The theoretical disengagement of a specifically criminal law from the body of delictual law is perhaps to be ascribed to Plato, *Laws* 862–863; see A. E. Taylor's translation (Everyman ed.) intro, at xlvii, and text at 250–252 (1960).

16. Elements of the following account will be found in Robert E. Rodes, Jr., "A Prospectus for a Symbolist Jurisprudence," 2 *Natural Law Forum* 88, 105–115 (1957). Supporting and contrasting material in recent German and American criminology will be found in Albin Eser, "The Principle of 'Harm' in the Concept of Crime: A Comparative Analysis of the Criminally Protected Interests," 4 *Duquesne University Law Review* 345 (1965–66). See also Walter Moberly, *The Ethics of Punishment*, chap. 8 (Faber, 1968).

individual injured by the crime, and the supporting value of respect for that welfare; there are the values directly or indirectly constitutive of human welfare — life, sociability, property, truth-telling, procreation, and so on; there is the value of doing as you would be done by, and the value of fairness to other members of society who put themselves out to uphold the social values; and there is the general value of giving priority in one's activity to the common good of which one's own good is a component.

The criminal law, with the penal process, is the symbolic drama by which the socially preferred range of values is vindicated against indifference and affront. Education is one of its principal aims, from which flow many of its characteristics. Thus it is not every killing of one human being by another that attracts the criminal sanction, but only those killings that are deemed to manifest an indifference to the value of human life (that is, by intention or negligence). This attention to the value-choices and value-rejections symbolized by individual actions, rather than to the actions simply as movements-plus-consequences,[17] is a classical instance of Western rationality reflecting upon the grounds for social reaction to undesired events. Again, the grading of crimes and punishments signifies the approved ranking of the values threatened by crime; and the grading of degrees of culpability recognizes that while negligence symbolizes little more than human weakness, direct intention and willfulness are assertions and expressions of available alternative horizons of values. "Evil communications corrupt good manners," [18] and intentional and successful crime tends to bring the law into contempt.

It is, of course, a main aim of the criminal law to eliminate undesired conduct. But the criminal law is not futile if it succeeds in doing little more than manifesting society's continuing commitment to its preferred values. Examples of such laws are many: laws against speeding, against perjury, against domestic murder, against prostitution, once upon a time against duelling, and now against certain forms of racial discrimination. Such laws are to be contrasted with laws that not only fail to eliminate the forbidden conduct, but also are so widely and publicly flouted by respected

17. See H. L. A. Hart, *Punishment and Responsibility*, chap. IV (Oxford U. P., 1968).
18. I *Cor.* 15:33.

men that they lose even the character of symbolizing a real societal commitment to the values they purport to uphold. These laws are pointless, and their limping continuance symbolizes the impotence, not the supremacy, of the officially approved values. Prohibition was such a case.

The first scheme of abortion regulation, then, is an effort to suppress abortions in all but a few cases, and to witness society's commitment to the value and inviolability of human life. (The very nature of the admitted exceptions [19] witnesses an effort to distinguish between life as such — the life of the mother — and mere qualities of life such as peace of mind, standard of living, avoidance of shame, and so forth.) The basic commitment, jurisprudence itself cannot evaluate; jurisprudence is a partner in Western rationality, not a summation of it. Nor can jurisprudence itself comment on the minor premise: that early fetal life is simply a modality of human life. Suffice it to say that the fully self-conscious jurist may feel the attraction of both premises. It was no accident that the first great theoretical jurist, Plato, also first elaborated the Western idea of the immaterial soul as the center of what we now call personality. For jurisprudence is a sustained and questioning reflection on certain human performances, and a fully reflective jurist will include his own performance as a jurist within the scope of his reflections. So doing, he may well apprehend that the mysterious organizing center of his life's work, of his concern for truth, of his actual insights, and of his will to reflect, lies beyond the capacities of his merely material constitution, however much the latter may be a *sine qua non*. He may conclude that what makes him the person he is, and confers on him any worth he may have, is in the last analysis not a mere function or correlate of his size or shape, of the rhythm of his sleeping and waking, growing and fading.

Still, it is schemes of regulation, not their premises, that lie within the competence of jurisprudence, and we have now sufficiently set the stage for a jurisprudential evaluation of the rationality of the first scheme of abortion regulation.

Is this scheme effective in suppressing abortion? An unbiased

19. That is, respecting the life of the mother; it is at this point that the compatibility of the eugenic and "ethical" indications with the first scheme is put in question.

answer to this question will be very circumspect. On the one hand, there is much reason for saying, No. At this point we must venture on the first of a number of statistical discussions, and it is as well to point out that the figures for illegal abortions are everywhere unreliable, and inferences from any abortion statistics rather uncertain.[20] For example, the great majority of commentators in recent American law journals[21] accept that 1,200,000 is a plausible estimate of the number of abortions *per annum* in the United States. But on examination it appears that this figure is based on a study published in 1934[22] — according to which it may be assumed that there is one illegal abortion for every 3.55 live births. And this latter figure is an extrapolation from the case histories of 10,000 women who attended the Margaret Sanger birth control clinic in New York City between 1925 and 1929! Another widely accepted figure for the United States is 600,000 *per annum* — this by extrapolation from the case histories of the women who volunteered the information in Kinsey's famous study of female sexuality (a group which included a negligible proportion of blacks and Catholics, and which was unrepresentative even of urban white women.)[23] The statistics committee at a 1958 conference called by Planned Parenthood agreed that the number may be between 200,000 and 1,000,000, and that there is no way of determining the number more closely than that.[24] Similarly, estimates of illegal abortions in the United Kingdom before the Abortion Act of 1967 ranged between 50,000 and 100,000 (250,000 was occasionally mentioned); but on the basis of fairly

20. See the remarks in Christopher Tietze, "Induced Abortion and Sterilization as Methods of Fertility Control," 18 *Journal of Chronic Diseases* 1161 (1965).

21. There is a good bibliography in 40 *University of Colorado Law Review* 297, Appendix B (1968).

22. M. E. Kopp, *Birth Control in Practice* (Robert M. McBride and Co., 1934), quoted by Frederick Taussig, *Abortion: Spontaneous and Induced* 368 (The C. V. Mosby Co., St. Louis, 1936), and used as the basis of his calculations at 25–26.

23. See the comments of the Statistics Committee of the 1957 Planned Parenthood Federation of America Conference on Abortion on the Kinsey Institute's study (Paul H. Gebhard, Wardell B. Pomeroy, Clyde E. Martin, and Cornelia V. Christenson, *Pregnancy, Birth and Abortion* [Harper and Hoeber, 1958]) in Mary Calderone, ed., *Abortion in the United States* 178 (Hoeber, Harper, 1958). For further discussion of the figures see David Louisell and John T. Noonan, Jr., "Constitutional Balance," sec. II *infra*.

24. Comments of the Statistics Committee, Calderone, *Abortion in the United States supra* n. 23 at 180; Christopher Tietze and Sarah Lewit, "Abortion," 220 *Scientific American* 21, 23 (1969)

reliable statistics for maternal deaths, C. B. Goodhart was able to argue plausibly that the figure might in fact be as low as 10,000 *per annum*.[25] Still, whatever figures are accepted, the fact remains that the numbers everywhere are very high. Moreover, Herbert L. Packer and Ralph J. Gampell have shown that, before the reforms of 1967,[26] reputable California hospitals regularly went beyond the law,[27] and Harold Rosen has opined that 80 to 90 percent of the illegal abortions in the United States are performed by qualified physicians.[28]

On the other hand, before examining other aspects of the abortion figures, it will be in order to offer a few general cautions about the apparent effectiveness of the criminal law in this age. For in this age the overflowing of criminality has affected all parts of Western civilization. In the United States, and even in England, the number and the rate of serious crimes known to the police have multiplied much more than tenfold in the past sixty years; yet in 1965 Leon Radzinowicz was willing to hazard that "crime fully brought into the open and punished represents no more than about fifteen percent of the total." [29] But would it not be perhaps a little hasty to declare the criminal law, as a whole, redundant or simply futile? [30]

One can accept any of the previously quoted estimates of the

25. "The Frequency of Illegal Abortion," 55 *Eugenics Review* 197, 200 (1964). Criticism in Dickens, *Abortion and the Law supra* n. 7 at 79–80. The Minister of Health estimated that in 1964, 75,000 cases of abortion were treated at National Health Service hospitals, of which 3,300 were therapeutic and 3,000 septic: [1967], 1 *Brit. Med. J.* 577. In that year there were about 850,000 live births. As is explained in Appendix B *infra*, a number of miscarriages, corresponding to about 12½%, at most, of all conceptions, might be expected to be treated in hospital. Sir Dugald Baird, "A Fifth Freedom?" 58 *Eugenics Rev.* 195, 204 (1966) estimated that the incidence of therapeutic abortion in Aberdeen, with a very liberal medical profession, was about 2% of all maternities; clandestine abortions he thought very few, because septic abortions were very rarely seen in Aberdeen. In 1964 legal abortions in Denmark numbered about 5% of live births; in Hungary they were about 135%.

26. *California Health and Safety Code*, secs. 25950–25954.

27. Packer and Gampell, "Therapeutic Abortion: A Problem in Law and Medicine," 11 *Stan. L. Rev.* 417, 447 (1959).

28. "Psychiatric Implications of Abortion: A Case Study in Social Hypocrisy," 17 *W. Res. L. Rev.* 435, 436 (1965).

29. *Ideology and Crime* 64 (Columbia University Press, 1966).

30. Herbert Packer has said: "We can have as much or as little crime as we please, depending on what we choose to count as crime": Packer, *The Limits of the Criminal Sanction* 364 (Stanford University Press, 1969). As a response to the problem of social life and order in this age, the slogan is less than adequate.

incidence of abortion in countries using the first scheme of regulation, and yet find reason to believe that the scheme is effective in suppressing, though not eliminating, abortion. It is agreed that when in 1939 Denmark and Sweden adopted the second scheme (legal abortion by official permission under fairly wide conditions), there was a sharp increase in the number of both legal and illegal abortions. Twenty years later, while the number of live births in Denmark was about 25 percent higher than in 1939, and the population about 20 percent higher, the number of legal abortions had multiplied tenfold, and the number of illegal abortions seemed to be anywhere between two and fifteen times as high as in 1939.[31] And where the third scheme (virtually unconditional permission of all abortions performed by qualified physicians) has been adopted, as in Eastern European countries during the last decade, the total number of abortions has risen so sharply that the increase is generally agreed to be responsible for at least part of substantial, even dramatic, decreases in the birthrate.[32] Thus in Hungary, a steady or rising birthrate of 23.0 per 1,000 population in 1954 was converted, after full legalization of abortion in 1955, to one that dropped about one point each year until 1962 it was only 12.9.[33] In 1964 the number of *lawful* abortions was over 184,000 (in a population of about 10 million) — far above any estimate of the number of all legal and illegal abortions under the old regime of rigorous regulation.[34] Similar,

31. See Vera Skalts and Magna Norgaard, "Abortion Legislation in Denmark," 17 *W. Res. L. Rev.* 498, 505, 519 (1965); Gebhard, Pomeroy, Martin, and Christenson, *Pregnancy, Birth and Abortion supra* n. 23 at 221–229; D. V. Glass, "The Effectiveness of Abortion Legislation in Six Countries," 2 *Modern Law Review* 97, 117 (1938), quoting estimates of the Danish Governmental Committee on Abortion (1936). In 1964 there were 3,936 legal and an estimated 12,000 to 15,000 illegal abortions, in a population of just over 4,600,000. See also Appendix B *infra*.

32. Tietze, "Abortion and Sterilization" *supra* n. 20 at 1167; K.-H. Mehlan, "Combating Illegal Abortion in the Socialist Countries of Europe," 13 *World Medical Journal* 84, 87 (1965).

33. See Appendix B, Table D *infra*. Martin J. Buss, "The Beginning of Human Life as an Ethical Problem," 47 *Journal of Religion* 244, 252 (1967) thinks this is due to social dissatisfaction and the loss of young emigrés; but forementioned sources base their opinion that the abortion laws are a causal factor on the occurrence of the same phenomena in other Eastern European countries. Competent observers of Japan have come to the same conclusion: C. P. Blacker, "Japan's Population Problem," 48 *Eugenics Rev.* 31 (1956); T. J. Samuel, "Population Control in Japan: Lessons for India," 58 *Eugenics Rev.* 15, 19 (1966).

34. See Tietze, "Abortion and Sterilization" *supra* n. 20 at 1167; and Mehlan, "Combating Illegal Abortion" *supra* n. 32 at 87.

John M. Finnis

though not so marked, effects are observable in countries such as Poland,[35] Bulgaria, Czechoslovakia, and Russia, not to mention Japan. After nine years under the third scheme, Rumania reverted to a version of the first scheme in 1966; the effect was staggering: within nine months the birthrate (per 1,000 population) had risen from 13.7 to 38.4.[36] Making all allowances for the difficulty of isolating causal factors, it can hardly be doubted that the transition from the first to the second or third schemes of legal regulation is liable to be accompanied by marked increases in the *total* number of abortions.

Is this scheme effective in symbolizing society's commitment to protecting the value of human life against deliberate or negligent affront? It seems clear that the answer must be: Yes. Unless one were to contemplate a prohibition of all abortions whatever, it is difficult to conceive of any other symbolic treatment of the sphere of maternity that could witness this commitment to the value of human life. One cannot expect empirical sociology to produce decisive estimates of the effectiveness or ineffectiveness of such symbols.[37] What is at stake is the long haul of civilization. Even in retrospect the cultural historian can assess such development only by a wisdom that must do without checks or control groups and an apparatus designed to produce a deceptive appearance of scientific certainty.[38]

It is, however, permissible to wonder whether the lower num-

35. On Poland, see Appendix B, Table D *infra;* see also Helena Wolinska, "Assumptions Faced with Reality: Marginal Remarks on the Conditions of Permissibility of Abortion Act of 27th April, 1956," 15 *Państo I Prawo* 282 (Polish Academy of Sciences, 1960; English summary, 1960 [1], 5-7).

36. Tietze and Lewit, "Abortion" *supra* n. 24 at 23. The preamble to the law of 1966, restoring a version of the first scheme, referred primarily to "the great prejudice to the birth-rate and the rate of natural increase," secondarily to "severe consequences for the health of the woman." See Christopher Tietze, "Abortion in Europe," 57 *American Journal of Public Health* 1923, 1931 (1967).

37. Cf. Arnold M. Rose, "Sociological Factors in the Effectiveness of Projected Legislative Remedies," 11 *Journal of Legal Education* 470 (1959), stressing the lack of research, but opining that even widespread violation of law need not, in certain circumstances, diminish respect for law, *id.* at 474. Also Per Sternquist, "How Are Changes in Social Behaviour Developed by Means of Legislation?" in *Legal Essays: A Tribute to Frede Castberg* 153-169 (1963).

38. On the Scandinavian debate about the law's effect in creating an "abortion mentality," see U. Borell and L. Engstrom, "Legal Abortions in Europe," 13 *World Med. J.* 72, 74 (1966); Mögens Ingerslev, "The Danish Abortion Laws," 7 *Medical Science and Law* 77, 81 (1967); Tietze, "Abortion in Europe" *supra* n. 36 at 1927, and works there cited.

bers of abortions under the first scheme than under the second or third schemes are kept down only by the purely deterrent effect of the legal sanctions, so relatively rarely invoked.[39] or whether the symbolic weight of the law's denunciation is perhaps contributing too. In countries where the first scheme still holds, reformers have to agitate even to create the sense of a problem in the public mind, and people are shocked when they discover the supposed prevalence of illegal abortion.[40] The situation is indeed remote from the visible breakdown of the law's symbolic effectiveness under Prohibition. But all these considerations only touch the margin of the problem of symbolizing respect for life; further discussion must wait until we come to assess the civilizational implications of the second and third schemes of regulation.

Still, the value of human life may provoke someone to ask, *How effective is this scheme in suppressing the maternal mortality and morbidity caused by bungled abortions?* Again, the answer must be very circumspect. It would be reasonable to suppose that maternal death is diminished by adopting the *third* scheme of regulation, which encourages any woman desiring an abortion to approach properly qualified persons.[41] On the other hand, the diminution is far from complete, since an element of risk pertains to this as to all operations, and the total number of operations tends, as we have said, to increase substantially.[42] The numbers of maternal deaths from abortions (lawful and unlawful) in Poland after six years of complete liberalization do not differ, when adjusted to population, from those for the United Kingdom under the first scheme of regulation.[43] The same is true of Czechoslovakia's experience of the third scheme; this experience is discussed

39. See the analysis of British statistics in Dickens, *Abortion and the Law supra* n. 7 at 73–106.

40. See Jerome E. Bates and Edward S. Zawadzki, *Criminal Abortion: A Study in Medical Sociology* (Charles C. Thomas Books, 1964) at 3, and Alan Guttmacher's Foreword, *id.* at viii.

41. See the analysis in Christopher Tietze and Hans Lehfeldt, "Legal Abortion in Eastern Europe," 175 *Journal American Medical Association* 1149, 1151 (1961). But see also Appendix B *infra*.

42. The total number of conceptions also rises: Tietze and Lehfeldt, *ibid.* It is interesting to note that the rate and proportion of abortions is higher among Japanese women who use contraceptives than among those who do not: Samuel, "Population Control in Japan" *supra* n. 33 at 21. On the risks of the operation see *infra* n. 84.

43. Compare Mehlan, "Combating Illegal Abortion" *supra* n. 32 at 86, with Goodhart, "The Frequency of Illegal Abortion" *supra* n. 25 at 198–200.

John M. Finnis

in Appendix B (Statistics on Abortion and Maternal Deaths after Illegal Abortion in Some European States). Swedish commentators on the second scheme of regulation have detected a fall in maternal deaths from abortion, but have been unable to say whether this is due to anything other than the increased availability of antibiotics.[44]

It is not the business of jurisprudence to offer opinions about the acceptability or unacceptability of the maternal death, officially somewhat under 300 in number (but doubtless slightly more), each year in the United States.[45] But it can offer the following reminders. First, the reduction of maternal deaths from bungled abortions, however desirable, is necessarily only a secondary aim of the first scheme of abortion regulation. Secondly, the number of such deaths, however calculated, is minute compared with deaths from other human and avoidable causes, and the feasible reductions in maternal deaths obtainable by abandoning the first scheme of regulation are doubtless only a small fraction of the reductions in road deaths obtainable by keeping the speed of vehicles to (say) 50 miles per hour or by regulating the consumption of tobacco. Thirdly, no woman need go to her death at the hands of bunglers. To speak of the law driving women to their deaths is none too enlightening. As the studies of Packer and Gampell[46] and the testimony of the Royal College of Obstetricians and Gynaecologists indicate, no woman whose life is in any way endangered need suppose that her gynecologist will de-

44. Borell and Engstrom, "Legal Abortions in Sweden" *supra* n. 38 at 74.
45. Most commentators in American law journals continue to accept a figure for annual maternal mortality from abortion of 5,000–10,000. This figure has been denounced by every competent enquirer as, in Tietze's words, "unmitigated nonsense." Tietze, a statistician for the Population Council of New York and by no means opposed to abortion, estimated that the number was 500–1,000: see *New York Times*, 28 January 1968, 28, col. 3. Tietze and Lewit, "Abortion" *supra* n. 24 at 23. The higher figures so widely and irresponsibly publicized seem to have no other basis than a claim, itself fancifully arrived at, by Taussig in 1936: see Taussig, *Abortion supra* n. 22 at 26–28. In 1934 there were 4,000 registered deaths from abortion p.a.; in 1968 there were about 400. See Robert E. Hall, "Commentary" in Smith, ed., *Abortion and the Law supra* n. 12 (Hall, passionately in favor of free abortion, thinks 500 a reasonable estimate). See also the careful analyses of deaths in Minnesota, Michigan, and Tennessee in Alex Barno, "Criminal Abortion Deaths, Illegitimate Pregnancy Deaths, and Suicides in Pregnancy — Minnesota, 1950–1965," 98 *American Journal of Obstetrics and Gynecology* 356–370 (1967); from these one can conclude that the figure for the U.S. can hardly be higher than 600 p.a. and may well be nearer 400.
46. "Therapeutic Abortion" *supra* n. 27.

186

cline to operate for fear of legal sanctions under the first scheme of regulation.[47] Even if gynecologists were less liberal than they are, it would remain true, as is universally admitted, that the cases where abortion is needed to save life or health from serious and lasting impairment are today remarkably rare.[48] A society which has not surrendered to what Maurice Hauriou scathingly called *"l'instinct du moindre effort"* [49] would consider measures to alleviate poverty, to disseminate sexual and birth-control information, and to publicize the dangers of amateur abortion, rather than abandon or radically modify the symbolizing of its civilizational ideals and norms in order to accomplish a rather small diminution in a category of mortality much less numerous and no more sad, unpleasant, or unavoidable than many others.

II. THE "RIGHTS OF THE MEDICAL PROFESSION":
BROADER MEDICAL CRITERIA AND CONTROL
BY PRIOR AUTHORIZATION

The second model scheme of regulation is that which, broadly speaking, has obtained in Denmark and Sweden.[50] In this scheme, as has been shown, the inducing of abortion is permitted when previously authorized by official personnel, who must be satisfied

47. The Report of the Council of the Royal College of Gynaecologists and Physicians, "Legalized Abortion" [1966], 1 *Brit. Med. J.* 850, begins by saying that "the present situation [i.e., the first scheme as it obtained in England before 1967] commends itself to most gynaecologists in that it leaves them free to act in what they consider to be the best interests of each individual patient . . . We are unaware of any case in which a gynaecologist has refused to terminate pregnancy, when he considered it to be indicated on medical grounds, for fear of legal consequences."

48. There is an extensive review of medical literature on this point in Quay, "Justifiable Abortion" *supra* n. 6 at 173–241. The matter is no longer disputed, even in the polemical literature.

49. In *Précis de Droit Constitutionnel* xi (2nd ed., Sirey, Paris, 1929), commenting on Kelsen's jurisprudence.

50. It should be emphasized that the Scandinavian systems only approximate to the second model scheme, since (1) the medical boards are only partly representative of the medical profession, and (2) some of the grounds for abortion are only partially medical. See Skalts and Norgaard, "Abortion Legislation in Denmark" *supra* n. 30; Ingerslev, "Danish Abortion Laws" *supra* n. 38; Henrik Hoffmeyer, "Medical Aspects of the Danish Legislation on Abortions," 17 *W. Res. L. Rev.* 529 (1965). Norway's system, since 1960, approximates to the British and thus to the third scheme: see Ruth Roemer, "Abortion Law: The Approaches of Different Nations," 57 *Am. J. Pub. Health* 1906, 1914 (1967). On recent relaxations of procedures in Sweden, see Tietze and Lewit, "Abortion" *supra* n. 24 at 24.

that the case falls within one of a number of categories specified by ample but not indefinite criteria of a medical, psycho-medical or quasi-medical nature. Criteria and method of control are, of course, independent variables; but we may say that usually control by boards goes along with criteria wider than in most versions of the first scheme.

This is the place to emphasize that the difference between the three schemes is not to be read off the face of the relevant statute; the accepted interpretation in each jurisdiction is the crucial determinant. If medical boards generally interpret the permitted categories so as to allow abortions in all cases of inconvenience, the scheme being followed must be counted as approximating to the third, not the second, of our categories. One can even conceive a statute intended to effect the third scheme being so interpreted by a united medical profession that it approximated in practice to the first scheme. The only legislative guarantee against such a breakdown in the third scheme would be to enact that, where a woman persists in her demand, the physician shall be obliged to perform an abortion. (Such appears now to be the law in Hungary.) [51] Short of this, legislatures cannot themselves define the limits of their scheme (whichever it is) with complete adequacy and security. Nevertheless, legislation is irrational if its aims are not clear and distinct, and our three model schemes do correspond to distinct sets of aims of abortion regulation.

What are the aims of the second scheme? Three are commonly identified: (1) to preserve the dignity, rights, and freedom of action of the medical profession; (2) to recognize the right of the woman over her own body; (3) to suppress unskilled abortions.

Each of these objectives is obviously aimed against a real or supposed implication of the first scheme. Indeed, only hostility to that scheme could prevent intelligent men from seeing that these three objectives cannot all be maintained together. For in the first place, if the woman has the supposed right over her own body, the medical profession (as represented by the authorizing board) has no right to deny her the opportunity of getting a lawful abortion: so the first and second objectives do not cohere. In the second place, there is no natural necessity for the medical pro-

51. Tietze, "Abortion and Sterilization" *supra* n. 20, at 1149–1150; Mehlan, "Combating Illegal Abortion" *supra* n. 32.

fession to share the reformers' enthusiasm for reducing unskilled abortions at all costs; medical ethics may be so restrictive that many women will seek out unskilled abortionists: the first and third objectives do not cohere. As we shall see, these observations are not abstract quibbles; they delineate the main features of the Scandinavian experience.

Let us consider the first objective, often rendered as: "setting free the medical profession." [52] At the outset, an ambiguity must be brought to light. It is one thing to set free the medical profession by giving its accredited representatives, on carefully selected and balanced medical boards, the right to interpret medical criteria in terms of medical science and professional ethics. It is quite another thing to set "the profession" free in the sense of permitting any licensed practitioner (or pair of practitioners) to carry out an abortion when "in good faith" [53] he considers certain criteria fulfilled. In the former case, one is permitting the reinforcing of the standards of the profession by the profession, by providing formal mechanisms for authoritative expression of those standards. In the latter case, one is subjecting those standards to a powerful solvent; for if the profession were to attempt to take disciplinary action against a physician who was acting within the penal law but outside the canons of medical ethics and practice, the accused physician could with reason reply that the policy of the law and society was precisely to set him free to act according to his own conscience.

These broadly opposed tendencies, corresponding to the two broadly distinct senses of the ambiguous notion of "professional freedom," will remain effective, though in varying degrees, as complicating components are added to one legal setup or the other. For example, one could settle for medical boards and thus for the maintenance of general professional standards; but the strengthening effect on those standards would vary according as the boards were exclusively or only partly obstetrical, exclusively or only

52. The phrase, with all its ambiguities, is employed in Glanville Williams, "Euthanasia and Abortion," 38 *U. Col. L. Rev.* 178, 196 (1966). Cf. also Michael S. Sands, "The Therapeutic Abortion Act: An Answer to the Opposition," 13 *University of California at Los Angeles Law Review* 285: "The Therapeutic Abortion Act [Calif.] . . . attempts to allow the medical profession to practise according to its highest standards in spite of restrictive religious views."
53. This is the phrase in the Abortion Act 1967 (U.K.) s.1(1).

partly medical, centrally or locally selected, representative of State commissions or representative only of hospital managements, and according as the criteria for decision were exclusively medical, or partly psychiatrical, or partly "social," and according as the decisions were required to be unanimous or only by majority. On the other hand, one could settle for setting free individual physicians or hospitals; but the solvent effect of this on professional standards would vary according as the decision was left with individual physicians, or pairs of physicians, or committees of hospitals, or exclusively gynecologists and obstetricians, or generally all practitioners, and according as a "reasonable" or only a "good faith" decision was required, and according as the onus of proving conformity with the legal criteria rested with the prosecution or with the defendant physician.[54]

But one characteristic may be observed of any scheme which leaves the decision (in ordinary as well as in emergency cases) to anything other than centrally appointed medical boards acting by unanimous decision on substantially medical grounds:[55] such a scheme will approximate the third rather than the second of our three model schemes.[56] For the brute fact is that standards *within*

54. On onus of proof, see George, "Current Abortion Laws" *supra* n. 12 at 392; Marvin M. Moore, "Antiquated Abortion Laws," 20 *Washington and Lee Law Review* 250, 259 (1963); Quay, "Justifiable Abortion" *supra* n. 6 at 241; David W. Louisell, "Abortion, the Practice of Medicine and the Due Process of Law," 16 *U.C.L.A. L. Rev.* 233 (1969).

55. Provided that the scheme is introduced specifically to liberalize the first scheme. As to uses of the second scheme to tighten up a sagging first scheme, see text *infra* at nn. 69–71.

56. The Abortion Act 1967 (U.K.) and the *Model Penal Code* s.230.3 both leave everything to the good faith of two doctors. This similarity is more important than the difference which appears from the fact that the *Model Penal Code* authorizes abortion only where there is substantial risk of grave injury to the mother (*infra* n. 72), whereas the Abortion Act specifically distinguishes between grave injury and other injury, and authorizes abortion in the latter as well as the former case: compare s.1(1) (a) with s.4(2). Packer and Gampell's scheme, "Therapeutic Abortion" *supra* n. 27 at 452–453, is announced as an attempt to substitute "the institutionalized exercise of responsible medical judgment for the hit-or-miss application of the criminal law," *id.* at 455. The hospital committee scheme has been adopted in the 1967–68 abortion legislation in Colorado (*Revised Statutes* 40-2-50 to 40-2-53), Maryland (*Annotated Code,* art. 43, sec. 149E), North Carolina (*General Statutes,* sec. 14–45.1) and California (*Health and Safety Code,* secs. 25950 to 25954). But the institutionalization is basically feeble, in that the authorizing committees are subject to no central appointment, direction, or control; a hospital out to make money would need to do no more than constitute itself a committee with "humane and progressive" standards. Note that the great Japanese liberalization of 1952 was effected not by extending the

the medical profession (not to mention the psychiatric profession), as distinct from the representative standards *of* the profession, vary so widely in relation to the relevant questions of medical and ethical propriety that getting an abortion would depend on no more than a woman's eye for the liberal practitioner or hospital.[57] She need only persist in seeking an "authoritative" consent to her request after any number of refusals (since, unlike consents, refusals could never be authoritative or final in such a scheme). Or perhaps the determining factor would be no more nor less than her wealth.[58]

Scandinavian experience in these matters may now be considered. Vera Skalts and Magna Norgaard state that under the 1937 Danish legislation (which came into force in 1939), hospital physicians, gynecologists, and surgeons often considered that the decisions of the official boards were too liberal, while many women and their families and doctors considered the boards too restrictive. The physicians, gynecologists, and surgeons saw only the cases in which consent was given by the boards, and not the cases in which consent was refused. The tension is said to have disappeared with the introduction of regulations requiring the submission of all cases to the boards, including those cases ending in a refusal.[59] This explanation of the tension must be taken along with the fact that in 1964, for example, only 54 percent of applicants

---

grounds for abortion in the Eugenic Protection Law of 1948, but by removing the control of the District Eugenic Committees over individual doctor's decisions: Blacker, "Japan's Population Problem" *supra* n. 33 at 35.

57. When Packer and Gampell put eleven hypothetical case histories to California hospitals, in only four did a majority of hospitals say that they would approve an abortion, but in nine a majority of the hospitals thought that other reputable hospitals would approve. On the difference in standards between family doctors and gynecologists, see Skalts and Norgaard, "Abortion Legislation in Denmark" *supra* n. 31 at 506. For the difference between psychiatrists and gynecologists, compare the report of the R.C.O.G., "Legalized Abortion" *supra* n. 47 with the *Report of the Royal Medical-Psychological Association,* 199 *J. Am. Med. Ass.* 199 (1967). On the alarming differences among psychiatrists, see Kenneth R. Niswander, "Medical Abortion Practices in the United States," 17 *W. Res. L. Rev.* 403, 414 (1965). For the effect of putting psychiatrists and social workers on authorizing boards, see Ingerslev, "Danish Abortion Laws" *supra* n. 38 at 78.

58. H. L. A. Hart has attacked the unfairness of the first scheme, under which the obtaining of an illegal but skillful abortion depends on one's wealth: *The Morality of the Criminal Law* 47 (Magnes Press, Jerusalem, and Oxford U. P., 1965). How much more unfair would be the system under which the obtaining of a *legal* abortion depended on wealth!

59. "Abortion Legislation in Denmark" *supra* n. 31 at 506, 511; Ingerslev, "Danish Abortion Laws" *supra* n. 38 at 81.

were granted their request for abortion.[60] Indeed, during the later 1950s, there is evidence of "a more restrictive practice of author-ization," [61] presumably reflecting changing assessments of medical and psychiatric realities in relation to the permitted categories of indication.[62] Moreover, Henrik Hoffmeyer has recognized that the liberalizations he desires meet with "the problem . . . that doctors are not specifically qualified to apply them ["social cri-teria"] and would certainly refrain from participating . . . and many surgeons and gynecologists certainly would refrain from performing the operations." [63]

In short, the Scandinavian concern has to some extent been to set free the medical and psychiatric professions to apply represen-tative, not individual or merely local, standards of judgment; and change in the law is feared because it would involve the division of the profession and a clear threat to the maintenance of those very standards.

Clearly, the Swedish and Danish legislation does not recognize any distinct "right of women to dispose of their bodies as they see fit." The boards' refusals to terminate pregnancy are authori-tative, and the criteria do not include the wishes of the woman. So we can turn to the implications of the Scandinavian experience for the third of the objectives commonly proposed for this scheme of regulation: the suppression of unskilled abortions.

It is not generally denied that during the first ten years after the introduction of an approximation to the second scheme in Sweden and Denmark, the number of illegal and presumably of unskilled abortions rose appreciably.[64] No one asserts that during the subsequent decade there was any greater decline in the number of such illegal abortions than was experienced during a similar period in countries, such as Holland, under the rigorous first scheme.[65] Nor is this surprising. The strict application of medical

60. Skalts and Norgaard, *ibid. supra* n. 31 at 513.
61. Tietze, "Abortion and Sterilization" *supra* n. 20 at 1163.
62. Thus Hoffmeyer, "Danish Legislation on Abortions" *supra* n. 50 at 536, comments on the development during the 1950s of "a more objective and sober attitude on the part of officials . . . adopted as it was realized that suicides and the development of chronic psychopathology were rare" in many cases once supposed to provide indications for abortion.
63. *Id.* at 551.
64. *Supra* n. 31.
65. Skalts and Norgaard, "Abortion Legislation in Denmark" *supra* n. 31 at 519, opine that the number of illegal abortions may have declined by 10–14%

and psychiatric professional standards by the medical boards must be well known in Denmark and Sweden; it cannot escape the notice of women that only about a half of those who apply will be granted an abortion. The formalities necessary to secure a sound judgment according to national standards are not trivial; there is red tape.[66] So a great many women do not apply, and of those who do so unsuccessfully, it is known that over 15 percent subsequently obtain illegal abortions, despite the general aid and dissuasive counsel which they have received from the Mothers' Aid Centres in connection with their application.[67]

It is as well to be realistic here. The conception of an unwanted child represents a failure for the woman and is a source of humiliation to her. Studies in Amsterdam indicate that these failures in birth-control methods frequently result from lack of communication between the spouses, manifesting a disturbed family structure.[68] It is in this context of failure, mental isolation, shame, and dilemma that many women will decide to act. Formalities, the requirement of informing the husband, the fear of being "talked out of it" by professionals [69] — all these must weigh in favor of an approach to unauthorized abortionists.

So the use of the second scheme to protect representative professional standards is incompatible with the aim of reducing unskilled abortions. The second scheme, therefore, stands or falls with its aim of setting the profession as a whole, through its representatives, free from all legal restrictions save those generated by the representative professional conscience. To use this scheme for other ends as well would be irrational, since it would in all probability follow that none of its ends would be secured and all would be prejudiced. The scheme often attracts favor as a moderate, pragmatic compromise between the "extremes" of the rig-

between 1954 and 1964; a similar decline took place during the postwar period in Amsterdam, where the first scheme is in force: P. E. Treffers, "Abortion in Amsterdam," 20 *Population Studies* 295, 299–300 (1966–67).

66. On Swedish red-tape, see Tietze and Lehfeldt, "Legal Abortion in Eastern Europe" *supra* n. 41 at 1152.

67. Skalts and Norgaard, "Abortion Legislation in Denmark" *supra* n. 31 at 516.

68. Treffers, "Abortion in Amsterdam" *supra* n. 65 at 308–309, contains a very detailed analysis and demonstration of these facts by many of a variety of statistical *indicia*.

69. The Danish Mothers Aid Centres claim to talk a lot of women out of getting an abortion: see Skalts and Norgaard, "Abortion Legislation in Denmark" *supra* n. 31 at 516–517.

orous first scheme and the permissive third scheme. But the compromise is illusory; the essence of the scheme is to set aside all the aims of the first and third schemes, and to replace them with the distinct aim of preserving representative medical-psychiatrical standards. If this point is not firmly grasped by legislatures, the resulting schemes will simply get the worst of all worlds. It must be said that the point was not grasped by many of the British and American legislators of 1967–68. Academic American commentators, too, have almost all proposed schemes which structurally approximate the second model scheme (in more or less unstable versions), but which profess all the aims of both the first and third schemes as well.[70]

Moreover, it is not clear that even a regulatory scheme which firmly and precisely sought to liberate and strengthen representative medical ethics would succeed — at least if it were adopted expressly as an alternative to a functioning first scheme. For the primary object of the first scheme is the protection of innocent human life against deliberate or careless attack. So the adoption of the second scheme might be taken to represent a judgment that the free operation of professional standards is to be preferred to the foregoing objective of the first scheme. This judgment would be particularly undisguised if society continued to impose its own standards on the medical profession in respect of life other than fetal life, and operations other than abortions.

What would be the effect of such a judgment on the professional standards themselves? At present, those standards happen to include the objective of the first scheme. Would not some members of the medical profession be tempted to conclude that society, in seeming to prefer the liberty of the medical profession to the protection of fetal life, was willing to follow professional ethics

70. On Packer and Gampell's scheme see *supra* n. 56. Compare the scheme in Moore, "Antiquated Abortion Laws" *supra,* n. 54 at 259. On the Model Penal Code scheme, see *Model Penal Code* s.207.11 (*Tentative Draft No. 9,* 1959); s.230.3 (*Proposed Official Draft,* 1962); Thomas H. Barnard, Jr., "An Analysis and Criticism of the Model Penal Code Provisions on the Law of Abortion," 18 *W. Res. L. Rev.* 540 (1967). The principal criterion is "substantial risk that continuance of the pregnancy would gravely impair the physical or mental health of the mother." This weakens without clarifying the principle of the first model scheme, provides none of the institutionalized safeguards or advantages of the stable versions of the second scheme, and on the admission of the draftsmen themselves does not meet the problem of illegal amateur abortions to which the third scheme is a plausible answer.

however they developed, even if they abandoned concern for fetal or other categories of human life? Would not such conclusions, whatever their justifiability, be likely, and might they not inspire attempts to revise medical ethics, not in the light of the immanent norms of those ethics, but in accordance with presumptions about "social opinion?" Would not such attempts threaten the very value which the second scheme seeks to realize, namely, the orderly development and functioning of an autonomous and respected body of medico-ethical standards? All these questions are distinct from the further question, which I shall not here pursue: Would society be happy with a medical profession which held itself free to dispose of human life according to the criteria of professional ethics, or which was encouraged to believe it had a general right to develop its standards in these matters without any legal restrictions imposed from outside the profession?

The symbolic significance, and hence the consequences, of the second scheme would be quite different if it were adopted in order to prevent a development observable in many Western societies: an uncontrolled drift from the first scheme to the third by a process of official and unofficial interpretation and practice, together with a breakdown in the unity of medical ethics. In such a situation, the second scheme would be an attempt, not merely to support medical ethics against the wayward consciences of individual physicians, nor merely to liberate respectable practitioners from fear of the variable rigors of nonmedical prosecutors, but also to strengthen a particular tenet of existing medical ethics, namely respect for fetal life. In other words, the second scheme could conceivably be adopted specifically to strengthen, rather than to depart from, the primary objective of the first scheme. In this case, to ensure its success, the adoption of the scheme would have to be generally recognized as clarifying and tightening up "the law," and not as liberalizing or "humanizing" it. The boards would have to be selected largely from those representatives of the medical profession known to favor the traditional medical standards; more weight would have to be given to gynecologists than to psychiatrists and social workers, and decisions to abort would have to be unanimous. The point could be reinforced by appointing a public defender of the unborn child's interests, whose duty would be to present to the board those facts about the applicant's circumstances which otherwise might be suppressed by the woman's anxious advocacy of her own cause. The consent of the husband would need to be required, in order to stress the point that the law was not dealing with a mere adjunct of the woman's body, but with the living, human fruit of a familial enterprise.[71] Emergency operations without the permission of a board would, of course, need to be lawful — but to prevent abuse of this facility, it might perhaps be necessary to put the onus of proving reasonable belief in the existence of such an emergency on the doctor or hospital concerned.

Whether the second scheme were adopted as a liberalization of the first or as a tightening up, many of the foregoing technical questions would need careful resolution. Given clear and coherent aims, technicalities are the law's means of securing substantive rationality. The symbolic and practical significance of technical devices is immense; most people see the aims and significance of the law only through its technical operations. Onus of proof, unanimity of decision, representation of competing interests, verification of *ex parte* assertions, consent of interested parties — the determination of these factors one way or another will govern the efficacy of any version of the second scheme. One may add that, if the liberalizing version of the second scheme (or, indeed, the third scheme) be adopted, some further technical questions will need clear solution: Will it be an implied term in a medical practitioner's contracts with his employers (if any) and his patients that he will perform abortions in all situations where the law permits abortion? Will it be actionable negligence not to suggest to a patient the possibility of an abortion in those situations where a considerable number of practitioners would be willing to perform an abortion? Should, for example, a surgeon be entitled to plead conscientious objection to the performing of any authorized abortion, for purposes of criminal, civil, and professional liability? The first scheme may be somewhat hard on medical practitioners because of its want of precision (in some versions) and its uncertain application in the hands of police and prosecutors. Is there not as great injustice in any version of the other schemes which,

71. The husband's consent is not required under the Abortion Act 1967 (U.K.). Cf. *supra* n. 12. It is required under the Colorado statute of 1967 *supra* n. 56.

through failing to distinguish between the permitted and the compulsory, leaves the practitioner with conscientious objections uncertain of his legal right to act according to his conscience? [72]

III. THE "RIGHT OF THE WOMAN": UNCONTROLLED APPLICATION OF INDETERMINATE CRITERIA

The third scheme of regulation is that which, broadly speaking, obtains in the United Kingdom, Japan, Russia, and Eastern Europe. Here, abortion is either formally or in practical effect permitted whenever it is performed by a qualified physician.[73] The limiting case is where the physician or authorizing board must perform or authorize an abortion if the woman persists in her demand (Hungary). But there are many variants short of this. The first scheme is liable, as we said, to change gradually into the third wherever qualified physicians are in practice permitted to perform abortions at will without fear of prosecution or professional disciplinary proceedings. The second scheme is liable to be converted into the third by extension of the grounds on which the boards may authorize abortion, so as to include considerations remote

72. The Abortion Act 1967 (U.K.) s.4(1) contains a conscience clause which extends only to "participation in any treatment authorized by this Act," but which does not protect a physician in respect of any duty to advise his patient nor in respect of "any duty to participate in any treatment which is necessary to save the life or to prevent grave permanent injury to the physical or mental health of a pregnant woman": s.4(2). In both these respects the conscience clause in Moore, "Antiquated Abortion Laws" *supra* n. 54 at 259 is preferable. The *Model Penal Code* has no conscience clause. The proposed Humane Abortion Act of 1967 (New York) would, it seems, have required courts to order abortion in certain cases. "Comment," 31 *Albany Law Review* 290, 294 (1967). Could a judge plead conscientious objection?

73. The Japanese Eugenic Protection Law 1948, as amended, provides that an abortion can be performed whenever in the judgment of a single physician "it is feared that continued pregnancy or childbirth will for physical or economic reasons markedly injure the health of the mother's body." In some ways this is formally stricter than the Abortion Act 1967 (U.K.). Since Parliament expressly rejected any special qualifications for the required second opinion, it must be regarded as the merest formality. See also Appendix A, par. 1 *infra*. Note that in East European states, abortions must be approved by a board, and in some countries about 10% of applications are refused; but the fundamental fact remains that "medical reasons for termination are uncommon, contributing 6% of cases in Slovenia, 10% or under in Czechoslovakia, approximately 4% in Hungary and only 1% in Rumania": Malcom Potts, "Legal Abortion in Eastern Europe," 59 *Eugenics Rev.* 232, 239 (1967).

from medical or psychiatric indications. Within the third scheme it is possible for there to be central boards, or no boards; permissive or mandatory indications; fee-paying requirements, or free service;[74] stipulations of authorized hospitals, or no such stipulations; compulsory sterilization as a condition of first, second, third, or subsequent abortions, or no such requirement; compulsory instruction in birth-control procedures, or no such provision; and other similar variations, including many of those mentioned in discussing versions of the second scheme. In Appendix A, *infra*, I have given a detailed account of the new English scheme, its operation, and its already visible effects.

The aims of the third scheme are two: (1) to give effect to the rights of the mother over her own body; (2) to eliminate unskilled abortions.[75] Neither of these aims need be regarded as primary or secondary; each is by itself a sufficient explanation of the scheme.

What is the meaning of the first aim? In both the first and the second model schemes, recognition is given to the rights of the mother as against any rights which the unborn child may have. But these schemes preserve the impression that the problem is one of balancing competing rights; it is only where the mother is medically gravely threatened that her rights are given precedence. In the third scheme, on the other hand, the fetus has no rights as against the mother, since its existence is strictly by her sufferance or at her will and pleasure, subject only to her finding compliant physicians. Indeed, under the third scheme the fetus is likely to be less protected as against the mother than are other portions of the mother's anatomy. For by the Anglo-American common law,

74. If abortions are cheaper than contraceptives, the results are predictable: on the Japanese experience, see Blacker, "Japan's Population Problem" and Samuel, "Population Control in Japan" *supra* n. 33. In 1964, one-third of the 184,000 Hungarian women legally aborted had had two or more previous legal abortions: A. Klinger, "Abortion Programs" in Bernard Berelson et al., ed., *Family Planning and Population Problems* 471 (U. of Chicago Press, 1966). (Proceedings of the International Conference on Family Planning Programs, Geneva, 1965.)

75. An orthodox but nuanced account of current doctrine in Communist states is Vladimir Solnar, "Contribution à la Question de la Criminalité de l'Avortement Provoqué," in *Les Principaux Aspects* . . . cited *supra* n. 10 at 171. Also Tietze and Lehfeldt, "Legal Abortion in Eastern Europe" *supra* n. 41 at 1149; Wolinska, "Assumptions" *supra* n. 35; Potts, "Legal Abortion" *supra* n. 73 at 232, and Mehlan, "Combating Illegal Abortion" *supra* n. 32 at 87, both citing the preamble to the Russian legislation of 1955; Klinger, "Abortion Programs" *supra* n. 74 at 465.

no one may consent to an assault upon himself; consent is relevant only as a precondition of the lawfulness of physical interventions within the context of lawful games or of medically indicated treatment.[76] To ask a surgeon to cut off one's leg in order to win a bet, or the better to beg, or for no reason other than that one wants it off, does not legally entitle the surgeon to perform the operation. This is not in itself a criticism of the third scheme, but underlines its novelty and scope.

Sometimes it is argued that to adopt the third scheme would contradict the recently developed legal rules conferring conditionally enforceable rights upon unborn children, even nonviable fetuses, in respect of negligently caused antenatal injuries.[77] The argument, as it stands, is not cogent. The law can, without contradiction or legal-logical absurdity, confer legal personality on whatever it wishes, human or nonhuman, and under whatever restrictions and conditions it sees fit. For example, the law could coherently confer a right of action upon a child as against its parents for conceiving it in face of known risk of malformation. To say that legally the child had a right not to be conceived would in no way carry the implication that the child had in any sense existed prior to its conception. Similarly, it would not be legal-logically absurd for the law to say that a nonviable fetus had no right, as against its mother and her physicians, not to be aborted, but did have a right, as against third parties, not to be negligently injured.[78] Of course, legal-logical coherence and legal legitimacy

76. Patrick Devlin, *The Enforcement of Morals* 6 (Oxford U.P., 1965); Rollin M. Perkins, *Criminal Law* 853 (Foundation Press, 1957). Cosmetic operations doubtless fall under a kind of *de minimis* principle.

77. On these developments see David A. Gordon, "The Unborn Plaintiff," 63 *Michigan Law Review* 579 (1965); Note: "A New Theory in Prenatal Injuries: The Biological Approach," 27 *Fordham Law Review* 684 (1957–58); Note: "The Impact of Medical Knowledge on the Law Relating to Prenatal Injuries," 110 *U. Penn. L. Rev.* 554 (1962). All the authors predict the general triumph of the new extension of tort and other civil rights to the nonviable fetus.

78. Indeed, the law which grants a child an action in respect of negligent injuries caused while it was still nonviable, need not be expressed in terms of "rights of the non-viable foetus" at all. It can be expressed, after the fashion of the civil law systems in this matter, in terms of nothing more than a causal link between the plaintiff child's condition and the defendant's wrongful act: see Gordon, "The Unborn Plaintiff" *supra* n. 77 at 590–591. Similarly, under existing law, the young fetus is protected against abortion, but has no right to legal interment, can be handled as a pathological specimen, and its untimely birth need not be registered.

John M. Finnis

are to be distinguished — the latter concept, unlike the former, involves considerations of the law as a project for social order, as a scheme of living, of coordinating human ends, and ends with means. Even so, to point to the developing common law civil rights of the unborn child does not of itself establish that the third scheme lacks substantive legal legitimacy.

But the recent developments of the law on antenatal injuries by third parties are not irrelevant. For the developments have been provoked by, and are striking witness to, a growing sense of the arbitrariness of the distinction between viability and nonviability. To more and more judges it has seemed that there is no meaningful stage, in the development of the child after conception, at which the child could in common sense be said to change from a "part" into something more than a part of the mother.[79] The conferment of rights and personality has in large measure been due to a judicial sense that, as a matter of fact, not of legal logic, the nonviable fetus is as distinct from the mother as the viable fetus.

This development provokes the question: What are the symbolic implications, for society at large, of adopting the third scheme in preference to the first or second? Such an adoption seems symbolically to devalue the primary objective of the first scheme: the unconditional protection of human life in the womb, save where another human life is involved. Now this objective has two components: The major premise is that human life is to

79. In *Smith v. Brennan*, 31 N.J. 353, 157 A.2d 497, 502 (1960) the Supreme Court of New Jersey said: "The third reason for the rule denying recovery was the theory that an unborn child was a part of the mother, and therefore not a person in being to whom a duty of care could be owed. All the courts that have permitted recovery for prenatal injuries have disagreed with that theory. They have found that the existence of an infant separate from its mother begins before birth . . . Medical authorities have long recognized that a child is in existence from the moment of conception, and not merely a part of its mother's body . . ." See also, for example, *Sylvia v. Gobeille*, 220 A.2d 222, 223 (R.I. 1966). In *Sinkler v. Kneale*, 401 Pa. 267, 164 A.2d 93, 94 (1960), the Supreme Court of Pennsylvania said of Justice Holmes's doctrine in *Dietrich v. Inhabitants of Northampton* 138 Mass. 14 (1884): "Judge Holmes's real point d'appui for decision was that the unborn child was part of its mother. This was undoubtedly the medical view accepted by the law at the time, and it is precisely the view that has altered since." The court approved *Bennett v. Hymers*, 101 N.H. 483, 147 A.2d 108, 110 (1958), in which the Supreme Court of New Hampshire said that "the fetus from the time of conception becomes a separate organism and remains so throughout its life." Holmes's doctrine was overruled in his own State, in respect of a nonviable fetus, in *Torigian v. Watertown News Co.*, 225 N.E. 2d 926 (Mass. 1967).

be protected unconditionally, save where other human life is involved; the minor premise is that fetal life is human life. One or other of these premises must be undermined by adoption of the third scheme. Which will it seem to be? Will it not be the major premise? The minor premise is protected by the strong trend of modern thought, in the light of improved biological knowledge of antenatal development and of the chromosomal determination of human characteristics at the moment of conception, in favor of recognizing the distinct humanity of the fetus after conception, and in favor of denying the relevance (long since denied by medical science)[80] of "viability" or "quickening" or any other notional stage in antenatal growth.[81] It is to this trend that the developments in the law about antenatal injuries bear witness.

The symbolic form of Western civilization is in large part what we have called Western rationality, in which the generality of rules is highly valued. We see this form of thought in the following passage from the contemporary moralist, Joseph Fletcher: "There are common exceptions to the rule against medical homicide. If one can be made at the beginning of life (abortion) why not also at the end of life (euthanasia)? The one situation is no more absolute than the other. There is no more stigma in the one than in the other." [82] It so happens that Fletcher is arguing in favor of euthanasia; but the symbolic form and movement of his argument is what is of interest here. The dialectic moves in the ambit of the rationalist symbols: "rules" — "exceptions"; "if this, why not that?"; "the one, so the other." Once Western rationality had differentiated itself from the traditional and charismatic symbolic forms, it became a dynamic system with a low tolerance of the arbitrary and anomalous. "Common exceptions" must be

---

80. See "Note," 110 *U. Penn. L. Rev. supra* n. 77 at 554, 556n. 17.

81. It is not clear why a full-blooded exponent of the third scheme, like Glanville Williams, should wish to use the criminal law to prevent abortions after the first 16 weeks of pregnancy: "Euthanasia and Abortion" *supra* n. 52 at 196. Donald Giannella raises the sensible (rationalist) question how it can be consistent (that is, just) to allow the destruction of three or four healthy fetuses in order to prevent one defective, while convicting the doctor who kills an unexpected defective after birth: "The Difficult Quest for a Truly Humane Abortion Law," 13 *Villanova Law Review* 257, 271 (1968).

82. *Morals and Medicine* 205 (Princeton, 1954). Compare the title of Glanville Williams' article, "Euthanasia and Abortion" *supra* n. 52.

restated as a new "rule," even if the old rule fares rather badly in the process. So, given the increasingly apparent humanity of the fetus, it must be assumed that the consequence of shifting to the third system of abortion regulation will be the gradual displacement of the old rule, often expressed as "the sanctity of human life." The eventual content of a stabilized new rule, no one can predict.

Some, preferring not to draw attention to the question of rights (which, however, arises whether one likes it or not), rely on the alternative objective of the third scheme: the elimination of unskilled abortions. Indeed, of all the schemes the third seems best fitted for attaining this end. But quick results and complete satisfaction, as we have seen, are not to be expected. A decade after adoption of the third scheme, the hospitals of Eastern European states have to deal with many thousands of cases consequential on illegal abortions.[83] Mortality and morbidity are probably lowered; but they are far from eliminated, not least because the total number of abortions is considerably increased, and even lawful operations are not free from risk of complications and sequelae.[84]

Advocates of the third scheme must consider a further issue: How great is their devotion to the rights of the mother or the elimination of unskilled abortions, or both? The unrestricted availability of abortion may well lead, as it has in Hungary, to a fall in the birthrate so great that the population begins to decline quite rapidly. At a certain point such a fall in population brings hardships and threatens the common economic and social good.[85] Is the availability of abortion then to be restricted, with consequential limitations on the rights of the mother and probable increases in the number of unskilled abortions? Does the abortion question ultimately involve no more than shifting considerations of social welfare, or does it involve human rights, and if so, whose? On the answer to those questions, too rarely pressed, depends the clarity of

83. See Appendix B *infra*.

84. R.C.O.G., "Legalized Abortion," *supra* n. 47 at 851; Carl Müller, "The Dangers of Abortion," 13 *World Med. J.* 78 (1966); Yoshio Koya, "The Harmful Effects of Induced Abortion," 13 *World Med. J.* 170 (1966).

85. The Report of the Inter-departmental Committee on Abortion (1939: U.K.) recommended against extension of the grounds for abortion largely for fear that it would lead to underpopulation: s.232.

aim, and consequential precision of means, which are the essence of legal rationality.

IV. THE PROPER SCOPE OF PENAL LAW

"He who violently bloweth his nose bringeth forth blood." [86] To the proverbial wisdom of Israel were added the words of Christ: "Neither do men put new wine into old bottles, else the bottles break, and the wine runneth out, and the bottles perish." [87] With a fanciful but vivid sense of relevance, the Christian legal philosopher drew from these sayings support for the conclusion that the law should not lay too severe a moral burden on weak men.[88] Crime should not be coterminous with vice. I do not think that any of the three model schemes of abortion regulation conflict with this jurisprudential canon. In the current phase of Western mores, a criminal law which forbade abortion in all circumstances whatever would perhaps offend against the maxim; but the form of the first scheme operative in the law and practice of all relevant countries now permits abortions wherever the life of the mother is in danger. Of course, this scheme is too severe for many women, and they break the law. But there is no evidence of widespread resentment against the law, spilling over as a result into more general lawlessness. There seem to be no general criminal rackets flourishing on the basis of illegal abortions and extending into other areas of crime.[89] Unlike Prohibition, the abortion law has not led to any split in the wineskin of the criminal law as a whole.

Are there then any further jurisprudential doctrines, considerations or debates relevant to the problem of legally regulating abortion? There seem to be two candidates: (1) the doctrine of

86. *Prov.* 30:33.
87. *Matt.* 9:17.
88. Both the texts were cited by Thomas Aquinas, *Summa Theologica* I–II, q. 96, a.2, to support the view that the law should not suppress all vices.
89. The reasons for this lack of connection between abortion and organized crime are analyzed by Thomas C. Schelling, "Economic Analysis and Organized Crime" in the President's Commission on Law Enforcement and Administration of Justice, *Task Force Report: Organized Crime* 114, 121, 124 (1967). Edwin M. Schur, *Crimes Without Victims* 61 (Prentice-Hall, 1965) cites no pertinent evidence for his assertion that existing abortion law has caused serious problems of police corruption.

the American Law Institute that to use the criminal law against a substantial body of decent opinion is contrary to basic American traditions;[90] (2) the questions raised in the "Hart — Devlin" debate about the proper scope of the criminal law.[91]

This is not the place to offer a full discussion of the American Law Institute's opinion: on its face it is a proposition within the ideology of American democracy, not within jurisprudence. However, a few questions may be raised in passing: What is the body of decent opinion referred to in the context of abortion? Is it the representative opinion of the medical profession? Or is it the opinion of those women and practitioners who consider they have a human right to demand and perform abortions at will? If it is the latter, why does the *Model Penal Code* not contain a straightforward version of the third scheme? If it is not the latter opinion, what is indecent about that body of opinion? But more important, how conscientiously is the American Law Institute willing to apply its principle in other areas? Would it have eliminated the law against duelling, during the centuries before the law's eventual triumph? Is the opinion of decent racialists to be protected by the principle? Looking at the Bill of Rights, we are inclined to believe that American democratic principles are somewhat richer than the ALI would have us believe. As Edmond Cahn remarked of the desegregation decision in *Brown v. Board of Education:* "Here again we see the falseness of the popular belief that with regard to moral values, the law imposes only 'minimum standards'." [92]

In the beginning of the debate between Professor H. L. A. Hart and Lord Devlin, the principle that society has the right to punish immorality as such was opposed by Hart to John Stuart Mill's principle that "the only purpose for which power can be rightfully exercised over any member of a civilized community,

90. *Model Penal Code* s. 207.11 at 151 (Tent. Draft No. 9, 1959); also Leavy and Kummer, "Criminal Abortion" *supra* n. 10 at 138. This view seems to lie behind another very popular, but weak and obscure, argument: that the law should not "make hypocrites of law-abiding citizens": see Monroe Trout, "Therapeutic Abortion Laws Need Therapy," 37 *Temple Law Quarterly* 172, 173 (1964); "Comment," 15 *Journal Public Law* 386, 399 (1966).

91. Devlin, *Enforcement of Morals supra* n. 76 (which contains a bibliography of the debate to 1964); Hart, *Morality of the Criminal Law supra* n. 58; Mitchell, *Law, Morality and Religion supra* n. 9; J. R. Lucas, *The Principles of Politics* 172–175, 344–351 (Oxford U.P., 1966).

92. "Jurisprudence," 30 *New York University Law Review* 150, 156 (1955).

against his will, is to prevent harm to others." [93] At the end of the day, Lord Devlin's advocacy of the former view had been reformulated: "Whether society should have the power to restrain any activity depends on the nature of the activity. Whether it should exercise the power at any given time in its history depends on the situation at that time and requires a balance to be struck between the foreseeable danger to society and the foreseeable damage to the freedom and happiness of the individual." [94] Meanwhile, Professor Hart's advocacy of the other view had been shifting, too: for him, Mill's principle comes down to little more than "that the issue should be calmly viewed as one to be decided by consideration of the balance of harm done by the practice and the harm done by the existing law." [95] Between this "principle" of balancing and the "principle" of balancing quoted from Lord Devlin, I find it difficult to see any difference. In the absence of critical clarification of the concept common to both, namely "danger," "damage," or "harm," I feel free to say that the debate has neither strengthened nor weakened the analysis here advanced of the functions of the criminal law.

John Stuart Mill himself was able to recognize that the problem is not as simple as some of his uncritical followers have supposed. One hundred years ago, progressive and humanitarian thinkers in England were agitating for state registration and certification of prostitutes.[96] The primary object of this scheme was analogous to a main aim of the third model scheme of abortion regulation: the prevention of venereal disease. But in his evidence to the Royal

93. John Stuart Mill, *Essay on Liberty* 72–73 (Everyman ed., 1910).
94. *Enforcement of Morals supra* n. 76 at 113.
95. Hart, *Morality of the Criminal Law supra* n. 58 at 47; also 48–49.
96. Sheldon Amos, *Laws for the Regulation of Vice* (Stevens and Sons, 1877); Ann Stafford, *The Age of Consent* (Hodder and Stoughton, 1964). State-controlled facilities or licensing provisions obtained in almost every European country and, in practical effect, in English military districts. In 1870 a Royal Commission was appointed to inquire into the possibility of extending the quasi-licensing provisions to all parts of England. At the outset, most of the Commissioners, who included T. H. Huxley and F. D. Maurice, were in favor of such an extension. But at the end of the day the Chairman was to say: "So far as the medical testimony was concerned, there can hardly be a doubt that the system of the periodical examination was the most efficacious for the restriction of diseases. On the other hand, there were many considerations of morality and decency which rendered the Commission unwilling to recommend it." Amos, *ibid.* at 16, 47. For the conclusions of the Commission, *id.* at 478–496. On the Contagious Diseases Act 1864, *id.* at 423–471. On the Royal Commission, Stafford, *ibid.* at 43–51.

John M. Finnis

Commission on Contagious Diseases, in 1871, it was Mill who said that a licensing law

facilitates the act beforehand, which is a totally different thing, and is always recognised in legislation as a different thing, from correcting the evils which are the consequences of vices and faults. If we were never to interfere with the evil consequences which persons have brought upon themselves, we should help one another very little. Undoubtedly, it is true that interfering to remedy evils which we have brought on ourselves has in some degree the same bad consequences, since it does in the same degree diminish the motive we have to guard against bringing evils on ourselves. Still, a line must be drawn somewhere, and a marked line can be drawn there. You may draw a line between attacking evils when they occur, in order to remedy them as far as we are able, and making arrangements beforehand which will enable the objectionable practices to be carried on without incurring the danger of the evil. These two things I take to be distinct and capable of being kept distinct in practice. As long as hospitals are not peculiarly for that class of diseases, and do not give that class of disease any favour as compared with others, they are not liable to objection, because their operation consists in remedying the effects of past evils; they do not hold out a special facility beforehand to practising illicit indulgence with a security which it would not otherwise enjoy. The interference is not preventive but remedial.[97]

And then Mill was asked: "You think that the tendency of the Act is to do moral injury?" He said: "I do think so, because I hardly think it possible for thoughtless people not to infer, when special precautions are taken to make a course which is generally considered worthy of disapprobation safer than it would naturally be, that it cannot be considered very bad by the law, and possibly may be considered as either not bad at all, or at any rate a necessary evil." [98] It is this more supple and farseeing conception of harm that is relevant in jurisprudence.[99]

The problem of abortion, like that of prostitution, is not to be solved by any legislative scheme alone; but almost throughout Europe experience of the progressive and humanitarian scheme for

97. Quoted in Amos, *ibid. supra* n. 96 at 53–54.
98. *Ibid.*
99. Registration of prostitutes is condemned by the Convention for the Supression of the Traffic in Persons and of the Exploitation of the Prostitution of Others, approved by United Nations General Assembly Resolution of 2nd December 1949. The Contagious Diseases Act 1864 (U.K.) was repealed in 1875.

regulating prostitution showed that if society regards something as a vice, it will generally be better to treat it as a vice and not merely as a problem of health regulation like the sale of milk. If the law speaks with a clear voice, it is easier to set in motion the educative and alleviative programs which are essential if the vice is to be checked at its root.

To anyone who shares what have been the fundamental values of Western society, an abandonment of the universal respect for the value of human life must seem a harm — a change for the worse — not only to those whose lives are lost as a result but also to those who are persuaded to commit the unjust killings. At the root of Western moral thought is the conviction of Socrates that the man who does an injustice harms himself more than he harms his victim; he makes himself less of a man, and thus altogether worse off.[100] On the other hand, to someone who disputes these values in their application to abortion, the first and even the second scheme of abortion regulation must seem pointless and harmful. Between the two ranges of opinion there need be no further jurisprudential issue; it is just that the calculations or balances of harm are drawn up with different weights.

The jurisprudential questions remain, whatever the fundamental values in balance. Ends must be carefully clarified, and means related strictly to mutually compatible ends, not to vague hopes, nor to compromises which in pursuit of the immediately attainable lose sight of both the ultimately and the immediately desirable. The most popular schemes in current discussion happen to be compromises that muddle together aims and elements of all three model schemes, and so more or less obviously diverge from the jurisprudential ideal of rational coordination of means with clear and coherent ends. "Pragmatism" and "moderate reform" are not synonyms for rationality; in much recent thought, they are substitutes.

100. Plato, *Gorgias* 469 and *passim*.

Appendix A

NOTES ON THE ABORTION ACT 1967 (U.K.)

1. The Act draws a sharp distinction between two types of lawful abortion. Emergency abortions are lawful when performed by a medical practitioner who is of the opinion, formed in good faith, that an abortion is immediately necessary to save the life or to prevent "grave permanent injury to the physical or mental health" of the pregnant woman: s.1(4). Other abortions are lawful when performed by a medical practitioner, if any two medical practitioners are of the opinion, formed in good faith, that the continuance of the pregnancy "would involve risk to the life of the pregnant woman or of injury to the physical or mental health of the pregnant woman or any existing children of her family, greater than if the pregnancy were terminated," or that there is "substantial [1] risk that if the child were born it would suffer from such physical or mental abnormalities as to be seriously handicapped": s.1(1).

Not only (a) may the medical practitioners take into account a risk to the health of persons other than the pregnant woman (and the unborn child), but also (b) in determining such risk to health, "account may be taken of the pregnant woman's actual or reasonably foreseeable environment": s.1(2). When people speak of "the social clause" they may be referring to either (a) or (b) and very often to both.

It is the existence of the so-called social clause that perhaps more than any other feature of the Act gives the average citizen, doctor, and parliamentarian the impression that the Act considerably relaxes or liberalizes the law on abortion. This impression is of great social significance, and no doubt of itself profoundly affects the working of the Act's scheme of abortion regulation. But the fact is that in the first 13 months of the Act's operation, only 3.9 percent of lawfully notified abortions were stated to be on the grounds of risk to the health of existing chil-

1. In considering the meaning of "substantial," and the effect of the Act on medical ethics, it will be noted that an editorial in the *Lancet* for 12 July 1969, p. 89, commended abortions at the 24th week of pregnancy in certain cases wherever the risk of congenital abnormality is 1 in 10 or greater.

dren.[2] Far more significant than the "social clause" in this sense, is the fact that the Act, by drawing the sharp distinction already mentioned, sanctions abortion where the anticipated injury to health[3] is not grave and permanent but slight and transient, and where the risk of such injury is not substantial or serious but merely "greater than if the pregnancy were terminated." This fact is emphasized by the printed form provided for certification in accordance with the Abortion Regulations 1968.[4] The certifying doctors need do no more than sign the form, having ringed a number: for example, "2. the continuance of the pregnancy would involve risk of injury to the physical or mental health of the pregnant woman greater than if the pregnancy were terminated;" or "3. the continuance of the pregnancy would involve risk of injury to the physical or mental health of the existing child(ren) of the family of the pregnant woman greater than if the pregnancy were terminated."

As C. B. Goodhart has said: "Since the almost non-existent risk to the life of a healthy woman in an abortion properly performed early on in pregnancy is indeed likely to be less than the present very low, but not wholly negligible, risk in childbirth, it is hard to see how any doctor could justify a refusal to give such a certificate. Whatever Parliament may have intended, this is in effect abortion on demand, subject only to a doctor's right to refuse to participate if he can prove a genuine conscientious objection."[5]

2. The Act (which does not apply to Northern Ireland) came into force on 27 April 1968. From time to time since then, Ministers have supplied Parliament with statistics based on the notifications required by the Act. These statistics relate to England and Wales; Scottish figures are issued separately, and are not included in Table A and commentary. The appropriate graph of the figures in columns IV and V

2. Sec. of State for Social Services, *Parliamentary Debates* (*House of Commons*), 16 June 1969, col. *9–13*.

3. Note that in 1960, the World Health Organization defined "health" as "a state of complete physical, mental, and social well-being, not simply the absence of illness and disease." See 41 *Bulletin New York Academy of Medicine* 410 (1965). Note also the looseness of the English requirements as against those in the California legislation of 1967, where what is in question is "mental illness to the extent that the woman is dangerous to herself or to the person or property of others, or is in need of supervision or restraint" (Cal. Health and Safety Code sec. 25954). Even so, however, 86% of the abortions lawfully performed in California during the first eleven months under the new law were performed on grounds of "mental health": Phyllis B. Thurstone, "Therapeutic Abortion: The Experience of San Mateo County General Hospital and the State of California," 209 *J. Amer. Med. Ass.* 229, 230 (1969).

4. Statutory Instruments, 1968 No. 390, Schedule 1.

5. [1968], 2 *Brit. Med. J.* 298.

John M. Finnis

Table A. Abortions lawfully notified, England and Wales, 1968–1969.

I Period	II Cumulative total at end of period	III Notifications within period	IV Average daily rate within period	V Equivalent annual rate
27 April–24 June 1968	3,863	3,863	65	24,000
24 June–8 October	13,042	9,179	87	32,000
8 October–31 December	22,256	9,214	110	40,000
31 December 1968–25 February 1969	28,849	6,593	118	43,000
25 February–27 May	41,496	12,647	139	51,000
27 May–1 July	46,714	5,218	149	54,000

SOURCE: Figures supplied by Ministers: see *Parl. Deb.* (*H.C.*) vol. 767, col. *184;* vol. 770, col. *84;* vol. 771, col.192; vol. 776, col. *137;* vol. 780, col. *10;* vol. 781, col. *199;* vol. 785, col. *9; Parl. Deb.* (*H.L.*) vol. 304, col. 252.

produces an ascending and rather strikingly straight line. If the established and uniform trend were to continue, the average daily rate in April 1970 would be about 220, corresponding to 80,000 per annum, and the number of abortions performed in the second year of the Act's operation would be about 67,000, as against about 39,000 in the first year.

It is possible that some of the notable increase in the rate of lawful abortions observable during the first 15 months of the Act's operation has been due to an increased influx of women from outside the United Kingdom. However, it seems unlikely that this is the major cause of the increase. In the period from 27 April to 31 December 1968, 5 percent of women aborted in England and Wales gave a place of residence outside the United Kingdom.[6] In the period from 1 January to 1 July 1969, the number rose, but only to 7.3 percent of the total.[7] Perhaps more significant (since it is impossible to estimate how many women give false addresses) is the fact that the proportion of abortions performed in National Health Service hospitals has remained virtually constant at about 60 percent of all abortions being performed in England and Wales. Since it is most unlikely that many foreign women, coming to England to be aborted, would find it possible or desirable to

6. *Parl. Deb.* (*H.C.*), 16 June 1969, col. *12.*
7. Calculation based on ministerial figures in *Parl. Deb.* (*House of Lords*), 15 July 1969, col. *252.*

attend N. H. S. hospitals, one would expect any considerable increase in the influx of such women to be reflected by a fall in the proportion of abortions performed in these hospitals relative to the total number of abortions being performed. A very slight fall is observable, but it is from 60.8 percent in mid-1968 to 59.2 percent in mid-1969,[8] a change which seems quite insufficient to support the hypothesis that the 100 percent increase in the total abortion rate over the same period is owing largely to an increased influx of foreign women.

3. It is commonly supposed that the majority, even the great majority (the most popular figure is 80 percent), of women seeking abortion in modern Western societies are married women living with their husbands. Many supporters of reform use this supposition to support an argument that reform would not occcasion sexual promiscuity and a change in sexual *mores*.[9] Whatever the merits of this argument, which is not in question in this article, the supposition has not been borne out by the evidence available, for the first time, since the Abortion Act 1967 came into force.

During the first nine weeks of the Act's operation, only 45 percent of women aborted were married and living with their husbands. During the 13 weeks ended 31 December 1968, the proportion had fallen to a little over 43 percent, and over 47.5 percent of the women aborted were single (the remainder being widowed, divorced, or separated).[10]

4. In a letter to the *Lancet* in 1968, Harold Frederiksen and James W. Brackett stated: "From data presented for countries in which contraception is already practised by a substantial proportion of the population, it appears that permissive abortion laws may contribute more to a diminution of the effective practice of contraception than to a reduc-

8. *Parl. Deb.* (*H.C.*), 16 June 1969, col. *12*.

9. See, e.g., Taussig, *Abortion supra* n. 22 at 388; Dickens, *Abortion and the Law* 111 (1966); Roy Lucas, 46 *N. Carolina Law Review* 730 (1968); "Comment," 14 *Wayne Law Review* 1006, 1019 (1968); Marvin M. Moore, "Antiquated Abortion Laws," 20 *Washington and Lee L. Rev.* 250, 256 (1963); "Note," 7 *Journal of Family Law* 496 (1967); etc. Note that the *Report of the Inter-Departmental Committee on Abortion* (H.M.S.O. 1939) stated, in par. 37, that "both the mortality statistics and the figures of cases treated in hospital show that the overwhelming majority of abortions occur among married women."

10. See Registrar-General's *Quarterly Returns for England and Wales*, for quarter ended 31 March 1969 (H.M.S.O. 1969), 23; *Parl. Deb.* (*H.C.*), 16 June 1969, col. *12*. These figures correspond strikingly to the experience of California and Colorado since this relaxation of abortion law in 1967: see Thurstone, "Therapeutic Abortion" *supra* n. 3 at 230; William Droegemueller, E. Stewart Taylor, Vera E. Drose, "The First Year of Experience in Colorado with the new Abortion Law" 103 *Am. J. Obstetrics and Gynecology* 694 (1969). See also, by the same authors, "Demographic Effects of Abortion" 83 *Public Health Reports* 999, 1008 (1968).

John M. Finnis

tion in the birthrate beyond the level already obtained by contraception before the enactment of liberal abortion legislation." [11] Be this as it may, since the Abortion Act came into force a good deal of evidence has become available concerning the birth-control practices of women seeking abortions.

Of one series of 1,000 women studied between 1964 and 1969, 30 percent normally used no method of birth control, and 48 percent used none on the occasion of the unwanted conception.[12] In a recent study of women who obtained lawful abortions through the Birmingham Pregnancy Advisory Service, 45.8 percent normally used no method and 73.5 percent used none at the time of conception.[13] Of the first 500 women aborted through the offices of the London Pregnancy Advisory Service, 42 percent normally used no method and 70 percent used none at the time of conception.[14] In the last-mentioned study, the Honorary Medical Secretary of the Service stated that 60 percent of the women were single, but "only 8% of the pregnancies resulted from a casual union. Many an intelligent young unmarried woman has admitted that she viewed taking oral contraceptives as a degree of commitment she was not prepared for." [15] Nearly 12 percent of the first-mentioned series of 1,000 women were doctors or nurses, a further 11 percent were students or teachers, and only 4 percent were schoolgirls who might, perhaps, be expected to be more ignorant of birth-control methods.[16] The President and Honorary Secretary of the Royal Society of Obstetricians and Gynaecologists stated in July 1969 that "evidence is accumulating that contraception among the young is an irrelevance." [17]

5. Under a scheme of abortion regulation as relaxed as that adumbrated by the Abortion Act, it might be expected that mortality (and morbidity) from unlawful abortion would decline appreciably. This does not appear to have occurred, as Table B indicates. Figures for such deaths after September 1968 are not yet publicly available, though it is known that the total number of notified deaths from all forms of abortion for the period 1 April 1968 to 31 March 1969 was 42, as against 36 for the same period in 1967–68.[18]

As for morbidity occasioned by unlawful abortion, no strong evi-

11. [1968] 2 *Lancet* 167.
12. P. L. Diggory, "Some Experiences of Therapeutic Abortion" [1969] 1 the *Lancet* 873, 875.
13. *Id.*
14. Sara R. Abels, [1969] 1 *Lancet* 1051.
15. *Id.*
16. Diggory, "Therapeutic Abortion" 873, 875.
17. Letter to the *Times*, 23 July 1969.
18. Sec. of State for Social Services, *Parl. Deb.* (H.C.), 16 June 1969, col. *12*.

Table B. Deaths notified as due to abortions induced for reasons other than medical or legal indications (England and Wales).

Year	No. of deaths
1961	23
1962	29
1963	21
1964	24
1965	21
1966	30
1967	17
1968 (January to April)	6
1968 (May to December)	15

SOURCE: Figures supplied by the Minister of Health, *Parl. Deb.* (H.C.) 18 October 1968, col. *192;* Registrar-General, *Quarterly Returns for England and Wales,* for quarter ended 31 March 1969 (H.M.S.O. 1969) at 21. All these figures exclude a category of deaths due to abortion notified to the Registrar-General without specifying whether induced or spontaneous. The *Report on Confidential Enquiries into Maternal Deaths in England and Wales 1964–1966* (H.M.S.O. 1969) confirms the substantial accuracy of the Registrar-General's statistics, but reveals that many of the deaths in the last-mentioned category are in fact due to illegal abortions. Thus a truer picture of the total number of deaths due to illegal abortion may be gained by adjusting each of the figures in the table upwards by about 30%.

dence is available yet. The sponsor of the Abortion Act stated in the House of Commons on 15 July 1969 that admissions to the London Emergency Bed Centre for spontaneous or incomplete abortions (a category which includes bungled criminal abortions) were 870 in the first quarter of 1969 as against 1363 in the first quarter of 1966.[19] However, the Emergency Bed Service Annual Report for 1964 indicated that many hospitals had a prejudice against abortion admissions, preferring to leave them to the Emergency Bed Service.[20] So the decline since 1966 may reflect a change in hospital attitudes now that hospitals are ready to perform twenty times as many abortions as in 1966.

The official Criminal Statistics for 1968 show that, while the annual average of *illegal* abortions "known to the police" was 235 between 1965 and 1967, the number in 1968 was 247.

6. Early in 1969, an unmarried student was aborted in a Scottish hospital. The certifying doctors ringed the clauses on the certificate which concern "greater risk to the mental or physical health of the pregnant woman . . ." and "substantial risk of abnormality." In fact the fetus

19. *Parl. Deb.* (H.C.), 15 July 1969, col. 414.
20. Dickens, *Abortion and the Law supra* n. 120 at 116.

was more than 28 weeks old and after the abortion lived for nine hours, being discovered to be alive when the porter carrying it to an incinerator in a paper bag heard its cries. At a public inquiry into the affair, the Procurator Fiscal, representing the Crown, suggested that, while the Act gave doctors a right to terminate pregnancy, it did not take away from them the duty to take every step to revive a child who might be viable. Not surprisingly, various medical witnesses opined that, since the object of abortion normally is to prevent the child's survival, resuscitatory measures might not be in place. But the jury unanimously recommended, not only (1) that legislation should be introduced prohibiting abortion when the fetus is approaching or has reached the stage of viability, but also (2) that in all cases where an infant of or approaching or about viable age or apparently or possibly viable is to be delivered by abortion, all facilities and resuscitatory measures applied in cases of ordinary birth should be adopted.[21]

The oddity, not to say downright absurdity, of this well-meaning recommendation may help to indicate how far the scheme of the Abortion Act 1967, as concretely understood in the society to whose order or disorder it contributes, diverges from substantive rationality.

21. "Death of a Baby — Inquiry in Glasgow," [1969], 2 *Brit. Med. J.* 704, 705. In a letter to the *Times* after the inquiry (2 June 1969), Professor Glanville Williams suggested that abortions after the 24th week of pregnancy should not be lawful except in a real emergency. Cf. *supra* n. 81. The 1967 California law draws the line at 20 weeks (*Col. Health and Safety Code,* sec. 25953).

Appendix B

STATISTICS ON ABORTIONS AND MATERNAL DEATHS AFTER ILLEGAL ABORTIONS IN SOME EUROPEAN STATES

In some of the tables which follow, there is a category termed "Other Abortions." This term refers to official figures for hospital admissions for all forms of incomplete, spontaneous, missed, or septic abortion. Thus it includes a certain number of bungled illegal abortions, as well as a number of spontaneous abortions (miscarriages). Is there any way of estimating how many of the total number of admissions are consequent on illegal abortions?

A very thorough recent study of births and abortions in Belfast (in Northern Ireland) indicates that not less than 12 percent nor more than 17 percent of all conceptions result in spontaneous abortions detectable by the woman concerned.[1] In this population, urban and well-serviced with state hospitals, just under 12 percent of all conceptions resulted in an abortion for which medical treatment was given; in nine cases out of ten, this treatment was given in hospital, even though of the women treated in hospital, only one in four passed any part of the fetus itself in hospital. The authors were confident that only a negligible number — at the outside 1 percent — of the women treated in hospital had had an illegally induced abortion. From this study it is reasonable to conclude, then, that *not more than* about 12½ percent of all conceptions in a population could result in abortion (other than induced abortion) calling for hospital treatment of any sort.[2]

1. A. C. Stevenson et al., "Observations on the Results of Pregnancies in Women Resident in Belfast," 23 *Annals Human Genetics* 395, 396 (1959). See also Donald Warburton and F. Clarke Fraser, "Spontaneous Abortion Risks in Man," 16 *American Journal Human Genetics* 1, 2 (1964); Christopher Tietze, Alan F. Guttmacher, and S. Rubin, "Unintentional Abortions in 1,497 Planned Pregnancies," 142 *J. Am. Med. Ass.* 1348, 1349 (1950).

2. In England and Wales in 1964, there were about 850,000 live births, an unknown number of illegal abortions (not less than 10,000), and 75,000 cases of abortion (of all kinds) treated in National Health Service hospitals, plus a small number treated in private clinics. These figures tally well with the Belfast depth-study, and suggest that the figure of 12½% (conceptions ending in hospital treatment for noninduced abortion) is a high maximum which in many areas and populations might be (as in Czechoslovakia and Poland it is known to be) considerably lower.

Table C. Legal abortions in Sweden and Denmark.

Year	Legal abortions (Sweden)	Legal abortions per 1,000 live births (Sweden)	Legal abortions (Denmark)	Legal abortions per 1,000 live births (Denmark)
1939	439	5	484	7
1940	506	5	522	7
1941	496	5	519	7
1942	568	5	824	10
1943	703	6	977	12
1944	1088	8	1286	14
1945	1623	12	1577	17
1946	2378	18	1930	20
1947	3534	28	2240	24
1948	4585	36	2543	30
1949	5503	45	3425	43
1950	5889	51	3909	49
1951	6328	57	4743	62
1952	5322	48	5031	65
1953	4915	45	4795	61
1954	5089	48	5140	67
1955	4562	43	5381	70
1956	3851	36	4522	59
1957	3386	32	4023	53
1958	2823	27	3895	52
1959	3071	29	3587	48
1960	2792	27	3918	51
1961	2909	28	4124	54
1962	3205	30	3996	51
1963	3528	31	3971	48
1964	4671	38	4527	54
1965	6245	51	5190	60
1966	—	—	—	—
1967	9,600	79		

SOURCE: Christopher Tietze, "Induced Abortion and Sterilization as Methods of Fertility Control," 18 *J. Chronic Diseases* 1161, 1163 (1965); Tietze, "Abortion in Europe," 57 *Am. J. Pub. Health* 1923, 1928 (1967); Tietze and Lewit, "Abortion," 220 *Scientific American* 21, 24 (1969).

This enables an estimate to be made of the proportion of the "Other Abortion" cases, in certain of the East European statistics, which should be ascribed to illegally induced abortion. The number of conceptions which might have ended in some kind of noninduced abortion is calculated by adding the number of live births to the whole of the number of "other abortions." (All conceptions assumed to have ended in induced abortion, legal or illegal, can be ignored because, in the event, these conceptions cannot have ended in noninduced abortion.) The proportion of this number of conceptions that might be expected to have ended in noninduced abortion calling for hospital treatment is, as a maximum, 12½ percent. (The resulting figure may in fact overstate the expected number of noninduced abortions calling for hospital treatment, since the number of conceptions used as the basis of the calculation in fact includes some conceptions which ended in illegally induced abortions calling for hospital treatment.)

Thus in Hungary in 1954, for example, with 132,100 live births and 34,300 "Other Abortions," one would expect that at most 20,000 women would have noninduced abortions calling for hospital treatment. So it is reasonable to suppose that the other 14,300 women who had hospital treatment for abortion (other than legally induced abortion) were victims of illegal abortions.

In respect to Czechoslovakia and Poland, no calculation can be made on this basis, since the figures for "Other Abortions" show that it has never been the case, in these countries, that 12½ percent of all conceptions ended in noninduced abortion resulting in hospital treatment; and there is no way of determining the relevant lower proportion. One can, however, observe that in neither country has the proportion of "Other Abortions" to conceptions (that is, to conceptions other than those known to have ended in induced abortion) fallen significantly, if at all, between 1953–54 and 1963–64, despite falling birthrates and legalization of abortion.

As regards deaths registered as due to illegal abortion in East Europe, Mehlan's figures[3] are often cited:

Poland:	1959	76
	1965	26
Czechoslovakia:	1959	53
	1962	11
Hungary:	1959	83
	1964	24

These figures cannot, however, be relied on. Malcom Potts, a passionate advocate of free abortion, has cited the analyses of the Czech figures

3. K.-H. Mehlan, "Combating Illegal Abortion in the Socialist Countries of Europe," 13 *World Med. J.* 84, 86 (1965); Ruth Roemer, "Abortion Law: The Approaches of Different Nations," 57 *Am. J. Pub. Health* 1906, 1912 (1967).

Table D. Births and abortions in Czechoslovakia, Poland, and Hungary.

Year	Live births (thousands)	Birthrate per 1,000 population	Legal abortions (thousands)	Other abortions (thousands)
		Czechoslovakia		
1953	271.7	21.2	1.5	29.1
1954	266.7	20.6	2.8	30.6
1955	265.2	20.3	2.1	33.0
1956	262.0	19.8	3.1	31.0
1957	252.7	18.9	7.3	30.2
1958	235.0	17.4	61.4	27.7
1959	217.0	16.0	79.1	26.4
1960	217.3	15.9	88.3	26.3
1961	218.4	15.8	94.3	26.0
1962	217.5	15.7	89.8	26.1
1963	236.0	16.9	70.5	29.4
1964	241.3	17.2	70.7	28.5
1965	231.6	16.4	79.6	26.2
		Poland		
1953	779.0	29.5	1.2	69.5
1954	778.1	29.1	—	—
1955	793.8	29.1	1.4	100.2
1956	779.8	28.0	18.9	85.4
1957	782.3	27.6	36.4	85.4
1958	755.5	26.3	44.2	82.2
1959	728.9	24.7	79.0	82.5
1960	669.5	22.6	150.4	73.4
1961	627.6	20.9	143.8	72.8
1962	599.5	19.6	140.4	70.3
1963	583.7	19.0	146.5 (?) 190.0	113.8 (?) 70.3
1964	560.9	18.1	177.5 (?)	69.3
		Hungary		
1950	195.6	20.9	1.7	34.3
1951	190.6	20.2	1.7	36.1
1952	185.8	19.5	1.7	42.0
1953	206.9	21.5	2.8	39.9
1954	223.3	23.0	16.3	42.0
1955	210.4	21.4	35.4	43.1
1956	192.8	19.5	82.5	41.1
1957	167.2	17.0	123.4	39.5

Table D. *Continued.*

Year	Live births (thousands)	Birthrate per 1,000 population	Legal abortions (thousands)	Other abortions (thousands)
		Hungary		
1958	158.4	16.0	145.6	37.4
1959	150.8	15.2	152.4	35.3
1960	146.5	14.6	162.2	33.8
1961	140.4	14.0	170.0	33.7
1962	130.1	12.9	163.7	33.9
1963	132.3	13.1	173.8	34.1
1964	132.1	13.1	184.4	34.3
1965	133.0	13.1	180.3	33.7
1966	—	—	—	—
1967	148.9	—	187.5	—

SOURCE: Christopher Tietze and Hans Lehfeldt, "Legal Abortion in Eastern Europe," 175 *J. Am. Med. Ass.* 1149, 1150 (1961); Tietze, "Methods of Fertility Control" at 1166; and "Abortion in Europe" at 1928; Potts, "Legal Abortion in Eastern Europe" *supra* n. 6, App. B; Mehlan, "The Socialist Countries of Europe," in Berelson, *Family Planning and Population Programs supra* n. 74 at 207, 209; Klinger, "Abortion Programs," *ibid.* 465 at 475; Tietze and Lewit, "Abortion" *supra* n. 24 at 25.

made by J. Lukás[4] and by A. Černoch.[5] Potts states that Černoch's are based on the more thorough analysis.[6]

Lukás' figures are:
    Czechoslovakia: 1959   14
                             1962   15
Černoch's figures are:
    Czechoslovakia: 1959   10
                             1962   9

The contrast drawn by Mehlan thus evaporates.

It will also be noticed that in Czechoslovakia, in 1962, the ratio of these deaths to live births (assuming only 9 deaths, rather than 15) was 1:24,000, and in England (where the first scheme still prevailed), about 1:28,000. The third scheme had then been in force in Czechoslovakia for five years.

4. J. Lukás, "Abortion in Czechoslovakia" in *Sex and Human Relations* (International Planned Parenthood Federation Conference: 1965), 93.

5. A. Černoch, "Les Autorisations d'Interruptions de Grossesse en Tchécoslovaquie," 160 *Gynaecologia* 293 (1965).

6. Malcom Potts, "Legal Abortion in Eastern Europe," 59 *Eugenics Rev.* 232, 242 (1967).

DAVID W. LOUISELL AND
JOHN T. NOONAN, JR.

Constitutional Balance

Moral argument, jurisprudential theory, and social and medical facts intertwine in a consideration of the constitutional issues posed by abortion. In this paper we propose to examine the twin questions: Is it constitutional for the State to regulate abortion? Is it constitutional for the State not to regulate abortion? As a start to answering both questions, we shall examine the status accorded to the fetus by Anglo-American law. Although cases which answer a legal question in one context do not necessarily provide answers to other questions, there is a fund of experience, tested by reason, in the developing attitude of the courts to the being within the womb.

I. THE FETUS IN THE LAW

The Fetus in the Law of Property

The English courts, beginning in the late eighteenth century, held that a fetus is within the description in a devise to "children living at the time of his [life tenant's] decease"[1] and is also within the description of a testamentary disposition to children "born in her [testatrix] lifetime."[2] The case of *Wallis v. Hodson* allowed a posthumous child to have an accounting of her father's intestate estate years after her birth where her mother and second husband

1. Doe *dem. Clarke v. Clarke*, 2 H.Bl. 399, 126 Eng. Rep. 617 (C.P. 1795). Language in the case indicates that it was the court's unequivocal opinion that the unborn child was a human being: "[A]n infant *en ventre sa mere*, who by the course and order of nature is then living, comes clearly within the description of 'children living at the time of his decease.'" *Id*. at 401, 126 Eng. Rep. at 618.
2. *Trower v. Butts*, 1 Sim. & Stu. 181, 57 Eng. Rep. 72, 73 (Ch. 1823).

held the property.[3] The unborn child was also considered to be a life in being for purposes of the perpetuities rule even where it was not to the benefit of the unborn child to be so considered.[4]

The American cases, based upon English common law rules, reached much the same results. Faced with the necessity of making decisions involving considerations of the existence of prenatal life and given the uncertain knowledge of embryology, American courts chose, uniformly, to treat the unborn child as a human being. A posthumous child is able to take under a will description bequeathing property to those "living at my (testator's) decease." [5] The unborn child can also take, under a will, as a tenant in common with its own mother.[6] It can have a sale of land set aside where the sale involves descendant land a portion of which is held to vest in the unborn child prior to its birth.[7]

3. 2 Atk. 114, 117, 26 Eng. Rep. 472, 473 (Ch. 1740). The Lord Chancellor states that "both by the rules of the common and civil law, she [the unborn child] was, to all intents and purposes, a child, as much as if born in the father's lifetime."

4. *Thellusson v. Woodford*, 4 Ves. 227, 31 Eng. Rep. 117 (Ch. 1798). J. Buller, in replying to the contention that the unborn child is a nonentity, said: "Let us see, what this non-entity can do. He may be vouched in a recovery, though it is for the purpose of making him answer over in value. He may be an executor. He may take under the Statute of Distributions. [citation] He may take by devise. He may be entitled under a charge for raising portions. He may have an injunction; and he may have a guardian." *Id.* at 322, 31 Eng. Rep. at 163. In answer to the contention that an unborn child is to be considered as being alive only in those cases when it is to its own benefit, he replied: "Why should not children *en ventre sa mere* be considered generally as in existence? They are entitled to all the privileges of other persons." *Id.* at 323, 31 Eng. Rep. at 164.

5. *Hall v. Hancock*, 32 Mass. (15 Pick.) 255 (1834). Chief Justice Shaw quoted with approval the language of the Lord Chancellor in *Wallis v. Hodson*, quoted in parts in *supra* n. 3. *Accord, Barnett v. Pinkston*, 238 Ala. 327, 191 So. 371 (1939); *Cowles v. Cowles*, 56 Conn. 240, 13 A. 414 (1887); *McLain v. Howald*, 120 Mich. 274, 79 N.W. 182 (1899). In *Hall* the court also explicitly negates the applicability of the "quickness" requirement found in certain of the criminal law cases, to cases involving issues of descent and distribution. *See* the section on The Fetus in the Criminal Law infra, this essay. CAL. PROB. CODE § 250 (West, 1956) provides: "A posthumous child is considered as living at the death of the parent." Section 255, amended as recently as 1961, provides that an illegitimate child is the heir of his mother, whether the child is "born or conceived."

6. *Biggs v. McCarty*, 86 Ind. 352 (1882).

7. *Deal v. Sexton*, 144 N.C. 110, 56 S.E. 691 (1907). The court recognized that constitutional rights of the unborn child are at stake when it stated: "If we hold, as we must, that the inheritance vested immediately in the plaintiff, while *en ventre sa mere*, upon the death of the father, the conclusion must follow that such inheritance ought not to be divested . . . [A] person must have an opportunity of being heard before a court can deprive him of his rights, and . . . an unborn child, not having been made a party, can recover from those claiming his title." *Id.* at 110-11, 56 S.E. at 692.

David W. Louisell and John T. Noonan, Jr.

The suggestion that the unborn child is a legal nonentity was clearly rejected in *Industrial Trust Co. v. Wilson*.[8] Here the court held that a posthumous child was to begin sharing in the proceeds of a trust at the date of her father's death rather than upon the date of her subsequent birth. Thus, the child was an actual income recipient prior to the event of her birth.

The state of the law in American courts is fairly well summed up in *In re Holthausen's Will*, where a New York court states, "It has been the uniform and unvarying decision of all common law courts in respect of estate matters for at least the past two hundred years that a child en ventre sa mere is 'born' and 'alive' for all purposes for his benefit."[9]

The requirement, stated in certain cases,[10] that the courts recognize prenatal existence only for the benefit of a child subsequently born alive, has been suggested by some to indicate that the courts have merely developed a rule of construction and that these cases are no authority on the question of whether or not the unborn child does, in fact, have any legal rights.[11] But when a lawsuit is commenced on behalf of an unborn child on the theory that property rights accrued to him while he is still in gestation, almost inevitably that child will have proceeded to term and been successfully born or will have miscarried or been stillborn before the case which decides his rights is adjudicated and the opinion written. Thus at the time the court speaks, the child, by his representative, is actually before the court requesting some kind of relief. Similarly, where a lawsuit is based on accrual of property rights to a child prior to his birth, but is commenced after his birth, he is likewise before the court when the opinion is written. Under such circumstances it is understandable, but really gratuitous and superfluous, for the court to observe that the child must have been born alive. The observation is only dictum; it does not necessarily require a different result in those cases where the observation is inappropriate.

8. 61 R.I. 169, 200 A. 467 (1938).
9. 175 Misc. 1022, 1024, 26 N.Y.S.2d 140, 143 (Sur. Ct. 1941).
10. *In re Well's Will*, 129 Misc. 447, 221 N.Y.S. 714 (Sur. Ct. 1927). The court states: "It is well settled that a child en ventre sa mere, *which is subsequently born alive* and capable of living, is considered a child living, so as to take a beneficial interest in a bequest or devise when the description is 'child living.'" *Id.* at 451, 221 N.Y.S. at 719 (emphasis added).
11. *See In re Scanelli*, 208 Misc. 804, 142 N.Y.S.2d 411 (Sur. Ct. 1955).

The property rule which recognizes human life in the unborn child prevails whether or not it inures to his personal benefit, and even where it works a detriment to him. Thus, in *Barnett v. Pinkston*[12] a child born two months after the death of his father was held to be a "living child" at the death of his father. The child lived only several hours, leaving its mother as its sole heir. She died a few days later. The remainder that had vested in the child was held to have passed to her and through her to her heirs. The court's recognition that a child en ventre sa mere is a child in esse, thus produced no personal benefit to the child. In *In re Sankey's Estate*[13] a child conceived but not born was held bound by a decree entered against the living heirs.

These property cases have established this proposition: the ordinary person when he uses "children" in a will means to designate by the term "children" those who are conceived but not yet out of the womb. This interpretation has, to our knowledge, never been criticized as fanciful or arbitrary or imposed by a court in the service of some theological scheme. It has been generally accepted as a fair interpretation of the ordinary use of language and of the ordinary person's notion of who are indeed "children."

The Fetus in the Criminal Law

The first reference to abortion in English criminal law occurs in Bracton. He transposed the canon *Sicut ex* to England by saying that aborting a woman by blow or poison is homicide if the embryo "were formed and especially if it were ensouled."[14] This language was repeated early in the seventeenth century by Coke in a passage which begins, "If a woman be quick with child . . . this a great misprision and no murder."[15] Later in the seventeenth century "quick" is clearly identified with "developed pregnancy." Hale says, "If a woman be quick or great with

12. 238 Ala. 327, 191 So. 371 (1939).
13. 199 Cal. 391, 249 P. 517 (1926). *See also Orange v. State Farm Mut. Auto. Ins. Co.*, 443 S.W. 2d 650 (Ky. Ct. App. 1969) (a viable unborn child is a legal person with a separate existence of its own so that he is a member of a class excluded from coverage by a "family" or "household" exclusion clause of an automobile liability policy).
14. Henry de Bracton, *De legibus et consuetudinibus Angliae*, 3.2.4 (London, 1640).
15. Edward Coke, *The Third Part of the Institutes of the Laws of England* (London, Printed for E. and R. Brooke, 1797), sec. 50.

child . . . it is not murder or manslaughter by the law of England, because it is not yet in *rerum natura,* tho it be a great crime." [16] The statutory law, 43 Geo. III c. 58, which became effective in 1803, made it a felony punishable by death to administer poison "to cause and procure the miscarriage of any woman then quick with child," and a felony punishable by fine, imprisonment, pillory, whipping, or transportation to attempt by drug or instrument to procure the miscarriage of any woman "not being or not being proved to be quick with child." In *Rex v. Phillips* in 1812, the doctors disagreed as to when a fetus could be said to be quick, and the court ruled that it was quick when the mother felt the fetus move.[17] In later nineteenth-century America, "quick" was defined in the same way, despite doubts as to the medical significance of the term and a tendency to interpret abortion statutes as applicable to any stage of the pregnancy.[18]

Medical writers were critical of the retention of the distinction by the courts. Thus, criticizing the increase of abortion "especially among the higher classes," Isaac M. Quimby in the *Journal of the American Medical Association* for 1887 wrote, "This fallacious idea that there is no life until quickening takes place has been the foundation of, and formed the basis of, and has been the excuse to ease or appease the guilty conscience which has led to the destruction of thousands of human lives." [19] Several times in the course of the nineteenth century the House of Delegates of the American Medical Association called on the states to reform their laws and to prevent abortion.[20] In 1859 Horatio R. Storer of Boston reported for the Committee on Criminal Abortion, and obtained unanimous adoption of a resolution condemning the act of procuring abortion at every period of gestation except as necessary for preserving the life of either mother or child. The

16. Matthew Hale, *The History of the Pleas of the Crown,* 1st American ed. vol. 1. Notes and references to later cases by W. A. Stokes and E. Ingersoll. (Philadelphia: Robert H. Small, 1847), p. 432.

17. William O. Russell, *A Treatise on Crimes and Misdemeanors,* vol. 1 (London: J. Butterworth and son, 1819), p. 797.

18. Joel P. Bishop, *Commentaries on the Law of Statutory Crimes,* 2nd ed. (Boston: Little, Brown, 1883), sec. 746.

19. "Introduction to Medical Jurisprudence," 9 *Journal of the American Medical Association* (August 6, 1887); 164; *see also* N. C. Markham, "Foeticide and Its Prevention," *ibid.,* 11 December 8, 1888), 805.

20. American Medical Association, *1846–1958 Digest of Official Actions,* ed. F. J. L. Blasingame (1959), p. 66.

reason for the resolution was stated to be the increasing frequency "of such unwarrantable destruction of human life." [21] This nineteenth-century history indicates both that the medical objection to abortion was the physician's defense of the human life of the fetus and that the medical objection to existing law was the medical unsoundness of the attempted distinctions earlier made on the basis of the age of the fetus.

Even at common law, some nineteenth-century courts refused to deny protection to the unborn child during the stage of development prior to quickening and held that abortion was just as illegal at that time as at a later period.[22] Other courts expressed dissatisfaction with the common law requirement but stated that it was up to the legislature to abolish the "quickening" element.[23]

As the legislatures of the various states began to codify existing law during the nineteenth century, the anticipated change in the abortion laws occurred. The quickening requirement often was abolished [24] so that the fetus was protected from the moment of conception throughout the entire period of gestation. Some jurisdictions extended protection by the means of a feticide statute[25] which made destruction of the fetus at any stage of development a criminal act and in some cases, where the fetus was "quick," made such destruction a capital offense.[26] States which prohibited abortion by specific statutes aimed at feticide abolished "quickening" as an element of the crime, while those states which utilized regular homicide (manslaughter) statutes generally retained that element.[27] But there was a minority view under which a convic-

21. American Medical Association, Minutes of the Annual Meeting, 1859, 10 The American Medical Gazette (1859), 409. "Abortion" to save the life of the child meant surgical removal of the child in a premature delivery.

22. Mills v. Commonwealth, 13 Pa. 630, aff'g 13 Pa. 633 (1850).

23. Mitchell v. Commonwealth, 78 Ky. 204 (1879). The court stated: "That the child shall be considered in existence from the moment of conception for the protection of its rights of property, and yet not in existence, until four or five months after the inception of its being, to the extent that it is a crime to destroy it, presents an anomaly in the law that ought to be provided against by the lawmaking department of the government." Id. at 209-10.

24. See, e.g., Cal. Penal Code § 274 (West 1954).

25. Hans v. State, 147 Neb. 67, 22 N.W.2d 385 (1946).

26. See Passley v. State, 194 Ga. 327, 21 S.E.2d 230 (1942).

27. Thus Wisconsin held that where the death of the mother resulted from an illegal abortion it was immaterial whether the fetus had quickened, but where the prosecution was for the death of the child he must have quickened. State v. Walters, 199 Wis. 68, 225 N.W. 167 (1929); State v. Dickinson, 41 Wis. 299 (1878).

tion of manslaughter could be sustained for destruction of the fetus at any stage of gestation.[28] The trend, however, was to protect the fetus by specific antiabortion laws rather than by application of homicide statutes, and, with the former, distinctions based on the various stages of fetal development were not generally made.

Historically the common law had recognized the inviolability of the unborn child by providing for suspension of execution of pregnant women under death sentence, at least when "quick."[29] This solicitude continues in modern statutes without regard to the stage of pregnancy.[30] Statutes imposing criminal sanctions protective of children's right of support from their parents also apply to the unborn child. These statutes also apply to the child at any stage of the pregnancy.[31]

In summary, starting from a misinterpretation of the canon law and treating quickening as a decisive moment to confer protection, English and American criminal law in the nineteenth century moved to a protection of the fetus throughout his life in the womb. Impetus for change came from informed medical opinion. The purpose of the change was not to protect the life of the mother but the life of the fetus. The response of the legislators and then of the courts to the new medical data was a response to data which showed the unreality of distinctions based on differences in the stage of fetal development.

The Fetus in the Law of Torts

Perhaps no other area of the law has undergone such a dramatic reversal as that of the law of torts in recognizing the legal existence of an unborn child.[32] Until World War II most American courts denied recovery in tort to the child who had been harmed by negligent injury to his mother while she carried him. This denial

28. See *State v. Atwood*, 54 Ore. 526, 102 P. 295 (1909).
29. 1 W. BLACKSTONE, *Commentaries* *456 (ed. W. Jones at 651, 1916); M. HALE, PLEAS OF THE CROWN vol. 2, pp. *413–14 (1st Am. ed. at 412–13, [1847]). *See generally* Geoffrey Hazard & David Louisell, "Death, the State, and the Insane: Stay of Execution," 9 *University of California at Los Angeles Law Review* (1962), 381.
30. *E.g.*, *Cal. Penal Code* §§ 3705–06 (West 1954).
31. *E.g.*, *id.* § 270 (West Supp. 1968): "A child conceived but not yet born is to be deemed an existing person insofar as this section [child neglect] is concerned."
32. *See* W. PROSSER, *Handbook of the Law of Torts* § 56 (3rd ed. 1964).

was predicated upon several factors, including the difficulty of proving causation in view of the then deficient state of medical knowledge. The primary reason for denying recovery, however, was reliance upon the statement of Justice Holmes in *Dietrich v. Northampton*,[33] that "the unborn child was a part of the mother at the time of the injury." [34] Since the rejection of this view in 1946, in the case of *Bonbrest v. Kotz*,[35] the law has proceeded apace to recognize the unborn child as a human being in this area as it had in others.

Many of the early cases required that the unborn child have reached the stage of viability at the time the injuries were inflicted in order to maintain an action.[36] The modern trend, however, has been to reject viability as a criterion and to allow recovery whenever the injury was received, provided that the elements of causation are properly established.[37] Where the child has died due to injuries received while in the womb, the cases have allowed recovery based on wrongful death actions where the fetus has

33. 138 Mass. 14, 17 (1884).

34. *Compare* with the statement made by Justice Holmes, the holding which appears to have been the settled rule, in *Prescott v. Robinson*, 74 N.H. 460, 69 A. 522 (1908), that the mother could not recover on her own behalf for injuries sustained by her unborn child. The mother had, unsuccessfully, claimed that the unborn child was a part of her.

35. 65 F.Supp. 138 (D.D.C. 1946).

36. *Id.; Scott v. McPheeters*, 33 Cal. App. 2d 629, 92 P.2d 678 (1939) (CAL. CIV. CODE § 29 [West 1954] expressly provides that the fetus is to be deemed an existing person); *Tursi v. New England Windsor Co.*, 19 Conn. Supp. 242, 111 A.2d 14 (1955); *Damasiewicz v. Gorsuch*, 197 Md. 417, 79 A.2d 550 (1951); *Keyes v. Constr. Serv., Inc.*, 340 Mass. 633, 165 N.E.2d 912 (1960); *Williams v. Marion Rapid Transit, Inc.*, 152 Ohio 114, 87 N.E.2d 334 (1949); *Mallison v. Pomeroy*, 205 Ore. 690, 291 P.2d 225 (1955); *Seattle-First Nat'l Bank v. Rankin*, 59 Wash. 2d 288, 367 P.2d 835 (1962).

37. *Hornbuckle v. Plantation Pipe Line Co.*, 212 Ga. 504, 93 S.E.2d 727 (1956); *Daley v. Meier*, 33 Ill. App. 2d 218, 178 N.E.2d 691 (1961); *Bennett v. Hymers*, 101 N.H. 483, 147 A.2d 108 (1958); *Smith v. Brennan*, 31 N.J. 353, 157 A.2d 497 (1960); *Kelly v. Gregory*, 282 App. Div. 542, 125 N.Y.S.2d 696 (1953); *Sinkler v. Kneale*, 401 Pa. 267, 164 A.2d 93 (1960); *Sylvia v. Gobeille*, 220 A.2d 222, 223–24 (R.I. 1966), where the court said: "While we could, as has sometimes been done elsewhere, justify our rejection of the viability concept on the medical fact that a fetus becomes a living human being from the moment of conception, we do so not on the authority of the biologist but because we are unable logically to conclude that a claim for an injury inflicted prior to viability is any less meritorious than one sustained after." W. PROSSER, *supra* note 32, § 56. "Viability" of a fetus is not a constant but depends on the anatomical and functional development of the particular baby. J. MORISON, FOETAL AND NEONATAL PATHOLOGY 99–100 (1963). The weight and length of the fetus are better guides than age to the state of fetal development, and weight and length vary with the individual, Peter Gruenwald, "Growth of the Human Fetus," 94 *American Journal of Obstetrics & Gynecology* (1966), 1112.

reached to stage of viability. At first, recovery was limited to those cases in which the child was born alive and then died due to injuries received prior to birth.[38] But perhaps the most significant cases for establishing the legal existence of a child prior to birth have been those very modern decisions which allow the parents, or survivors, to maintain such an action where the child is stillborn.[39] Thus, the unborn child, to whom live birth never comes, is held to be a "person" who can be the subject of an action for damages for his death.

In *Porter v. Lassiter*,[40] such an action was allowed even where the child had not reached the stage of viability at the time the fatal injuries were received. In 1967 the Supreme Court of Massachusets[41] allowed recovery where the child had not reached that stage

38. *Worgan v. Greggo & Ferrara, Inc.*, 50 Del. 258, 128 A.2d 557 (1956) (not certain whether child was born alive or was stillborn); *Steggall v. Morris*, 363 Mo. 1224, 258 S.W. 2d 577 (1953); *Cooper v. Blanck*, 39 So.2d 352 (La. Ct. App. 1923); *Hall v. Murphy*, 236 S.C. 257, 113 S.E.2d 790 (1960); *Shousha v. Matthews Drivurself Serv., Inc.*, 210 Tenn. 384, 358 S.W.2d 471 (1962); *Leal v. C. C. Pitts Sand & Gravel, Inc.*, 419 S.W.2d 820 (Tex. 1967) (child lived two days; question of liability when stillborn left open).

The jurisdictions which persist in the notion that recovery in tort for injury to the fetus is conditioned on the child being born alive, do so for policy reasons: difficulty of proof, danger of double recovery if the mother also sues for miscarriage, or the peculiarity of language of the wrongful death statute involved. *See generally* W. PROSSER, *supra* n. 32 § 56. The requirement of survivorship as a condition to redress tortious injury does not detract from jural recognition that a right came into existence at the time of the injury. Survivorship may be a condition precedent to an enforcement of a right, but hardly confers retroactively rights not in existence at the time of the injury. The common law was replete ·with instances of torts not remediable because the victim died before enforcement of his rights. "If it were conceded that killing the plaintiff was a tort toward him, he was none the less dead, and the tort died with him." *Id.* § 121, at 923. Who would have contended that the law did not recognize a tort in trespass, for assault and battery, or for medical malpractice simply because none of the actions survived if the victim died?

39. *Gorke v. Le Clerc*, 23 Conn. Supp. 256, 181 A.2d 448 (1962); *Hale v. Manion*, 189 Kan. 143, 368 P.2d 1 (1962); *Mitchell v. Couch*, 285 S.W.2d 901 (Ky. 1955); *State v. Sherman*, 234 Md. 179, 198 A.2d 71 (1964); *Verkennes v. Corniea*, 229 Minn. 365, 38 N.W.2d 838 (1949); *Stidam v. Ashmore*, 109 Ohio App. 431, 167 N.E.2d 106 (1959); *Poliquin v. MacDonald*, 101 N.H. 104, 135 A.2d 249 (1957); *Panagopoulous v. Martin* 295 F. Supp. 220 (D.C. W.Va. 1969); *White v. Yup*, 458 P. 2d 617 (Nev. 1969). *See also Wendt v. Lillo*, 182 F. Supp. 56 (N.D. Iowa, 1960); *Valence v. Louisiana Power & Light Co.*, 50 So. 2d 847 (La. Ct. App. 1951); *contra, Estate of Powers v. City of Troy*, 380 Mich. 160, 156 N.W.2d 530 (1968) and *Endresz v. Friedberg*, 24 N.Y.2d 478, 248 N.E. 2d 901, 301 N.Y.S. 2d 65 (1969) (strictly limited meaning of "person" under wrongful death statute); *Padillow v. Elrod*, 424 P.2d 16 (Okla. 1967), *criticized in* Note, "Torts: Prenatal Injuries—Viability and Live Birth," 21 *Oklahoma Law Review* (1968), 114.

40. 91 Ga. App. 712, 87 S.E.2d 100 (1955).

41. *Torigian v. Watertown News Co.*, 352 Mass. 446, 225 N.E.2d 926 (1967).

and died a few hours after birth. The court, after noting that it had allowed recovery for wrongful death following prenatal injury to a viable child, said:

> In the case at bar, where the fetus was not viable, we must decide whether there is a sound distinction from the situation where the fetus is viable . . .
> In the vast majority of cases where the present issue has arisen, recovery has been allowed . . . To the extent that the views of text-writers and legal commentators have come to our attention, they are unanimously of the view that nonviability of a fetus should not bar recovery . . .
> We are not impressed with the soundness of the arguments against recovery [alleged lack of precedents, the avoidance of speculation or conjecture as to causation, and the encouragement of fictitious claims]. They should not prevail against logic and justice. We hold that the plaintiff's intestate was a "person" within the meaning of [the wrongful death statute of Massachusetts].[42]

One could predict, confidently so before the current pressures for abortion liberalization,[43] that actions for the wrongful death of unborn children generally would be allowed without regard to the stage of fetal development at the time of death.

Other areas of tort law have also recognized the civil rights of the unborn child. Thus, an unborn child has been held to be a "child" or "other person" allowing him to bring an action for the death of his father where the death occurred prior to the child's birth.[44] The fetus has also been held to be an "existing person"[45] and a "surviving child"[46] under various wrongful death statutes.

In this development of tort law the courts overcame cultural lag to get abreast of scientific realities. As put in *Scott v. McPheeters*: "The respondent asserts that the provisions of section 29 of the [California] Civil Code are based on a fiction of law to the effect that an unborn child is a human being separate and distinct from its mother. We think that assumption of our statute is not a fic-

---

42. *Id.* at 448, 225 N.E.2d 927.
43. Cf. *Estate of Powers v. City of Troy*, 380 Mich. 160, 156 N.W.2d 530 (1968).
44. *La Blue v. Speker*, 358 Mich. 558, 100 N.W.2d 445 (1960).
45. *Herndon v. St. Louis & S.F.R.R.*, 37 Okla. 256, 128 P. 727 (1912).
46. *Texas & P. Ry. v. Robertson*, 82 Tex. 657, 17 S.W. 1041 (1891).

David W. Louisell and John T. Noonan, Jr.

tion, but upon the contrary that it is an established and recognized fact by science and by everyone of understanding." [47]

The tort law is not simply a guide to the status of the fetus in one branch of the law. It is a reflection of how judges responding to changing medical knowledge and attempting to do justice have come to regard the being in the womb. In the words of Dean Prosser summarizing the revolution in tort law, "All writers who have discussed the problem have joined in condemning the old rule and in maintaining that the unborn child in the path of an automobile is as much a person in the street as the mother." [48] We shall see if the unborn child can become less than a person if he stands in the path, not of a negligent motorist, but of a surgeon who would take his life.

II. THE CONSTITUTIONALITY OF REGULATING ABORTION

Since in a variety of ways the state recognizes the fetus as a center of legal rights, it would seem that the state could protect this locus of rights, this legal personality, against destruction unless there is some compelling reason why such protection should not be given. The prohibition of abortion, as a constitutional matter, thus becomes a question of weighing the life of the fetus against other interests that are asserted to require the taking of this life.

The Life and Health of the Mother

No American state has ever prohibited abortion. The states have always regulated abortion because they have always recognized that where a choice must be made between the life of the mother and the life of the child, it falls within the general rationale of self-defense if the mother seeks an abortion to preserve her own life. The typical state statute has permitted an abortion if "necessary to preserve" the mother's life, and the state has typically had the burden of proof that an abortion was not performed to save the mother's life or that the operating physician did not in good faith believe the abortion was necessary. [49]

47. 33 Cal. App. 2d 629, 634, 92 P. 2d 678, 681 (1939).
48. Prosser, *supra* n. 32 at 355.
49. *E.g., People v. Gallardo*, 41 Cal. 2d, 57, 257 P.2d 29 (1953); *Commonwealth v. Brunelle*, 341 Mass. 675, 171 N.E.2d 850 (1961).

Throughout the country, standards set by judicial interpretation of the statute have given a latitude to licensed practitioners operating within hospitals to exercise their professional judgment as to when an abortion was necessary to preserve the mother's life in the sense of preventing ill health from shortening it. In a survey of California practice, for example, it was found that 17 out of 21 hospitals would permit the performance of an abortion where there was a "substantial probability" that continuance of the pregnancy would affect the duration of the mother's life.[50] When it is questioned whether the state may constitutionally regulate abortion, the objections must be based on some interest or consideration other than the mother's life or longevity.

It has been maintained, however, that the laws regulating abortion do indirectly affect the life and health of women by forcing women who seek abortions not permitted by law to undergo criminal abortion with serious danger to their life or health. Thus, Alice S. Rossi has asserted that 8,000 women a year are killed in criminal abortions, and a similar estimate was accepted as a basis for action by the draftsmen of the proposed Model Code of the American Law Institute.[51] It has also been stated that criminal abortions are a serious cause of sterility in the women undergoing them.[52]

Maternal mortality as a result of abortion is known with some exactness in the United States. Approximately 250 women each year are known to have died as a result of abortions. The greatest expert on abortion statistics in the United States, Christopher Tietze, maintains that at the most this number might be judiciously increased to account for unreported or unanalyzed causes of death which would occur through abortion. As to the large figures in the thousands, customarily used by advocates of abortion before state

50. Herbert Packer and Ralph Gampell, "Therapeutic Abortion: A Problem in Law and Medicine," 11 *Stanford Law Review* (1959), 418, 444. Conferees at a 1959 conference on abortion held under the auspices of Planned Parenthood of America agreed that it was "virtually unknown" for an abortion performed under hospital jurisdiction to be the basis of criminal prosecution, *Abortion in the United States* ed. Mary S. Calderone (New York: Hoeber-Harper, 1958), p. 40.

51. Alice S. Rossi in *The Case for Legalized Abortion Now*, ed. Alan Guttmacher (Berkeley: Diablo, 1967), p. 27; American Law Institute, *Model Penal Code: Tentative Draft No. 9* (1959), Comment, p. 146.

52. S. J. Kleegman and S. A. Kaufman, *Infertility in Women* (Philadelphia: F. A. Davis Co., 1966), p. 301.

legislatures and courts, Tietze has described these figures as "un-mitigated nonsense." [53] It seems clear that not only the advocates of abortion but even the careful scholars of the American Law Institute have proceeded on the basis of serious inaccuracy, when the figures on which they based their recommendations could be described in this way and be in fact in the order of 1,000 to 2,000 percent off the mark.

The suggestion that a change in the abortion laws would elimi-nate even the 250 to 500 deaths, and also eliminate the danger of sterility undergone in an abortion, seems to be in good part wish-ful thinking. To some degree it is based on remarkably low statis-tics as to maternal mortality from some of the Eastern European countries.[54] These statistics are received with a credulity not often extended to other statistics provided by undemocratic regimes where there is no possibility of independent inquiry as to the truth of the statistics. The Eastern European countries including the prime case, Hungary, seem remarkably unenthusiastic about a method which is said to be so successful. At the International Con-ference on Family Planning programs held in Geneva in 1965, Andreas Klinger of the Central Office of Statistics of Hungary declared, "Induced abortion, however, cannot be viewed as a proper and suitable means of birth control. It can be regarded only as an interim, auxilliary method pending the adoption by the population of a proper means of birth prevention. Under present circumstances inasmuch as contraceptive measures are still primi-tive in most European socialist countries, induced abortion is ap-plied as one of the means of birth control." [55]

Caution has continued to prevail in countries of the West. At a

53. The *New York Times*, Sept. 7, 1967, p. 38. The National Center for Health Statistics reported that 235 deaths resulted from all forms of abortion in 1965, Christopher Tietze and Sarah Lewit, 220 *Scientific American* (January 1969), 5. Allowing for some failure to identify the cause of death, Tietze estimates that the number was still under 1000, *ibid.*, p. 5. In 1966, 189 maternal deaths were attributed to abortion, *Vital Statistics of the United States*. For the last five years known maternal deaths due to abortion have been at the rate of 0.1 percent per one hun-dred thousand, United States Department of Health, Education and Welfare, Public Health Service, *Vital Statistics of the United States 1967*, vol. II (Washington, 1969), pp. 1–19.

54. Christopher Tietze and Hans Lehfeldt, "Legal Abortion in Eastern Europe," 175 *J. Am. Med. Ass.* April 1, 1961), 1149–1154.

55. "Abortion Programs," in *Family Planning Population Programs*, Proceedings of the International Conference on Family Planning Programs, Geneva, 1965 (Chicago: University of Chicago Press, 1966). See also the statement of Dr. Vera

conference held by the Family Planning Association in Britain in 1966, Professor Keith Simpson stated, "The concern for the safety and health of the mother is as important and practical a reason for the control of abortion as it ever was." [56] On the basis of Danish figures for 1959 he noted that there was a 0.7 percent morbidity in abortion, and that this was true where the provisions of the law made sure that the women were in fairly healthy condition when they underwent an abortion. He estimated that without such regulation maternal mortality would be about one percent. He also estimated that the sterility resulting from induced abortion would run from one to two percent.[57] These cautious medical observations may be contrasted with the careless optimism of those discounting all danger to the mother in abortion.

Privacy

It has been suggested that the right of privacy of individuals is infringed by any law penalizing abortion. In behalf of this position there is invoked the decision of the United States Supreme Court invalidating the anticontraception law of Connecticut, *Griswold v. Connecticut*.[58] It is not clear, however, what relation *Griswold* has to the claim of privacy in this context.

The "zone of privacy created by several fundamental constitutional guarantees" which Justice Douglas, in the opinion for the Court, found violated by Connecticut's statute forbidding the use of contraceptives was the privacy of husband and wife in their relationship to each other. The aspect of that relation interfered with by the Connecticut statute was the sexual relationship. The state made it criminal for a married couple to have sexual intercourse using contraceptives. Enforcement of the statute would have required actual invasion of the marital bedchamber. The

---

Köblova of Prague: "The dangers attendant upon operative abortion are never wholly eliminated. Apart from an injury during the operation, and postoperative inflammatory troubles, complications in further pregnancies could arise, such as excessive bleeding during labor, incompetence of the cervix, dystocia of the uterus, or incompatibility in the ABO blood system." Köblova, Letter, 196, *J. Am. Med. Ass.* (April 25, 1966), 159.

56. In *Abortion in Britain*, Proceedings of a Conference held by the Family Planning Association, April 22, 1966 (London, 1966), p. 51.

57. *Id.*

58. 381 U.S. 479, 85 S. Ct. 1678, 14 L. Ed. 2d 510 (1965); cited as precedent in *Babbitz v. McCann* 69-C-548 (E.D. Wis., 1970) (Wisconsin abortion statute unconstitutional if fetus not quick).

Connecticut law challenged was more stringent and sweeping than any statute, civil or ecclesiastical, in the history of social efforts to control contraception.[59]

In contrast, a law against abortion does not interfere with the sexual relations of husband and wife. Pregnancy does not interfere with these relations except under some circumstances at limited times. Some women are more desirous of intercourse in pregnancy.[60] Prevention of abortion does not entail state interference with the right of marital intercourse. Nor does enforcement of a statute against abortion require invasion of the conjugal bedroom.

Determination of Family Size

It might be argued, however, that a right which the state must respect is the freedom of a married couple not to have, raise, and educate a child unwanted by them. Ability to obtain an abortion would be seen as the ultimate guarantee that this right was not infringed.

Proceeding from the undeniable fact that it is important for both the parents and the child that the child be wanted, this argument makes the parents' attitude toward their offspring the single criterion of that offspring's right to continue in existence. The right to determine family size is a right to practice contraception and to have access to the means necessary to practice contraception. This right is twisted when it is turned into a right to kill the child already conceived.

Historically, the movement for birth control in the United States had to defend itself against those who confused abortion with contraception, and the pioneers of birth control made clear their opposition to abortion. In her maiden public speech in favor of birth control Margaret Sanger spoke of women living in the past to whom "birth control does not mean what it means to us. To them it has meant the most barbaric methods. It has meant the killing of babies — infanticide — abortions — in one crude way or another." [61] Another early leader, Dr. William J. Robinson, declared in a very popular book, "I can truthfully say that one of

59. John T. Noonan, Jr., *Contraception* (Cambridge: Belknap Press of Harvard Univ. Press, 1965), p. 413.

60. Alan S. Guttmacher, *Pregnancy and Birth* (paperback ed., New York: New American Library, 1960), p. 86.

61. *My Fight for Birth Control* (New York: Farrar and Rinehart, 1939), p. 133.

the principal reasons, one of the strongest motives that makes us advocate contraception so persistently and assiduously is because we want to do away with the evil of abortion as far as we can; for we do consider abortion a terrible evil." [62]

In this area there has been a gradual evolution of civilized thought. In the Roman Republic the father by virtue of the *patria potestas* had the literal power of life or death over his children.[63] "Within the family the *paterfamilias* enjoyed a lifetime despotism." [64] In the Roman Empire this freedom to deal with one's children as one pleased was limited by the state. Infanticide, however, was still widely practiced, and abortion with the consent of the father was legal.[65] The basic concept of the law was that a fetus was "a part of the woman." [66] No protection was accorded to this being within the womb, and the law only guarded the father's right to determine this being's destiny.

Over a period of about 2500 years there has been built up a defense by the state in behalf of children, born and unborn, against the aggressive and the proprietary instincts of their progenitors. The problem of the "battered child" today is evidence, if evidence is needed, that the state must still by law restrain the freedom of conduct of parents. Parents who severely injure their children are sometimes sociopathic, sometimes socially established.[67] Whatever their relation to society, the law insists that they have no right to treat their children as "their thing." The statutes on abortion prevent the mother from treating the child in her womb as "her thing."

Self-Determination for a Woman

The argument is sometimes made that a woman has a right to destroy any fetus of her own that she, in the most literal sense,

62. *Birth Control or The Limitation of Offspring by Prevenception*, 32nd ed. (1929), p. 132.
63. Biondo Biondi, "La Patria Potestas" 3 *Il Diritto Romano Cristiano* (Milan: Dott. A. Giuffrè, 1954), 13.
64. W. W. Buckland and A. D. McNair, *Roman Law and Common Law* (Cambridge, Eng.: The University Press, 1936), p. 35.
65. Noonan, *Contraception supra* n. 59, pp. 85–86.
66. Justinian, *Digesta* 25.4.1.1, *Corpus juris civilis*, ed. T. Mommsen (Berlin, 1954).
67. Kempe et al., "The Battered-Child Syndrome," 181. *J. Am. Med. Ass.* (1962), 17.

finds "unbearable." It is contended that to force a woman to continue a pregnancy is to impose a kind of slavery upon her. It is added that the laws against abortion were enacted by men to constrain the behavior of women.

This argument seems to assert a self-evident legal right, if it means that a woman should be free to refuse sexual intercourse or should be free to practice contraception. A woman is not under the necessity of subjecting her body to the burden of pregnancy if she chooses either of these alternatives. But the further claim that a woman is free to destroy the being whom she has conceived by voluntarily having sexual intercourse makes sense only if that being can be regarded as part of herself, a part which she may discard for her own good. But at this point the evolution of social doctrine favoring freedom for women encounters the growth of scientific knowledge and recognition of the fetus as a living person within the womb.

It is true of the major provisions of the criminal law that they were enacted by male legislators because they were enacted in the nineteenth century when women were unable to vote. It is not evident how this general condition of political freedom influenced the abortion laws more than it influenced other parts of the criminal law. The suggestion that abortion laws are peculiarly the product of a male-dominated government seems completely inapposite in the states which have enacted abortion statutes within the last decade with electorates composed of both men and women.

Inequality

It has often been argued by advocates of abortion that the statutes directed against it discriminate against the economically deprived. It is suggested that there is an advantage to the class which is able to obtain abortions, and that this advantage is enjoyed by the wealthier persons in America.[68] Undoubtedly, persons who are poor find it harder to travel to a place where abortion might be legal, and often they cannot afford treatment by a private physician who might sympathetically find a legal reason for a therapeutic abortion.

It is a sad and harsh probability that a large number of criminal

---

68. *E.g.* Lawrence Lader, *Abortion* (Indianapolis: Bobbs, Merrill, 1966), p. 30.

236

laws bear with unequal severity in practice on the poor, who are more likely than the rich to be caught, to be prosecuted, to be unskillfully defended, to be convicted, and to be punished.[69] These de facto defects in the American system of the law are reasons to urge reform of the administration of criminal justice. When they are used as a reason for the selective invalidation of the criminal statutes, they appear to be put forward as a kind of special pleading. They are no more reason to believe that an abortion law is unconstitutional than they are reason to believe that any of the other portions of the criminal law are unconstitutional.

In general, it has always been recognized that not every inequality in fact is denial of equal protection of the law.[70] The statutes regulating abortion do not intend to discriminate by race, class, religion, sex, color, age, occupation, area, income, or on any other invidious basis. The persons who are punished under them are not the poor, but those practitioners of illegal abortions who profit from the activity condemned.

Vagueness

The Supreme Court of California, by a vote of 4–3, invalidated the old abortion statute of the state on the ground that the exception permitted by the statute for abortions "necessary to preserve the life of the mother" was too vague to be understood by men of common intelligence.[71] The court assumed that, since the phrase could not be understood, both a woman and her physician would be unable to determine when an abortion might legally be performed, and the right of a woman to obtain an abortion to preserve her life would be detrimentally affected by the vagueness of the standard.

The rationale of the court drew a strong dissent: "[O]ne would think that the English language which has been the sensitive instrument of our system of law for over 500 years has lost, by

69. *See, e.g.* Hugo A. Bedau, "Death Sentences in New Jersey, 1407–1960," 19 *Rutgers Law Review* (1964), 1, 37.

70. *Railway Express Agency v. New York,* 336 U.S. 106, 69 Sup. Ct. 463, 93 L. Ed. 533 (1949).

71. *People v. Belous,* 458 P.2d. 194, 80 Cal. Rptr. 354 (1969), criticized in McGrew, Note, 118 *U. Penn. L. Rev.* (1970) p. 643. *See also U.S. v. Vuitch,* 305 F. Supp. 1032 (D.C.D.C. Nov. 10, 1969). In the same year as *Belous,* a California Court of Appeal held that a fetus which has reached the stage of viability is a human being for purposes of the state's homicide statute. *Keeler v. Superior Court for County of Amador,* 80 Cal. Rptr. 865 (1969).

David W. Louisell and John T. Noonan, Jr.

the mere passage of time, all capacity for clarity of expression." [72] The statute which was invalidated in 1969 had been in substantially the same form for over a century. Countless criminal convictions had been sustained under it in California, in over 50 cases the statute had been applied by California appellate courts, and 15 cases had been heard on appeal by the Supreme Court of California without the court ever before adverting to the difficulty of understanding these words.[73] It is usual for a statute to be somewhat indefinite and to be progressively clarified by judicial decisions. The majority of the court in this case seemed to have thought that judicial decisions had made the statute progressively unclear so that finally there was nothing left but to say that it was unintelligible.

Historically, the invalidation of a statute on the ground of vagueness has been the technique for judges to use when they disagree with the rationale of a legislative determination, and when they can find no other way of rejecting what the legislature has done. In the first third of the century the conservative judges of the Supreme Court of the United States sometimes threw out legislative restraints of economic freedom which the judges found to disagree with their own philosophy of economic liberalism. In the second third of the century a liberal majority of the Supreme Court of the United States used the technique to invalidate some restrictions by legislatures on free speech which were repugnant to the liberal point of view of the judges.[74] The majority of the California court seems to have followed this pattern of judges permitting their own personal preferences to prevail over the legislature in the area of sexual behavior. One danger of such a technique is that it promotes cynicism among observers of courts as to the standards used by judges in measuring the constitutionality of statutes with which they personally disagree.

The words of Felix Frankfurter praising Justice Brandeis' large views of the province of the legislature are as apposite now as when they were written in 1932. Speaking of the veto power exercised in the 1920's by the Supreme Court over the socioeco-

72. 458 P.2d at 210, 80 Cal. Rptr. at 370.
73. *See* West's *California Penal Code Annotated* (1956), sec. 274.
74. *See* A. J. A. [Anthony J. Amsterdam], Note, "The Void-for-Vagueness Doctrine in the Supreme Court," 109 *University of Pennsylvania Law Review* (1960), 67.

nomic legislation of the states, he characterized this power as "undue centralization in its most destructive and least responsible form." It was "the least responsible" because "it so often turns on the adventitious circumstances which determine a majority decision, and shelters the fallible judgment of individual justices, in matters of fact and opinion not peculiarly within the special competence of judges, behind the impersonal authority of the Constitution." [75] Finding a well-tested statute to be vague is one form of this "least responsible" use of judicial power.

The historic rule for testing a statute is that if it has been on the books for some time, and especially if it has been construed authoritatively by a court, it presumably withstands a claim of impermissible vagueness. For example, in a new statute the words "unjust or unreasonable rate" were found too vague by the Supreme Court of the United States,[76] but, on the other hand, the Court found the statutory words of the income tax law, "reasonable deduction" sufficiently definite to sustain a criminal conviction after the law had been in force for some three decades.[77]

A second general rule laid down by the United States Supreme Court is that the vagueness of the statutory language must be such as to fail to give warning to the particular defendants charged with crime under the law. The thought of the Court is that "vagueness" is essentially objectionable because it is unfair. If a given defendant knows perfectly well that what he is doing under the statute is a crime, he may be convicted under it, even though some hypothetical case could be imagined where someone could genuinely be in doubt about the legality of his conduct. Thus, the Supreme Court in 1963 held that the phrase "unreasonably low prices" was not vague when applied to the criminal conduct of the defendant before it.[78] The same reasoning has recently been applied in upholding an abortion statute where it was contended that the statutory exception of "lawful justification" was vague.[79] In gen-

75. "Mr. Justice Brandeis and the Constitution," 45 *Harvard Law Review* (1931), 58.

76. *U.S. v. L. Cohen Grocery Co.*, 255 U.S. 81, 41 S. Ct. 298, 65 L. Ed. 516 (1921).

77. *U.S. v. Ragen*, 314 U.S. 513, 524 62 S. Ct. 374, 86 L. Ed. 383 (1942), *rehearing denied* 315 U.S. 826.

78. *U.S. v. National Dairy Products*, 372 U.S. 29, 83 Sup. Ct. 594, 9 L. Ed. 2d. 561, *rehearing denied* 372 U.S. 961, 83 Sup. Ct. 1011, 10L. Ed. 2d. 13 (1963).

79. *State v. Moretti*, 52 N.J. 182, 244 A. 2d. 499 (1968), *cert. denied* 393 U.S. 952 (1968).

eral, it may be said that the persons customarily charged with the crime of abortion — persons operating secretly in out-of-the-way, nonhospital locales — are fully aware that their behavior is condemned by the usual statute.

By the standard customarily invoked to measure definiteness, the usual statutory phrase "necessary to preserve life" is clear enough. About the same time that California invalidated its law, the Supreme Court of Massachusetts and the Supreme Court of New Jersey found parallel phrases in their statutes on abortion to be clearly understandable by ordinary persons.[80] It is difficult to believe that what is comprehensible to ordinary men in Massachusetts and New Jersey is not comprehensible to ordinary men in California.

Delegation

A separate ground for decision in the *Belous* case was that the statute constituted an unconstitutional delegation of authority to the physician who had to decide whether an abortion was necessary to preserve life. The court reasoned that the physician was interested in the decision because if he were wrong he risked criminal punishment, and the court invoked the rule that an interested person may not be given authority to decide whether an act is legal or illegal.[81]

This argument was surely put forward without much thought. Every time a surgeon performs an operation he engages in an act that may be a battery potentially subjecting him to severe damages, or that may constitute malpractice exposing him to the risk of loss of his professional license and even to a criminal charge of assault, if he has in fact proceeded without medical justification. He is an interested party in deciding whether there is justification or not. What the law has delegated to him in the first instance is this power to determine whether his own act is lawful or not.

It may be objected that it is one thing to delegate power to a physician to determine whether his own act is illegal and another to delegate it to determine whether someone else's act is illegal. But a comparable case is common. The self-interested decision of

80. *State v. Moretti, supra* n. 79 ("without lawful justification"), *Kudish v. Board of Registration in Medicine* 248 N.E. 2d. 264 (1969) ("unlawfully").
81. *People v. Belous,* 458 P. 2d. 194, 80 Cal. Rptr. 354 (1969).

the surgeon that an operation is justified for a child makes the child's parents immune from criminal liability for committing the child to a loss of an organ of his body. If the permissibility of the parents' act cannot constitutionally be determined by the operating physician, then the entire medical care of children must be put on a different footing from that on which it has existed from the beginning of the common law.

Unenforceability

It is often popularly argued that the abortion laws are obsolete because they are ineffective. The heart of this argument rests on statistics. Thus, for example, Lucille Newman of Mills College has written that "the reality, then, is a million illegal abortions a year." [82] She did not say where she obtained this information. In the same book Alice S. Rossi of the University of Chicago announced that there were 850,000 to 1,200,000 illegal abortions a year, and that one in every two or three married women between the ages of 30 and 50 would have had an abortion. [83] She did not say how she has arrived at these figures. If one goes back to some source which might give a basis for the estimates being used, one finds a book such as that published in 1964 by Jerome G. Bates and Edward S. Zawadzki. Here, too, it is said that there are one million criminal abortions a year in the United States. [84]

An examination of the basis for the Bates and Zawadzki statement is revealing. One source is a book by Frederick J. Taussig published in 1936, which estimated that there were 681,000 abortions in a given year. [85] Extrapolated to 1964, this guess might mean that then there were 1,000,000 abortions per year. But Taussig's estimate was made by reference to both spontaneous and induced abortions. Of course, a substantial number of pregnancies spontaneously fail to come to term. Taussig's figures provided no way of determining how many abortions he estimated to be criminally induced.

Another source for the one million figure is a study by Regine

82. In *The Case for Legalized Abortion Now*, ed. Alan S. Guttmacher (1967), p. 64.
83. Alice S. Rossi, *ibid.*, p. 27.
84. *Criminal Abortions* (Springfield, Ill.: Thomas 1964), p. 3.
85. *Abortion: Spontaneous and Induced* (St. Louis: The C. V. Mosby Co., 1936), pp. 25–26.

Stix published in 1935. The Stix study was based on 999 women attending a birth control clinic in the Bronx between January 1, 1931, and January 30, 1932.[86] Clearly it requires an enormous jump to go from these 999 women to the population of the United States, and to assume that the experiences reported as typical in this small community in 1931 are characteristic of the United States as a whole in the 1960's.

A third source is a work of Paul Gebhard done in connection with the Kinsey study of sexuality in women.[87] Here a sample of women was used, but a sample which has been much criticized. In 1959, under the auspices of Planned Parenthood of America, a conference was held to discuss abortion in America, and a committee on statistics was set up under the chairmanship of Christopher Tietze of the Population Council. The committee criticized the inadequacy of the data and reported, "We are therefore forced to conclude that the data collected by the Institute for Sex Research does not provide an adequate basis for reliable estimates of the incidence of induced abortion in the urban white population of the United States, much less in the total population." [88]

In contrast to these old studies is another study done in Indianapolis in 1941 and 1942 of married white Protestant couples. Of pregnancies in this group, 1.9 percent ended in illegal abortions.[89] If this figure were extrapolated and applied to the United States for the year 1940, it would have meant that there were 48,000 illegal abortions in the United States in that year. If this number were increased by 50 percent, to allow for population growth to 1969, there would be now roughly 72,000 illegal abortions per year.

In the 1960's an estimate was made of criminal abortions in England under a law similar to the law of most American states. Assuming that abortion was a serious operation as a result of which there would be inevitably a certain percentage of maternal deaths from its performance in nonhospital conditions, C. B. Goodhart

86. "A Study of Pregnancy Wastage," 13 *The Milbank Memorial Fund Quarterly* (October 1935), 347–365.
87. *Pregnancy, Birth and Abortion* (New York: Harper, 1958).
88. *Abortion in the United States,* ed. Mary Calderone (1958), p. 179.
89. P. K. Whelpton in *The Abortion Problem* (issued by The National Committee on Maternal Health, Howard C. Taylor, chairman, 1944) p. 18.

was able to go from the figures of known maternal mortality to an estimate of the number of criminal abortions in England. He arrived at the total of 10,000 criminal abortions a year.[90] If the English experience is a good guide to American experience, this number should be multiplied by five to account for the difference in population, and the estimate is reached of 50,000 criminal abortions annually in the United States.

Another way may be taken to confirm the estimate of 50,000. The draftsmen of the American Law Institute *Model Penal Code* accept a ratio of 1.2 percent maternal deaths to illegal abortions.[91] As we are reasonably certain that maternal mortality does not exceed 500, we could conclude that illegal abortions are between 40,000 and 50,000.

Is there any rational basis by which to choose between 40,000 or 50,000 annual abortions or 1,000,000 annual abortions? It would seem that the estimates favoring a smaller number have a little more to be said for them, but that essentially one is in the dark.[92] The act of abortion is not only criminal, but unlike a crime such as robbery its perpetration is secret. If it is successful, its accomplishment remains a secret. It is not easily subject to statistical survey. It became a matter of guesswork and extrapolation from fragmentary bits of information. It would seem unreasonable to declare a law obsolete because of guesses made as to the number of violations of the law — guesses made by persons often highly motivated to show that the law should be abolished.

Even if the wildest of the guesses made was correct, it is not clear that failure to enforce a law means that the law should be repealed. Who would advocate abandonment of the laws against perjury because of the lack of enforcement of these laws? The

90. "The Frequency of Illegal Abortion," 55 *Eugenics Review* (January 1964), 199ff.

91. American Law Institute, *Model Penal Code: Tentative Draft No. 9* (1959), Comment, p. 146. If we assume that illegal abortions in the United States are as safe as legal abortions in Sweden where the maternal mortality rate is now 39 per 100,000 and if we take the figure of 189 known number of maternal deaths from abortion in the United States in 1966 (*see* n. 53 *supra*), we reach an estimate of somewhat over 400,000 illegal abortions in the United States. But to assume that illegal American operations are as safe as legal Swedish ones is an admission that proponents of abortion are unlikely to make.

92. There is "no objective basis" for choosing between estimates of 200,000 and 1,200,000, according to the Statistics Committee at the Planned Parenthood Conference in 1958, *Abortion in the United States* (ed. Calderone), p. 180.

laws against theft were violated in 1966 by 762,352 cases of larceny of amounts over $50 known to the police, and by 486,568 cases of auto theft known to the police.[93] Unlike the case of abortion where there is an enormous range in the guesses, we have a known pattern of theft of which the police are aware. Does anyone argue from this enormous number of violations that there is something wrong with our laws on larceny, that the real trouble is with the victims whose property is taken, that we should reform the laws of larceny to accommodate the moral standards of those who steal from others? It seems fair to say that the only time that persons use guesses about the number of violations of law to urge the repeal of the law is when, for reasons very different from the law's ineffectiveness, they have already rejected the values preserved and protected by the laws.

III. THE CONSTITUTIONALITY OF NOT PROTECTING THE EMBRYO

Suppose that overnight a state abolished its statute regulating abortion. Would such an action be constitutional? The lines already pricked out by judicial decision indicate that such action would be a violation of the Constitution of the United States.

Judicial Precedents

The leading cases have developed in response to the advances of medicine in the science of fetology. Techniques have now been developed to make lifesaving transfusions of blood to fetuses who have developed acute anemia in the womb because of the incompatibility of the fetus' blood with the mother's blood.[94] A conflict of interest between child and parent has occurred where the parent by religious conviction has believed it sinful to accept a necessary transfusion of blood. In such a case where the hospital sought a court order authorizing the transfusion, Judge J. Skelly Wright observed, "The State as *parens patriae* will not allow a parent to abandon a child and so it should not allow this most

93. United States Census Bureau, *Statistical Abstract of the United States* (1967), p. 49. Similarly the laws against perjury are generally violated with impunity, McClintock, "What Happens to Perjurers," 24 *Minnesota Law Review* (1940), 727. Does anyone believe that there should be no statute against perjury?
94. Beth Day and H. M. I. Liley, *Modern Motherhood: Pregnancy, Childbirth, and the Newborn Baby* (New York: Random House, 1967 ed.), p. 48.

ultimate of voluntary abandonments. The mother had a responsibility to the community to care for her infant." [95]

Judge Wright's dictum was applied to a fetus in a New Jersey case, *Raleigh Fitkin–Paul Memorial Hospital v. Anderson.*[96] In this case there was again an assertion of the right to practice his religious belief by a Jehovah's Witness who believed that the Bible prohibited blood transfusions. The right not to have the state enforce its beliefs upon one's conscience, a "fixed star in our constitutional constellation," [97] might have led the court to subordinate the fetus' interest in survival to the constitutional right of the parents to practice their religion. Instead, the life of the fetus was treated as a value outweighing even a prized constitutional liberty. In a previous case the New Jersey court had ordered a transfusion, despite his parents' religious objections, to a "blue baby" suffering from a lack of oxygen after birth. The court composed of Chief Justice Weintraub and Justices Jacobs, Francis, Hall, Schettino, and Haneman found no difference between that case and the case now presented of a fetus likely to be aborted if denied blood. It declared in a unanimous *per curiam* opinion, "We are satisfied that the unborn child is entitled to the law's protection . . . We have no difficulty in so deciding with respect to the infant child." [98] Presented with a choice between a fetus' life and the most cherished of constitutional freedoms of the parent which were less than life, the court chose to prefer the life of the child.

The choice between the interests of the fetus and the civil rights of the parent has also been presented in the context of whether a father may be compelled to support a fetus conceived by him. A suit seeking support was begun by a fetus' guardian *ad litem* when the fetus was less than six months old. The court applied California Civil Code section 196a providing that "the father as well as the mother of an illegitimate child must give him support and education suitable to his circumstances." The court recognized the right of "an unborn child through a guardian ad litem to compel the right to support conferred by the code." [99]

95. *Application of President of Georgetown University Hospital,* 331 F. 2d. 1000 at 1008 (D.C. Cir. 1964), *cert. denied* 377 U.S. 985 (1964).
96. 42 N.J. 421, 201 A. 2d 537, *cert. denied* 377 U.S. 985 (1964).
97. Justice Jackson in *West Virginia State Board of Education v. Barnette,* 319 U.S. 624 at 642, 63 Sup. Ct. 1178 at 1187, 87 L. Ed. 1628 (1943).
98. *Raleigh Fitkin–Paul Memorial Hospital v. Anderson, supra* n. 96.
99. *Kyne v. Kyne,* 38 Cal. App. 2d. 122, 100 P 2d. 806 (1940).

245

It would be strange if a fetus had rights to support from his parents, rights enforceable by a guardian and sanctioned by the criminal law of neglect, and yet have no right to be protected from an abortion. It would be incongruous that a fetus should be protected by the state from willful harm by a parent when the injury was inflicted indirectly but not when it was inflicted directly. It would be odd if the fetus had property rights which must be respected but could himself be extinguished. The decisions recognize that where a choice must be made between the life of the fetus and the convenience or deep desires of the parent, the law will make the parent subordinate his rights in order to preserve the life in the womb.

Inaction by the State

The decisions reflect the conviction that the right of the parent must be subordinated to the right to life of the child. If the protection of the law were withdrawn from the child, then the life of the child could be taken at the will of the parent. If the state permitted this, it would be a discriminatory act barred by the Constitution. A long series of decisions supports the general proposition that for the government to withdraw protection from one class of its people is for the government to perform an act of discrimination against the group deprived of protection. In one of the classic older cases on this point, Chief Justice Taft had this to say, "Immunity granted to a class, however limited, having the effect to deprive another class, however limited, of a personal or property right is just as clearly a denial of the equal protection of the laws to the latter class as if the immunity were in favor of, or the deprivation of right permitted worked against, a larger class." [100] This fundamental principle has been recently affirmed in a variety of civil rights cases. In *Burton v. Wilmington Parking Authority*,[101] the United States Supreme Court found it unconstitutional state action for the operator of a restaurant in a building owned by the state to refuse to serve Negroes. The state, while taking no affirmative action to discriminate, by its "inaction" made itself a party to the refusal of service. Its failure to prevent the discrimination was itself treated as state action against one

100. *Truax v. Corrigan*, 257 U.S. 312, 42 S. Ct. 124, 66 L. Ed. 254 (1921).
101. 365 U.S. 715, 81 S. Ct. 856, 6 L. Ed. 2d. 45 (1960).

class of citizens. In *Reitman v. Mulkey*,[102] an amendment to the Constitution of California permitting discrimination in private housing was held to be unconstitutional. The state's action in permitting discrimination was itself found to be a form of action against one class of its citizens.

These cases have developed the concept of state discrimination by inaction in the context of discriminations based on race or color. But surely on the crucial question of whether mere inaction by the state can be regarded as unconstitutional state action they are conclusive. The cases do not decide whether a fetus falls within the class of citizens to whom the constitution extends protection. They do decide that if the fetus is regarded as a person the state may not justify its failure to protect the fetus by contending that absence of protection is without constitutional significance.

It may be objected that the state already discriminates against the unborn child by treating the killing in the womb as "abortion" rather than "murder," and by providing a lesser penalty for the crime of abortion than for the crime of murder. Undoubtedly, history and sentiment are the dominant reasons for this distinction. Historically, a difference was made in the social sanctions of the canon law and in the provisions of the common law between killing a child in the womb and killing someone outside the womb. Undeniably, in terms of human feeling there is a stronger repugnance to the act of killing a being who is already a visually perceptible person than there is to killing a being who has not yet appeared in the light of day. The law of homicide itself permits enhancement or mitigation of punishment depending on assessment of the crime's reprehensibility. This assessment is in part a function of the community's psychological reaction to the crime. The sanction afforded by the statutes against abortion has seemed proportionate and sufficient to defend the right to life of the unborn child. In a constitutional question it seems folly to demand an abstract consistency without attention to the history and feeling of mankind.

The New State Laws

It may then be asked how constitutional it would be for a state to adopt the draft prepared by the American Law Institute. Its

102. 387 U.S. 369, 87 S. Ct. 1627, 18 L. Ed 2d. 830 (1967).

statute, still in the form of a proposed draft which has not yet been acted upon by the Institute itself, provides that an abortion may be performed by a licensed physician "if he believes there is substantial risk that continuance of the pregnancy would gravely impair the physical or mental health of the mother or that the child would be born with grave physical or mental defect, or that the pregnancy resulted from rape, incest, or other felonious intercourse." [103] All illicit intercourse with a girl below the age of 16 is included within the definition of "felonious intercourse." Two physicians, one of whom may be the person performing the abortion, must certify in writing the circumstances which they believe to justify it. In the case of an abortion justified on the ground of felonious intercourse, the certificate must be submitted to the prosecuting attorney or the police.

The justification of the abortion involves no judicial process and no representation of the public interest or that of the father or unborn child. Justification is complete upon the request of the pregnant woman and certification of two physicians without involvement of any other agency or person. Except for the certificate to the prosecuting attorney or the police in the case of felonious intercourse, only the hospital need be informed of the abortion.

The constitutionality of such a statute is no longer purely an academic matter. As of September 1969, ten states have adopted statutes patterned to greater or lesser extent on the proposed "Model Code." Arkansas, Colorado, Delaware, Kansas, Maryland, New Mexico, and North Carolina permit abortion on grounds identical with those of the proposed Code — substantial risk to the physical or mental health of the mother; substantial risk that the child will be born with grave physical or mental defect; pregnancy resulting from rape or incest.[104] Georgia has made the danger to the mother "serious and permanent" injury and eliminated incest. California has recognized danger to mental health only if health would be impaired to the point of justifying com-

103. American Law Institute, *Model Penal Code: Proposed Official Draft* (1962) sec. 230.3.

104. *Arkansas Statutes*, c. 41–303 to 41–310 (1969); *Colorado Revised Statutes*, 40.2–50 and 51 (1967); *Delaware Statutes* (1969); *Kansas Laws*, c. 180. sec. 21–3407 (1968); *Laws of Maryland, 1968*, c. 470; *New Mexico Statutes Annotated, 1969*, sec. 40A-5-1-3; *North Carolina General Statutes*, 14-45.1 (1967).

mitment to an institution. It has also rejected the defective child provision. Oregon has gone even further than the proposed Code in relating the mother's health to "the mother's total environment, actual or reasonably forseeable." [105] Only Colorado and North Carolina require the consent of the husband if the mother is married.

The fact that a number of states have actually put the principles of the American Law Institute into legislation is, of course, not a reason to abstain from judgment as to the constitutionality of the principles. At one time over half of the states had enacted laws prohibiting marriage between persons of different races. For over a century the Supreme Court evaded passing on the constitutionality of these measures so offensive to human dignity. Only in 1967 in *Loving v. Virginia*[106] did the Court finally pronounce such state legislation to be invalid. It may be hoped that as long a wait will not be necessary for a clear constitutional ruling on the statutes which followed the proposed Code.

The principal draftsman of the American Law Institute proposal insists that the "legitimizing circumstances" for such abortions are "narrowly defined." [107] Yet the only factor limiting the discretion of the mother and the two certifying physicians is that the mother's or the child's physical or mental "health" must be gravely threatened. There is nothing in the statute which would aid the physician in making the determination. It would be fair to assume that, in the absence of any such guidelines, the area circumscribed by the word "health" will be broad. The World Health Organization, in 1960, defined health as "a state of complete physical, mental and social well-being, not simply the absence of illness and disease." [108] At the very least the statutory language

105. *Laws of Georgia, 1968,* 26.1102; *California Health and Safety Codes* (St. Paul: West Pub. Co., 1967), secs. 25951–25952; *Oregon Laws, 1969,* c. 684, sec. 17. The Hawaiian legislature passed a law in February 1970 repealing its old statutes against abortion and permitting operations "to intentionally terminate the pregnancy of a non-viable fetus." (*Honolulu Star Bulletin,* February 20 and February 21, 1970.)

106. 388 U.S. 1, 87 S. Ct. 1817, 18 L. Ed. 2d 1010 (1967).

107. Louis Schwartz, "Modernizing the Anti-Abortion Laws" (unpub. paper delivered to the International Conference on Abortion, Washington, D.C., September 5–7, 1967), p. 2.

108. World Health Organization, "Constitution" in Goodman, *International Health Organizations in the Theory and Practice of Health,* ed. Holson (1965), p. 384.

provides a fertile ground for the application of individual, subjective notions of what the requisite degree of gravity of risk ought to be in a given case.

In order to make the question of the legitimacy of an abortion solely a medical judgment it must be assumed that no human life, other than that of the mother, is involved in the termination of the pregnancy. The proposed Code accomplishes this by drawing a distinction between abortions which occur late in pregnancy and those which

occur prior to the fourth month of pregnancy, before the fetus becomes firmly implanted in the womb, before it develops many of the characteristic and recognizable features of humanity, and well before it is capable of those movements which when felt by the mother are called "quickening." There seems to be an obvious difference between terminating the development of such an inchoate being, whose chance of maturing is still *somewhat problematical*, and, on the other hand, destroying a fully formed viable fetus of eight months, where the offense might well become ordinary murder if the child should happen to survive for a moment after it has been expelled from the body of the mother.[109]

Not all of the states which have taken their inspiration from the proposed Code have been able to draw this kind of line. Georgia has used the system of the thirteenth century, and protected the fetus after "quickening." [110] Colorado, Kansas, New Mexico, and North Carolina have provided no cut-off point, and in these states the fetus is subject to being killed at any moment of existence in the womb.[111] For the first time in Anglo-American legal history there is in these states no protection for the six-, seven-, eight-, or nine-month old fetus. This trend, if it be a trend, may be contrasted with the 1967 revision of the New York Penal Law which, while maintaining a separate punishment for abortion, defines the killing of a fetus of six months as a species of homicide.[112]

109. American Law Institute, *Model Penal Code: Tentative Draft No. 9* (1959), sec. 207.11, Comment (emphasis added).

110. *Laws of Georgia, 1968*, sec. 26.1102.

111. *Colorado Revised Statutes*, 40.2-50 and 51 (1967); *Kansas Laws, 1968*, c. 180, sec. 21-3407; *New Mexico Statutes Annotated, 1969*, sec. 40-A-5-1-3; *North Carolina General Statutes, 1967*, 14-45.1.

112. *McKinney's Consolidated Laws of New York*, Penal Law 125.00; 125.40 (1967).

The variety in approaches by the states reflects the difficulty, if not impossibility, of drawing a line between different stages of the existence of the fetus in the womb. The line drawn by the proposed Code was arbitrary. It has been arbitrarily rejected. The difficulty arose from the draftsmen ignoring the medical and biological evidence which established the continuity of fetal life. How is the chance of maturing of the specified inchoate being "problematical" except as all life is "problematical"? Once spermatozoon and ovum meet and the conceptus is formed, in only 20 percent of the cases will spontaneous abortion occur. In other words, the chances are about 4 out of 5 that the new being will develop.[113] Implantation in the womb normally occurs within eight days of fruitful intercourse, and the fetus is no more "firmly implanted" four months later. A skilled embryologist can positively identify the humanity of the embryo shortly after conception, and human features can be recognized by the sixth week.[114]

Medical evidence would indicate that the various stages of development are merely labels which have been placed upon what is in fact the steady growth of the human being and are no more significant as tests of life itself than are the more commonly used labels of infancy, adolescence, maturity, middle age, and old age. The only real difference between the "inchoate being" and the eight-month-old fetus is that the latter is somewhat older than the former. This difference would hardly seem to justify the conclusion that one of the fetuses represents human life in its generally accepted form while the other does not. If we use the test of when an infant has personality as the criterion of when he is entitled to the law's protection, an infant five, six, or seven months after birth may be treated as his parents' thing. For example, a child psychologist describing the way an infant of this age becomes "a human person" declares "At this point (i.e., somewhere around six months after birth) we officially welcome the infant into the human fraternity." [115] If before this welcome as a personality the child cannot claim protection from society, the law on infanticide as well as on abortion needs revision.

113. Noonan, "An Almost Absolute Value in History" *supra* this book.
114. *Ibid. supra.*
115. Selma H. Fraiberg, *The Magic Years* (New York: Scribner, 1959), p. 45.

The recognition of the fetus as human life in a variety of other areas of law has been established. In recognizing the fetus the law has not engaged in some Pickwickian fancy. Its recognition of the fetus has not been fiction-making, but a response to the medical developments which have in the last quarter of a century made palpable the continuity between the being within the womb and the being outside the womb.

The great development which the American Law Institute draftsmen neglected to consider was the creation of a whole new science initiated by Dr. H. L. I. Liley. Of this science Allan C. Barnes of the Johns Hopkins Hospital writes, "Liley's pioneering work not only has opened new avenues in the treatment of erythroblastosis fetalis, but has inspired a new specialty of 'fetology' and created a need for fetological surgeons and fetological medical specialists of the future."[116] A popular magazine can coin a word and describe the advances now made in "embryiatics."[117] In the light of fetology, there can scarcely be a return to the Roman law theory that a parent has absolute dominion over his offspring or a return to the ancient notion that a fetus is "part" of his mother.

Organs and the blood of the fetus are his own. At six weeks, the features of his face are visible; they are the features of a human face.[118] Even the persistent belief that the placenta was part of the mother has been exploded.[119] "More than any living species," the fetus "dominates his environment."[120] "The head, housing the miraculous brain, is quite large in proportion to the remainder of the body, and the limbs are still relatively small. Within his watery world, however (where we have been able to observe him in his natural state through a sort of closed circuit x-ray television set), he is quite beautiful, perfect in his fashion, active and graceful. He is neither a quiescent vegetable nor a witless tadpole, as some have conceived him to be in the past, but rather a tiny human being, as independent as though he were lying in a crib with a blanket wrapped around him instead of his mother."[121] The med-

116. *Intra-uterine Development* (Philadelphia: Lea and Febiger, 1968), p. 455.
117. *Time*, September 19, 1969, p. 66.
118. Day and Liley, *Modern Motherhood supra* n. 94, p. 28.
119. *Ibid.*, p. 24.
120. *Ibid.*, p. 23.
121. *Ibid.*, pp. 30–31.

ical developments confirm the soundness of the law in treating the fetus as a being with rights not dependent on his parents.

In the light of this evolution of legal thought and medical knowledge, it would be to turn the clock back to hold that fetal life might be terminated whenever unwanted by the parents. The response of the civil law here is taken as a prime example of the effect of scientific development on judicial thought by Edwin W. Patterson in his analysis of the relationship between science and law. He observes "that the meaning and scope of even such a basic term as 'legal person' can be codified by reason of changes in scientific facts — the unborn child has been recognized as a legal person, even in the law of torts." [122]

The continuity now recognized between the embryo and the infant is such that today it is emphasized that the prenatal experiences of the child are critical to his future development. Ashley Montagu writes: "The nine months spent by the individual in the womb are fundamental. It is during these nine prenatal months that the individual's foundations are well and truly laid — or not. To an extent rather more profound than had hitherto been expected, the individual's prenatal past influences his postnatal future." [123]

In the light of that kind of continuity of experience it is difficult to understand how a line can be roughly drawn on the basis of age, and the being before birth or viability treated as nonhuman, as a thing which can be destroyed at his mother's pleasure. The rule which has hitherto been the law puts the life of the child above the welfare, convenience, or happiness of the parents: "The right of their child to live is greater than, and precludes, their right not to endure emotional and financial injury." [124]

In Anglo-American law the right to human life has been subordinate to no lesser claim than a superior right to life. A man may take the life of an assailant who threatens him with fatal or grave bodily harm, but he may not take the life of one who merely

122. *Law in a Scientific Age* (New York: Columbia University Press, 1963), p. 65.

123. *Prenatal Influences* (Springfield, Ill.: Thomas, 1962), p. 500.

124. *Gleitman v. Cosgrove*, 49 N.J. 22, 227 A.2d 689 (1967) (parents cannot recover damages from physician who did not abort their child and he was born defective).

threatens his automobile or other valuable possession.[125] Under the American Law Institute proposal, physicians may treat human life as subordinate to lesser interests. It is ironic that such a proposal should be put forward at a time when the taking of life by the state through capital punishment is being criticized and widely abandoned.

It seems fair to conclude that the new abortion statutes come not as a further evolutionary step in the law's perception of the value, intrinsic dignity, and essential equality of human life. To the contrary, they confront the law's evolution with a counter-movement. The unborn child, concededly morally blameless, may be sacrificed in the interest of the mother's mental health or the social interest in avoiding a defective person who might become a welfare charge, because those interests by the ethos of the day are regarded as more socially significant than the claim to life. The right to life becomes relative not only to others' right to life, but to others' health, happiness, convenience, and desires for freedom from avoidable burdens. The scales-master is to be not a neutral agent such as a court, but the person who desires to avoid the burden.

Procedural Protection for the Fetus

Could all objections be met by providing a neutral agent, a court, which would weigh the interest of the fetus in life against other interests urged as ground for taking that life? Some lawyers will feel that if easy abortion must be the wave of the future, they should at least construct dikes of due process against the most flagrant abuses in the threatening floods of the new permissiveness. They will contend that at a minimum they must prevent the orderly execution of the unborn from deteriorating into uninhibited lynching. Such due process instincts are laudable and attempts to construct machinery to effectuate them not wholly hopeless. The dilemma of course is that the crucial decision — that it is permissible for man to decide who shall live — will already have been made by the legislature. If the courts acquiesce in the

125. R. Perkins, *Criminal Law* (Brooklyn: Foundation Press, 1957), pp. 884–909; David Daube, "Sanctity of Life," 60 *Proceedings of the Royal Society of Medicine* (1967), 1235, 1237.

constitutionality of that decision, what is left to achieve under the rubric of due process?

Something may be left. Judicial inquiry might reveal that a mother's claim of grave injury to her mental health is under the facts of a particular case so trivial as to be sham in relation to the child's presumed desire to live. Fraudulent claims of rape or incest might be exposed. Fear of a gravely defective fetus might be shown by cross-examination of the proposing physician, and by other evidence, to be insubstantial.

To these suggestions objection may be made that the inexorable and rapid flight of the period in which abortion is medically feasible precludes such judicial inquiry; that due process is a luxury of leisure. If nature has itself ordained the impossibility of applying standards of fundamental fairness in appraising a claim to abortion, perhaps that is something of judgment on the intrinsic quality of the act. Perhaps what cannot be done fairly should not be done at all. The law, however, is steeped in experience of dealing with time emergencies and has in other areas been able to devise techniques of accommodating to emergency circumstances, for example, the temporary restraining order.

Appointment of a guardian to represent the fetus would seem feasible and would be the minimum starting point for any attempt at due process that is more than a sham. The guardian obviously would have to be one not under the domination of the mother or the recommending physician. The guardian would appear for the fetus at the judicial hearing on the petition for the abortion. Georgia has now enacted such a provision into law, permitting both a governmental official or "any person who would be a relative of the child within the second degree of consanguinity" to petition for a declaratory judgment and restraining order if "such abortion would violate the constitutional or other legal rights of the fetus."[126] It would seem that the constitutional right to life of

126. *Laws of Georgia, 1968*, sec. 26.1106(c). A bill submitted to the Colorado legislature goes further: "Any judge of a court of general jurisdiction of the state, or any district attorney of the judicial district in which a special hospital board as defined in section 40-2-50 meets or is scheduled to meet for the purpose of consideration of approval of a justified medical termination of a pregnancy as defined in section 40-2-50, or any child custody agency which is licensed by the state, or any person who would be a relative of the child within the second degree of consanguinity who has reason to believe that the constitutional or other legal

the fetus is violated by any abortion which is not justified by the necessary self-defense of the mother.

A possible alternative to a judicial hearing would be an administrative one before an interdisciplinary board with at least a limited right of judicial review. The board might consist of independent physicians, lawyers, sociologists, theologians, and lay persons. A model for the judicial review might be that recommended to review administrative determinations respecting alleged intervening insanity of those under death sentence. Provision for expedition would have to be made.[127] If experience proved that the foregoing ideas, rooted in common law experience and development, were not possible in the new area of legalized abortion, perhaps we could borrow from the extralitigious procedures of continental jurisprudence.[128] Under that approach a judge would be charged to make on his own initiative judicial inquiry into the substantiality of the claim for abortion under the statutory standard.

There would seem to be no inherent psychological or moral reasons for medicine to oppose attempts to construct for abortion applications a machinery of due process. The medical profession should be wary of preempting the abortion decisional prerogative by a statute that would formally ordain the legal right of two physicians to justify an abortion under the nebulous standards proposed.[129] Often in human affairs medical knowledge may determine aspects of a problem without purporting to be dispositive of the whole problem. In the case of the defense of insanity in a crim-

---

rights of the child or the pregnant woman may be, or would be, destroyed or substantially impaired by the performance of an abortion or justified medical termination as defined in section 40-2-50, may petition a court of general jurisdiction for a restraining order to prohibit the same for a period not to exceed fourteen days from the date of the order. Said petition shall be heard expeditiously by the court and may be granted after an ex parte hearing if said court believes there is probable cause that the aforesaid rights may be destroyed or substantially impaired" (Colorado Senate Bill 199, 1968).

127. *See* Hazard and Louisell, "Death, the State, and the Insane" *supra* n. 29; *see also* Luis Kutner, "Due Process of Abortion," 53 *Minn. L. Rev.* (1968), 25.

128. *See* Albert A. Ehrenzweig, "The Interstate Child and Uniform Legislation: A Plan for Extralitigious Proceedings," 64 *Michigan Law Review* (1965), 1.

129. "Mental health of the mother" is particularly nebulous and susceptible to subjective value judgments. Yet the first Report to the Legislature on Implementation of California's Therapeutic Abortion Act shows that out of 282 abortions approved, 238 were on the ground of the mother's mental health. Calif. Dep't of Public Health, *Report to the Legislature on California's Therapeutic Abortion Act,* Tab. 1 (January 1968).

inal prosecution, medical testimony is highly relevant to the issue of responsibility; but we do not submit the issue to the decision of a jury of psychiatrists. To the contrary, even where the problem appears predominately a medical one, a societal judgment is sought. If war is too important for the generals, the ultimate issues of life and death are too important for the surgeons. Medical defense committees and screening committees used in malpractice litigation utilize the services of clergy, lawyers, and other thoughtful persons in addition to physicians.[130] When kidney disease threatens to be fatal, and the possibilities for dialysis are limited, the choice of the beneficiaries is often left to a "jury" of lay people.[131] Even the strongest proponents of liberalized abortion admit that the potential, at least, for human life is present in the early stages of gestation. In principle, the medical profession should be reluctant to exchange its historic role of champion in the struggle for life, for the role of even a well-intentioned judge-executioner. Physicians as much as any men stand in need of the due process of law and should realize that the rights of any of us are secure only while those of all are secure.[132]

The best possible attempts at due process would be largely thwarted by the necessarily limited scope of inquiry permissible under a statute authorizing easy legal abortion. Hard questions would naggingly lurk in the background, pressing for their own resolution under historic notions of due process and equal protection. Frustratingly, they would be denied consideration. What type of evidence should be admissible where the very reason for the proceeding is a legislative judgment that innocent life is to be forfeited for reasons not necessarily having to do with the preservation of the mother's life? What criteria are to be relied upon in passing on the child's right to be born? Does a potentially defective child have a lesser claim on this right than a normal one who is the product of rape? An attempt to set up the machinery of due process for a weighing of interests under the standards

130. D. Louisell & H. Williams, *Trial of Medical Malpractice Cases* (Albany, N.Y.: Matthew Bender, 1960), ¶7.02.

131. Alexander, "They Decide Who Lives, Who Dies," *Life,* Nov. 9, 1962, at 102; Sanders & Dukeminier, "Medical Advance and Legal Lag: Hemodialysis and Kidney Transplantation," 15 *U.C.L.A. L. Rev.* (1968), 357, 371.

132. D. Louisell & H. Williams, *The Parenchyma of Law* 157, 165 (Rochester, N.Y.: Professional Medical Publications 1960).

of the American Law Institute has something of the element of the irrational or the absurd about it. To create a judicial model for such a balance is to bring out what it means to weigh the life of one against the self-interest of another.

IV. CONCLUSION

Easy legal abortion presents a genuine and disturbing reversal of the law's steady progress toward recognition of the dignity, value, and essential equality of human life. It is a negation of the constitutional guarantee of equal protection of the law. It is a loveless act offensive to the conscience of our common law tradition. Attempts to justify it on the ground that the fetus is not fully human want for logic. To pick any moment other than that of conception as the starting point of human life is artifical and arbitrary. All human life, whether fetal, infant, adolescent, mature, or aged, is in the process of becoming. Abortion can be justified only if society has the right to prescribe the conditions of continuing life and to authorize the weighing of the right to life against other values. The senile grandparent, the retarded child, the defective fetus and infant may be dire afflictions. Are they too heavy a burden for the richest country at its most affluent height?

Confronted with the threat of such a reversal of the law's posture, some lawyers would prefer that the law abandon the field rather than explicitly succumb to the threat. To take this escape, however, is to denigrate the function of law as teacher. By abandoning protection of the embryo the law would teach that nascent human life need not be respected.

If society insists on legal abortion, the law's last line of defense is to attempt to erect machinery calculated to bring as much due process as possible into the methodology of abortion. But the law must not pretend to do the impossible. The machinery of the most skilled proceduralists will hardly substitute for Albert Schweitzer's principle of Reverence for Life, or equivalently manifest that principle's ethical affirmation of life. As he put it: "Let a man once begin to think about the mystery of his life and the links which connect him with the life that fills the world, and he cannot but bring to bear upon his own life and all other life that comes within his reach the principle of Reverence for Life, and manifest this principle by ethical affirmation of life. Existence will thereby become harder for him in every respect than it would be if he lived for himself, but at the same time it will be richer, more beautiful, and happier. It will become, instead of mere living, a real experience of life." [133] Reverence for human life, at least, requires great sacrifices. The law as it has stood on abortion has asked the sacrifices and proclaimed reverence for each life.

The approach hitherto taken by the states of the United States is not some national aberration. The value protected has been a value generally recognized by civilized nations. In 1959 the United Nations adopted a "Declaration of the Rights of the Child" which supplemented the United Nations' statement entitled the "Universal Declaration of Human Rights." One reason for this supplementary declaration was stated in its preamble as this: "the child, by reason of his physical and mental immaturity, needs special safeguards and care, including appropriate legal protection, before as well as after birth." Thus the representatives of most of the civilized nations of the world acknowledged that the being before birth deserved recognition as a "child." They further agreed that a child, so defined, needed legal protection. The committee report on this declaration noted that "representatives of the most diametrically-opposed social systems find common ideals and aspirations in discussing the privileges of childhood." The rights asserted by the United Nations as applicable to the fetus represented a commitment which had commended itself to all of the various social systems represented within that worldwide body.[134]

In enumerating the ten principles which constituted the rights of the child including the child in the womb, the United Nations declared, "The child shall in all circumstances be among the first to receive protection and relief" (Principle 8). Further, "The child shall be protected against all forms of neglect, cruelty and exploitation" (Principle 9). Above all, the child "shall be entitled to grow and develop in health; to this end, special care

133. *Out of My Life and Thought* 179 (New York: Holt, Rinehart and Winston, 1963).
134. Third Committee of the General Assembly of the United Nations, *Official Records of the General Assembly*, 14th Session (1959), p. 593.

and protection shall be provided both to him and to his mother, including adequate prenatal and postnatal care" (Principle 4).[135] If the child in the womb is to be "among the first," if such child is not to be subjected to neglect or to cruelty, if the child is to receive prenatal care, then the child's life cannot be taken at the will of the child's mother.

The American constitutional guarantee of the equal protection of the law is rooted in the dignity of the individual and the inviolability of innocent human life. Historically the United States has been a professed defender of those values and has committed much to the effort to establish them internally and espouse them internationally. It would be tragic now by example to lead the world to the opposite view that human life is disposable, for utilitarian purposes, at the political will of those who hold power.

If the facts of modern society — population explosion, increasing longevity, environmental pollution — render obsolescent the old learning on innocent human life, those who take that position owe it to their fellow citizens to say so and forthrightly to press for constitutional amendment. Proponents of abortion who frankly contend that the old learning must pass, and that now society must have power to make life-death decisions, deserve credit for their intellectual candor. The discourse of a constitutional democracy presupposes the elemental intellectual honesty to present the claims for a "Brave New World" candidly. Against self-deception or the world of *1984* the equal protection clause still stands.

135. General Assembly of the United Nations, "Declaration of the Rights of the Child," *Official Records*, pp. 19–20.

Index   Table of Statutes   Table of Cases

Index

Abortifacients, 4, 17–18, 21, 65

Abortion

approved by: American Law Institute draftsmen, 248; American legislatures, 248–249; British Parliament, 208–210; De Sade, 37; Ellis, 43n.150

condemned by: American Medical Association, 224–225; American legislatures, 225; British Parliament, 224; common law, 223–225; Calvin, 169; Church Councils, 14, 17, 32, 40, 45, 124; Church Fathers, 11–18; Early Christians, 9–10; Greek Church, 18; Luther, 169; Margaret Sanger, 234; medieval theologians, 22–23; modern Catholic theologians, 40, 124; Hippocratic Oath, 5–6; New Testament, 8–9; Philo, 6; Popes, 32–34, 42–44

duty to remove causes of, 144

incidence of, spontaneous, 56, 215, 251

intentional, see Abortion, practice of

male preference for, 81n.27

means of: by accident, 6, 17; by blows, 31; by craniotomy, 41; by curettage, 78; by drug, 4, 6, 15–18, 21–22, 65, 224; by physical movement, 5, 21; other, 21, 29, 224

penalties for, 14, 20–21, 32–33, 40–41, 224

practice of: by clerics, 20, 33; by married, 6–7, 10, 43–44; by prostitutes, 33; by slaves, 14; by unmarried, 4, 14, 33, 211; in Amsterdam, 193n.65; in Belfast, 215; in Birmingham, 212; in Britain, 78n.22, 182n.25, 209–213, 215n.2, 242–243; in Bronx, 242; in Bulgaria, 184; in California, 182, 191n.57, 209n.3, 231; in Colorado, 211n.10; in Czechoslovakia, 217–219; in Denmark, 183, 191–193, 216, 233; in Eastern Europe, 183–185, 197n.73, 202, 232; in France, 37–38, 176n.10; in Greco-Roman world, 6–7, 235; in Hungary, 183, 197n.73, 217–219, 232; in Indianapolis, 242; in Italy, 37–38; in Japan, 44, 184–185; in Latin America, 134; in London, 212; in Northern Ireland, 215; in Norway, 187n.50; in Poland, 184, 217–219; in Rumania, 184, 197n.73; in Russia, 43, 197; in Scandinavia, 183, 187–188, 192–193; in Slovenia, 197n.73; in Sweden, 183, 216; in Switzerland, 37–38; in United States, 241–243; in Western Europe, 37–38

reasons against: assumption of God's lordship of life, 126; attack on creation of God, 11, 126; attack on image of God, 10, 12, 126; betrayal of human solidarity, 126; denial of parenthood, 126–127; departure from purpose of medical profession, 5–6, 126; destruction of the helpless, 75; failure of fiduciary responsibility, 12, 40; killing of human life, 11–16, 20–23, 34, 38, 39, 45, 126; infanticide, 85–86, 125; loveless act, 58–59, 125, 127; offense against marriage, 16, 22; parricide, 12; sadism, 16, 44; sin against nature, 23

reasons for: analogy to war, 25–26, 29–30, 122; anencephalia, 138; to baptize child, 24; to control population, 4, 150, 165; to eliminate probable defective, 138, 165–166, 248; to eliminate result of adultery, 4–5, 167–168; to eliminate result of fornication, 9–11, 14, 33, 117n.4; to eliminate result of incest, 83, 164–165; to eliminate result of rape, 28, 83, 107–112, 116, 141, 164–165, 248; to improve population, 44, 150, 165; to limit heirs of rich, 4, 7; to limit large family, 117, 248; to obtain re-

Index

Index

Criminal law: efficacy of, 182, 243–244; purposes of, 178–180, 203–206. *See also* Law

Curettage, 78

Curran, Charles E., 40n.138

Cyprian, St., 14

Czechoslovakia: abortion in, 197n.73, 217–219

Daube, David, 254n.125

Death: maternal due to abortion, 185–186, 212–213, 217–219, 231–232, 243; measurement by EEG, 76; permission of by physician, 94–100; right to, 97, 139; sentence of for pregnant woman, 226; sentence of, inequality in application, 237n.69; and belief in God, 94–96. *See also* Abortion

Decision, on abortion: participants in, 117, 163–164, 190–193

"Declaration of the Rights of the Child," 259–260

Decretals of Gregory IX, 20–21, 32

Deininger, Francis, 33n.113

Delegation: of authority to abort, 156–157; 256–257; constitutionality of, 240–241

Denmark: abortion in, 183, 216; abortion law in, 191–193; maternal mortality from abortion in, 233

Devlin, Patrick, 199n.76, 204n.91

Dialogue: on abortion, 144–145

Dickens, Bernard M., 174n.7, 182n.25, 211n.9

Didache, 9, 10

Digest (of Justinian), 6, 235n.66

Discrimination: in effect of abortion laws, 236–237

Dölger, Franz, 13n.29

Double effect: of moral act, 24–26, 29–30, 48–50, 115–116, 125

Douglas, William O., Justice, 233

Drinan, Robert F., S.J., 146n.2

Droegemueller, William, 211n.10

Due process: for fetus, 254–258; for mother, 230–237; for physician, 237–241

Eastern Europe: abortion in, 183–185; abortion law in, 197n.73; consequences of abortion in, 202; maternal mortality in, 232

ECG: of fetus, 73

Ectopic pregnancy, 42, 47–48, 137–138

Edelstein, Ludwig, 5

Elizabeth, mother of John, 8, 17

Ellis, Havelock, 43n.150

Elvira, Council of, 14

Embryo, *see* Fetus

Embryology, sacred, 161

Emotions: of women seeking abortion, 111–112, 115, 141, 193

England, *see* Britain

Ensoulment, *see* Soul

Epikeia, 121, 133n.20

Equal protection: and abortion laws, 236–237; violated by withdrawal of law, 246–247, 260

Equality: of fetus with other lives, 2–3, 56–57, 236–237, 253–254, 260

Equity, 121, 133n.20

Erasistratus, 13

Erythroblastosis, fetal, 245

Eschbach, A., 42n.147

Eser, Alvin, 178n.16

Ethics: as personal feeling, 108; as religion, 60–62; consequentialist, 89–90; juridical model of, 102–104; personal responsibility, 119; Protestant, 101

Eugenics, 165

Eustochium, 15

Euthanasia: Christian attitude to, 165; condemned by Barth, 91–93; distinctions in, 89–100; favored by Joseph Fletcher, Glanville Williams, 201; fetal, 91

Evans, Donald, 62

Exception: and effect on rule, 46–50, 201

Excommunication, 33, 39, 40–41, 128

Experience, legal: indications as to nature of fetus, 220–230; Protestant and fetology, 186; Scandinavian in abortion regulation, 191–193

Family: and state, 152–153

Family size: and right to abortion, 234–235

Father: consent to abortion, 6, 163–164, 196, 249; duty to support fetus, 226; emphasis on in Aquinas and Luther, 148; power over child in Roman Empire, 235; tort action by, 177n.12

Feminism, 150–151

Fetology, 99, 252

Fetus

chances of survival, 56, 215, 251; defective, 138, 165–166, 248; development of, 64–65, 69–79, 251; ectopic, 42, 47–48, 137–138; estimating age of, 78–79; experience of, 52–53; feelings toward, of mother, 141, of society,

266

53; formed, 6, 10, 15, 17, 20, 26–27, 31, 65. *See also* Soul
forgiveness of, 83
functions of: brain, 73, 76, 130; blood circulation, 252; heart, 72–73
implantation of, 64–65, 251; individuation of, 66–67, 131; in interpretation of wills, 220–223; as member of state, 150, 155; as part of mother, 6, 150, 196, 227, 235; as potential man, 56–57. *See also* Humanity
protection of: by advocate, 195, 255; by guardian, 255; by parents, 153
racial differences in, 52; relation to God, 10–12, 68, 126
rights of: to bring action for negligent injury, 226–228; to bring wrongful death action, 229; to care, 45, 258–259; to equal protection, 57, 246–247; to inherit, 220–223; to live after unsuccessful abortion, 214; to support by father, 226; in United Nations Declaration, 258–259. *See also* Abortion, reasons against
sensitivity to pain, 72–73, 99; unformed, 28–29; viability of, 51–52, 73–74, 87, 125, 250; visibility of, social, 54–55, 251
Fienus, Thomas, 34
Fletcher, Joseph, 201
Flood, Peter, 124n.3, 145n.38
Florentinio, Jeronimo, 35
Forgiveness: of fetus, 83
Fraiberg, Selma H., 251
France: abortion in, 18, 37–38, 176n.10
Frankfurter, Felix, Justice, 238–239
Frederiksen, Harold, 211
Freedom, personal: and abortion, 2; of medical profession, 194–195; religious and abortion, 163–164, 244–245; of women and abortion, 234–236

Gampell, Ralph J., 182
Gaudium et spes, 45–46, 124, 129, 134
Gebhard, Paul, 181n.23, 242
Gelasius, Pope, 154
Gemelli, Agostino, 47n.160, 48, 49
Genetic code, 56–57, 65–68, 112, 171
George, B. J., Jr., 177n.12, 190
Gerber, R. J., 129n.14
German measles, *see* Rubella
Germany: law on abortion in, 44
Giannella, Donald, 201n.81
Glass, D. V., 183n.31
God: creator of fetus, 69, 114, 126, 131; giver of life, 113; judge and avenger

of innocent, 44; lord of life and death, 126; redeemer of creation, 106; death as gift of, 91–92, 95; and limits on humans, 97; offense to in abortion, 10–11, 45, 131; purposes of, 106, 121–122; and sanctity of life, 10–12, 126; and value of suffering, 91
Goldblatt, D., 73n.16
Gonzalez, Constancio Palomo, 13n.29, 16n.40
Good faith: and abortion, 189; and sin, 120, 140
Goodhart, C. B., 182, 185n.43, 209, 242–243
Gordon, David A., 199n.77
Gottleib, Frederick J., 53n.180
Gousset, Thomas, Cardinal, 39
Gratian, 20, 22
Green, Ronald M., 80–81
Gregory IX, Pope, 20–21
Gregory XIV, Pope, 33, 129
Gribomont, J., 18n.47
Gruenwald, Peter, 52n.176, 227n.37
Guardian for fetus, 255–256
Gury, Jean, S.J., 38
Gustafson, James M., 131–132, 139–140, 142
Guttmacher, Alan, 185n.40, 231n.51, 234n.60, 241n.82

Hale, Matthew, 223–224, 226
Hall, Robert E., 186n.45
Hamlin, Hannibal, 76, n21
Häring, Bernard, C.SS.R., 39, 40, 121
Hart, H. L. A., 177–178, 191n.58, 204–205
Hauriou, Maurice, 187
Hazard, Geoffrey, 226n.29
Health: maternal, affected by abortion, 184n.36, 202; definition of, 249
Heart: of fetus, 72–73
Heimberger, 155n.7
Hellegers, André, 70n.11, 73n.18
Herod, 8
Hippocrates, 5, 13
Hippocratic Oath, 4, 5
Hippolytus, St., 14
History: organic view of, 1–2
Hitler, 139
Hoffmeyer, Henrik, 187n.50, 192
Holmes, Oliver Wendell, Jr., Justice, 200n.79, 227
Holy Office, 32n.109, 34, 40–42, 48
Homicide: abortion as, 223
Hospital committee, 155–157
Hospitals: abortions in, 231
Hostiensis, 22

Index

Index

Navarrus, *see* Azplicueta
Nazis, 165
Nephesh, 147
Neshamah, 147
Netherlands: abortion law in, 192–193
Newman, Lucille, 241
New York City, abortion, 181
Nider, John, O.P., 22
Nilsson, Lennart, 74
Noldin, Jerome, S.J., 48n.162
Nonfeasance: distinction from action, 89–90, 92–94, 139; in constitutional law, 246, 247
Noonan, John T., Jr., 7n.16, 19n.51, 33n.11, 55n.184, 127, 128n.10, 135n.23, 234n.59, 235n.65
Norgaard, Magna, 191
Northern Ireland: abortion in, 215
Norway: regulation of abortion in, 187 n.50
Novatian, 14

O'Connor, John, 55n.184
O'Donnell, Thomas J., S.J., 102n.2, 124 n.3
Oocytes: number of, 55
Organized crime: and abortion, 203
Organs, human: in fetus, 72
Osservatore Romano, 47
Ovum, fertilized: human status of, 46n. 158, 56, 65, 130

Pache, H. D., 130n.15
Packer, Herbert L., 182, 186, 190n.56, 194n.70, 231n.50
Palazzini, Pietro, 127n.6
Parents: as sovereigns of fetus, 153
Parricide: abortion as, 12, 14
Parsons, Talcott, 173n.4
Pastoral considerations, 107–118, 139–143
Patterson, Edwin W., 253
Paul VI, Pope, 45n.155, 46
Paul, St., 8–9, 17, 24, 44, 179
Paul the Jurist, 6–13
Pellegrino, Michele, Cardinal, 139n.28
Penance: for abortion, 14, 17, 19, 27
Penitentials, 19
Perjury: incidence of, 244n.93
Perkins, Rollin M., 199n.76
Person: definition of, 138–139; social determination of, 148–149. *See also* Humanity
Personality: dependence on position among siblings, 148–149

Pestalozzi, Ernesto, 47
Peter Cantor, 24n.82
Peter Lombard, 22–23
Pharmakeia, 8–11, 17–18
Pharr, Clyde, 8n.17
Philo, 6
Physician: conscience of, 144–145, 197n. 72; delegation of state's authority to, 240–241, 257; tort action against for not aborting, 196, 253. *See also* Medical Profession; Tort
Pill: "morning after," 65
Pilz, J., 124n.3
Pincus, Gregory, 55n.187, 65
Pius IX, Pope, 38
Pius XI, Pope, 43–44, 47, 134n.22, 135–136, 142–143
Pius XII, Pope, 45, 135–136, 169
Placenta, 71–72, 252
Plato, 4, 178n.15, 180, 207
Plautus, 7n.14
Plutarch, 6, 9, 10
Poland: abortion in, 184, 217–219
Popes: teaching on abortion, 32–34, 36. *See also* Calixtus; Clement X; Gelasius; Gregory IX; Gregory XIV; Innocent I; Innocent III; Innocent X; Innocent XI; Paul VI; Pius IX; Pius XI; Pius XII; Sixtus V
Population: abortion to restrict, 4, 5, 37, 150, 176n.10, 177n.12
Potter, Ralph B., Jr., 75, 150n.5
Potts, Malcom, 197n.73, 198n.75, 219
Prenatal influences, 253
Prenatal injuries: tort action for, 226–229
President's Commission on Law Enforcement, 203n.89
Privacy: right to and abortion, 233–234; zone of, 152
Probability: of birth of fetus, 56, 250–251
Prohibition of alcholic drinks, compared to abortion rule, 185, 203
Promise-keeping: and life of child, 80–81
Property: killing to defend, 40
Prosser, William, 226n.32, 227n.37, 228 n.38, 230
Prostitution: as reason for prohibition of abortion, 33; regulation of analogized to abortion regulation, 205–206
Protestant: counseling on abortion, 109–117; compared with Catholic, 119–121, 132; teaching on abortion, 169–170; view of fetus, 147–149
Prudence, virtue of in concrete, 121, 140

Index

Table of Statutes

BRITAIN

43 Geo. III c. 58 224
Abortion Act 1967 . . . . 189n.53
190n.56, 197nn.72, 73, 208–213

Contagious Diseases Act 1864 . . . .
205n.96, 206n.99

JAPAN

Eugenic Protection Act 1948 . . . .
197n.73

UNITED STATES

Arkansas Statutes c. 41–303 (1969) . . . .
248
California Civil Code
    sec. 196A 245
    sec. 29 . . . . 227n.36, 229
California Health and Safety Code
    secs. 25951–25952 248–249
    sec. 25954 . . . . 209n.3
    sec. 25950 . . . . 190n.56
California Penal Code
    sec. 270 . . . . 226n.31
    sec. 3705–3706 . . . . 226n.31
California Probate Code
    sec. 250 . . . . 221n.5
    sec. 255 . . . . 221n.5
Colorado Revised Statutes (1967), 40.2–
50 . . . . 190n.56, 248

Delaware Statutes (1969) 248
Hawaii Laws (1970) 248n.105
Kansas Laws c. 180 (1968) 248
Georgia Laws, 1968
    26.1102 248–249
    sec. 26.1106 (C.) 255n.126
Maryland Laws, 1968, c. 470 248
New Mexico Statutes, 1969, sec. 40A
    248
New York Penal Law 125.00 (1967)
    250
North Carolina General Statutes, 14–45.1
    (1967) 248
Oregon Laws, 1969, c. 684 248–
249

Table of Cases